# Gardens to Visit
## 2010

www.gardenstovisit.net

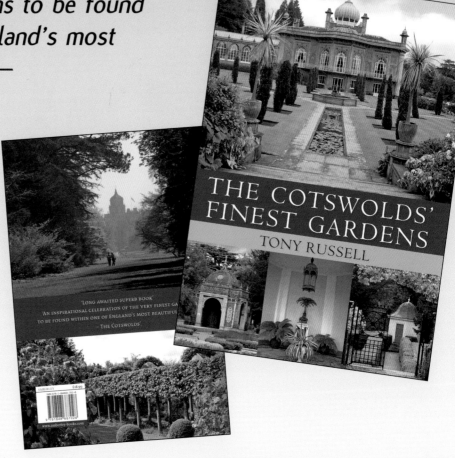

# Gardens to Visit 2010

Welcome to the 2010 edition of Gardens to Visit, which is once again packed with great ideas for all your garden visits in the forthcoming year.

As always we have tried to include gardens that you may not have come across before, as well as long standing favourites such as Exbury, Kiftsgate Court, Iford Manor, Trentham, the National Botanic Garden of Wales and the Royal Botanic Gardens Edinburgh.

New gardens for this year include the delightful south-coast gardens of Cadlands near Southampton and the Jekyll and Lutyens designed Secret Gardens at Sandwich in Kent; the fabulous National Trust gardens at Nymans; Hanham Court, home of Julian and Isabel Bannerman (garden designers to His Royal Highness The Prince of Wales) and Arley Arboretum in Worcestershire. That's just to whet your appetite, there are plenty more throughout these pages for you to enjoy!

It is interesting to note that during difficult times, such as the recession we are now experiencing, the number of visits to gardens tends to increase. Various explanations have been given for this. When the going gets tough, more people spend their holidays at home in the UK rather than going abroad. Gardens are generally great value for money with their admission charges amongst the lowest for any visitor attraction sector. Gardens offer peace and tranquillity in times of turmoil, a place of sanctuary away from the stresses and strains of modern day living. All undoubtedly true, however I would add a further reason for you to visit and enjoy Britain's wonderful gardens in 2010.

If we are finding the recession financially tough, then so are the garden owners and managers. I know of three gardens that have closed their doors to the public in 2009 and I hear that there may be more closures to follow. It is exactly at times like this that they need our support. Maintaining a garden for public enjoyment is neither easy nor cheap and there are very few that manage to make a substantial income from it. By visiting we are helping to support them and hopefully ensuring that Britain remains a country full of wonderful gardens that we can all enjoy.

**Tony Russell**
*BBC garden writer and broadcaster*

# Are you looking for new speakers
## to come and talk to your club?

If so, this leaflet may be of interest to you....

Each year BBC garden writer and broadcaster, former Head
Forester of Westonbirt Arboretum and editor of the annual publication **'Gardens
to Visit'**, Tony Russell, undertakes a series of entertaining talks and lectures to
garden clubs, horticultural societies and other groups around the country.

All lectures are illustrated with either transparencies or PowerPoint
presentation and last for a minimum of one hour plus questions.

'For details on Tony's talks and costs please visit
www.gardenstovisit.net or telephone 01453 836730

# Contents

# England

Leonardslee Lakes & Gardens - West Sussex

*'I hold the firm belief that the purpose of a garden is to give happiness and repose of mind, firstly and above all other considerations, and to give it through the representation of the best kind of pictorial beauty of flower and foliage that can be combined or invented.'*

**Gertrude Jekyll – 1905**

A simple statement made over 100 years ago and yet possibly even more pertinent today, given the need for all of us to be able to 'take time out' from our busy and all too often pressured lives. Gardens provide us with oasis of tranquillity and beauty, somewhere calm for reflection and a place to 'recharge our batteries' ready for our next foray into twenty-first century life.

In the pages that follow you will discover many such places; from Cornwall to Northumberland and from Kent to Cumbria, located within our busy cities and immersed in the countryside. We hope you enjoy our 2010 selection of the very best English gardens.

The Swiss Garden was created in the early nineteenth century. It contains picturesque features hidden in an undulating nine-acre landscape. The garden is planted with magnificent trees and ornamental shrubs which are arranged in a series of glades, lawns and winding walks, designed to provide unexpected vistas. The recently refurbished and replanted, subterranean grotto and fernery nestles in the centre. 'The Grand Tour' provided inspiration for the tiny thatched Swiss Cottage. The fashion for 'Swiss" architecture, so popular in the Regency period can be seen all around the Garden. Elegant floral arches and a network of ponds with decorative bridges and delightful islands complete the picture. Peafowl roam freely in the garden. Spring bulbs, rhododendrons and rambling roses are spectacular in season. Benches are located at frequent intervals. There is also an adjacent picnic area and a woodland lakeside walk.

## Fact File

| | |
|---|---|
| **Opening Times:** | November 1st to March 31st 9.30am - 4pm, April 1st to October 31st 9.30am - 5pm |
| **Admission Rates:** | Adults £5.00, Senior Citizen £4.00, Accompanied Children Free. |
| **Group Rates:** | Minimum group size: 20 but all groups welcome<br>Group Rate £3.50, Accompanied Children Free. |
| **Facilities:** | Visitor Centre, Restaurant, Toilets, Gift/Souvenirs and Plant Stall. |
| **Disabled Access:** | Yes, Toilet and parking for disabled on site. Wheelchairs on loan, booking advised. |
| **Tours/Events:** | Guided Tours and Group Bookings by appointment. |
| **Coach Parking:** | Yes. |
| **Length of Visit:** | 2 hours |
| **Booking Contact:** | Tony Podmore<br>The Swiss Garden, Old Warden Park, Old Warden, Biggleswade, Bedfordshire, SG18 9EP.<br>Telephone: 01767 627923 Fax: 01767 627949 |
| **Email:** | tony.podmore@shuttleworth.org |
| **Website:** | www.shuttleworth.org |
| **Location:** | Approximately 2 miles west of Biggleswade A1 roundabout signposted from A1 and A600. |

Please quote this
guide when
making a booking

World-renowned 35 acres of ornamental gardens and woodland, including National Collections and rare international species, The Savill Garden provides a wealth of beauty and interest in all seasons.

Do not miss the exciting new Rose Garden, which will be unveiled in June 2010. The contemporary design will create an intense sensory experience with roses especially chosen for their scent, strong colours and repeat flowering.

Spring in the Savill Garden is heralded by hosts of daffodils, marvellous magnolias and the wonderful perfume of the varieties of rhododendrons and azaleas. Summer brings a contrast of colour, with the vibrancy of the grand Herbaceous Borders and the tranquil, pastel shades of the Golden Jubilee Garden. The glorious displays of autumn in the Garden are a joy to behold, before attention turns to the striking new additions to the Winter Garden. The Queen Elizabeth Temperate House showcases original and unusual seasonal plant displays which offer continuous floral interest and vitality throughout the year.

Plus, the award-winning Savill Building offers excellent shopping, an art gallery, exhibitions and a restaurant, managed by Leith's.

## Fact File

**Opening Times:** 10am - 6pm March - October, 10am - 4.30pm November - February (last admission to the Garden is 30 minutes before closing).

**Admission Rates:** Adults: £8.00, Senior Citizens: £7.50, Child (6-16): £3.75, Family: £20.00.

**Group Rates:** £6.65 per person for groups of 10 or more.

**Seasonal Prices:** Prices shown are peak prices, (March 09 - October 09). Please contact The Savill Garden for off peak prices.

**Facilities:** Shop, Plant Sales, Teas, Restaurant.

**Disabled Access:** Yes.  Toilet and Parking for disabled on site. Wheelchairs available to loan.

**Tours/Events:** Guided tours are available, (please book your tour two week prior to visit)
Ongoing programme of events and exhibitions. Please visit www.theroyallandscape.co.uk or contact The Savill Garden for details.

**Coach Parking:** Yes.

**Length of Visit:** 3 - 4 hours

**Booking Contact:** Carla Hall
Crown Estate Office, The Great Park, Windsor, Berkshire, SL4 2HT
Telephone: 0845 603 6228 Fax: 01753 624107

**Email:** enquiries@theroyallandscape.co.uk

**Website:** www.theroyallandscape.co.uk

Please quote this guide when making a booking

A woodland garden on the grand scale; set beneath the canopies of beautiful mature trees with delightful views to Virginia Water Lake.  Over 200 acres of camellias rhododendrons, magnolias and many other flowering trees and shrubs provide visitors with breathtaking displays in March, April and May.

Massed plantings of hydrangeas are the highlight of the summer before a myriad of autumn tints from Japanese maples, birches, sweet gums and tupelos light up the woods.

Winter brings the flowers of witch-hazel and drifts of heathers amongst the dwarf conifers in the Heather Garden before swathes of dwarf daffodils stud the turf in the sweeping Azalea Valley.

Truly a garden for all seasons.

### Fact File

| | |
|---|---|
| **Opening times:** | Car park open: 8am - 7pm (4pm in winter) or sunset if earlier. |
| **Admission Rates:** | Car Park Charges: £6.00 |
| **Facilities:** | At nearby Savill Garden. |
| **Disabled Access:** | Limited. Toilet and parking for disabled on site. Wheelchair trail in the garden. |
| **Tours/Events:** | None. |
| **Coach Parking:** | Coaches by arrangement on weekdays only (Charge applies). |
| **Length of Visit:** | 2 - 3 hours |
| **Booking Contact:** | Carla Hall |
| | Crown Estate Office, The Great Park, Windsor, Berkshire, SL4 2HT |
| | Telephone: 0845 603 6228 Fax: 01753 624107 |
| **Email:** | enquiries@theroyallandscape.co.uk |
| **Website:** | www.theroyallandscape.co.uk |
| **Location:** | On the eastern boundary of Windsor Great Park ( off A30) |
| | Access to Valley Gardens car park via Wick Road. |

# Waltham Place Organic Farm & Garden Berkshire

Waltham Place Estate has often been described as "the best kept secret in Berkshire", and what you find here is a little oasis which has much to offer the visitor at all levels. There are beautiful gardens designed by Henk Gerritsen, which explore the boundaries between gardens and nature and are a haven for an array of flora and fauna.
The estate includes a farm, ornamental and kitchen gardens, with a lake and woodlands. It has been managed organically for over 20 years and has matured into a thriving environment.

Visitors can come and enjoy the gardens on their own or on a guided walk. Head Gardener Beatrice Krehl, takes groups around the gardens. She explains the principles of naturalistic planting used here, for example how the plants are allowed to run their natural cycle and therefore support the wealth of insect and bird life.

Next year the estate is celebrating the 100th anniversary of the Oppenheimer Family being at Waltham Place. There will be a number of special events to mark this occasion, Information is available on the website and from the estate.

## Fact File

**Opening Times:** NGS Open Day Sunday 30th May- 11am -4pm
Every Wednesday from 2nd June-29th September-Walks with the Gardener, 11am & 2pm
Every Friday from 4th June-24th September open in aid of NGS, 10am-4pm
Tuesdays and Thursdays- group visits by appointment only
Tea room and Farm Shop open June-September, Tuesday-Friday, 10am-4pm.

**Admission Rates:** Adults £4.00, Senior Citizen £4.00, Child £1.00. Group Packages available.

**Facilities:** Organic Farm Shop, Tea Room, Plant Sales, Education & Group Visits.

**Disabled Access:** Yes. Toilet and parking for disabled on site.

**Tours/Events:** Seasonal walks, group tours by arrangement.

**Coach Parking:** Not on site but very close by.

**Length of Visit:** 2 - 3 hours

**Booking Contact:** Estate Office
Waltham Place, Church Hill, White Waltham, Berks SL6 3JH
Telephone: 01628 825517  Fax: 01628 825045

**Email:** estateoffice@walthamplace.com

**Website:** www.walthamplace.com

**Location:** From M4 junction 8/9 take A404M and follow signs to White Waltham.
Turn left to Windsor and Paley Street and St Mary's Church.
Estate on left handside.

Please quote this guide when making a booking

# Hanham Court Bristol

This unexpectedly rural Court House with 13th Century Church and Tithe Barn was part of a monastic foundation. At the end of a tiny lane among fields it is half-way between the centres of Bristol and Bath. Here Julian and Isabel Bannerman, award winning garden designers, who most notably designed a 'Stumpery' for the Prince of Wales at Highgrove, have, over fifteen years, created a deeply romantic, highly scented garden. The formal part has luscious borders of old roses, tree peonies, lilies and fountains. The woodland garden has magnolias, ferns and tree ferns, stumpery, stream-fed pools and a cascade with a 'Dancing Crown' fountain. Beyond this lies a miniature wild meadow parkland and orchard, and by the barn a small vegetable and cutting garden.

## Fact File

| | |
|---|---|
| **Opening Times:** | Current times 11.30 a.m. – 5.30 p.m. |
| | Friday, Saturday, Sunday, Monday, April, Easter – end September. |
| **Admission Rates:** | Adults £6.50, Children under 14: £3.50 |
| **Group Rates:** | Minimum Group Size: 35 |
| | Adults: as above, Senior Citizens: as above, Children: as above |
| **Facilities:** | Plant sales, teas |
| **Disabled Access:** | Yes. |
| **Toilets On Site:** | Yes. |
| **Events:** | Weddings, lectures, etc. |
| **Tours:** | Yes. Booking required. |
| **Coach Parking:** | Yes. |
| **Car Parking:** | Yes. |
| **Length of Visit:** | 1-2 hours |
| **Booking Contact:** | Isabel Bannerman |
| | Hanham Court, Hanham Abbots, Ferry Road, Bristol BS15 3NT |
| | Telephone: 01179 610593, Fax: 01179 611202 |
| **Email:** | info@hanhamcourt.co.uk |
| **Website:** | www.hanhamcourt.co.uk |
| **Location:** | East Bristol, off A431 Bath to Bristol Road at Longwell Green. |

# University of Bristol Botanic Garden Bristol

The University of Bristol Botanic Garden cultivates four core collections illustrating: plant evolution, plants from the world's Mediterranean climate zones, useful plants and rare and threatened native plants to the Bristol area. The garden has a strong evolutionary theme including a sunken dell that charts the most important stages of plant evolution on land. A 'family tree' of flowering plant relationships inferred from the DNA sequencing of plant genes is the first display in the UK to show this new research. Chinese and European Herb Gardens contain medicinal plants.

A large glasshouse complex is home to many exotic cacti and succulents, subtropical ferns and orchids, while a tropical zone houses the giant Amazon waterlily, food, spice and medicine plants. New for 2010 is a South African and New Zealand plant display. Home made teas are served in the main house at weekends during the summer.

## Fact File

**Opening Times:** Open Wednesday, Thursday, Friday and Sunday 10am - 4.30pm plus special summer Saturday openings, see website for further details.

**Admission Rates:** Adults £3.50, children up to sixteen free

**Group Rates:** Minimum Group Size 10. Cost £4.50 per person for guided tour.

**Facilities:** Classroom/Meeting Room, Welcome Lodge, Toilets.

**Disabled Access:** Yes. Toilet and car parking on site. Bookable Wheelchairs available.

**Tours/Events:** Guided tours available at £4.50 per person. Jazz Concert and Theatre in Summer, educational activities, courses and study days.

**Coach Parking:** Yes on public highway.

**Length of Visit:** 1½ - 2 hours.

**Booking Contact:** Tours Administrator, University of Bristol Botanic Garden, Hollybush Lane, Stoke Bishop, Bristol. BS9 1JB
Tel: 0117 3314906  Fax: 0117 3314909

**Email:** botanic-gardens@bristol.ac.uk

**Website:** www.bris.ac.uk/Depts/BotanicGardens

**Location:** By car from city centre proceed across the Downs towards Stoke Bishop. Cross the traffic lights at the edge of the Downs, Stoke Park Road is the first turning right off Stoke Hill. The entrance to the Botanic Garden is opposite Churchill Hall. BS9 1JG

Please quote this guide when making a booking

# Cliveden                                               Buckinghamshire

Once the home of the fabulous Astors, Cliveden's Grade I listed garden has recently undergone, and continues to receive, major conservation and restoration works.

The spectacular south-facing parterre originally designed by John Fleming has been replanted for 2010 and offers magnificent views over the Thames Valley and beyond. The Long Garden with its extravagant topiary will be planted with 25,000 tulip bulbs for spring followed by a colourful scheme for summer. The lawns to the front of the Italianate mansion are flanked by great herbaceous borders providing summer-long colour.

Lunches and teas are served in the Orangery, with plants and a wide selection of interesting products available in the gift shop.

## Fact File

| | |
|---|---|
| **Opening times:** | 1 March – 30 October – daily, 11 a.m. – 5.30 p.m. |
| **Admission Rates:** | Adults: £8.00, Children: £4.00 |
| | NT Members Free. |
| **Group Rates:** | Minimum Group Size: 15  Adults: £6.80 – Not Sundays |
| **Facilities:** | Visitor Centre, Shop, Plant Sales, Restaurant, Teas, Audio-visual guide |
| **Disabled Access:** | Yes.  Wheelchair loan available |
| **Toilets on site:** | Yes |
| **Car Parking on site:** | Yes |
| **Coach Parking:** | Yes |
| **Guided Tours:** | Yes, booking required. |
| **Length of Visit:** | 2 – 3 hours |
| **Booking Contact:** | Gill Coop, Cliveden, Taplow, Nr. Maidenhead, Buckinghamshire, SL6 0JA |
| | Booking Tel No. 01628 605069.  Booking Fax No. 01628 669461 |
| **Email:** | cliveden@nationaltrust.org.uk |
| **Website:** | www.nationatrust.org.uk |
| **Location:** | M4 Junction 7 to A4 or M40 Junction 4 to A404 and follow brown signs. Coach entrance on Bourne End Road |

Please quote this guide when making a booking

Waddesdon Manor and Gardens were bequeathed to the National Trust by the Rothschilds in 1957. The garden today is essentially the one laid out by Baron Ferdinand de Rothschild and his French, landscape designer, Elie Lainé.

It is considered one of the finest Victorian gardens in Britain with a parterre, seasonal displays, colourful shrubs, carpet bedding, statuary, fountains and parkland. At its heart lies the rococo-style Aviary housing exotic birds and known for breeding endangered species. The Aviary glade is the location of a new acquisition called Perceval by Sarah Lucas, a life-sized, bronze horse and cart. Sarah is of the same generation of artists as Damien Hirst and the late Angus Fairhust, whose gorilla sculpture can be seen in an area called the Tulip Patch.

The garden can be enjoyed at any season. Guided walks take place from April to September.

## Fact File

| | |
|---|---|
| **Opening times:** | Gardens, Aviary, Woodland Playground, Shops and Restaurant - 10.00-5.00 |
| **Admission Rates:** | Winter Season, 2 Jan-28 Mar (weekends only), Adult: £7.00, Child: £3.50, Family: £17.50 |
| | Peak & Christmas Season, 31 Mar-31 Dec (Weds-Fri), Adult: £5.50, Child: £2.75, Family: £13.75 |
| | 31 Mar-31 Dec (weekends & BHs), Adult: £7.00, Child: £3.50, Family: £17.50, |
| | (Including Mondays & Tuesdays 20, 21 & 27 28 December) |
| | NT members free. RHS members free, gardens only, September and October only |
| **Group Rates:** | Minimum Group Size: 15. |
| | Group rates available see www.waddesdon.org.uk or phone the booking contact (see below). |
| **Facilities:** | Shops, Plant Centre, Restaurant, Woodland Playground |
| **Disabled Access:** | Yes. Wheelchair loan available. |
| **Toilets on site:** | Yes |
| **Car Parking on site:** | Yes |
| **Coach Parking:** | Yes |
| **Guided Walks:** | Yes |
| **Length of Visit:** | 1 – 4 hours |
| **Special Events:** | Yes |
| **Booking Contact:** | Deborah Read, Waddesdon Manor, Waddesdon, Nr. Aylesbury, Buckinghamshire HP18 0JH |
| | Booking Tel No.01296 653226. Booking Fax No. 01296 653212 |
| **Email:** | deborah.read@nationaltrust.org.uk |
| **Website:** | www.waddesdon.org.uk |
| **Location:** | 20 minutes from Junction 7 (northbound) and 9 (southbound) off the M40, off the A41 between Aylesbury and Bicester. |

Please quote this guide when making a booking

# Anglesey Abbey, Gardens & Lode Mill
## Cambridgeshire

A passion for tradition and style inspired one man to transform a run-down country house. The glorious Jacobean-style country house is now set amidst a magnificent landscape. At the age of 30, the 1st Lord Fairhaven sought to inspire and surprise. He created a spectacular garden, encompassing 114 acres of rolling lawns, sweeping avenues, formal gardens, classical statuary, wildflower meadows, wildlife discovery area and a working watermill.

Throughout the year, changing colours and scents provide a unique experience. Rare varieties of snowdrops create a popular display in January and February; thousands of hyacinths highlight spring, while summer is celebrated by colourful herbaceous borders and dahlias. Magnificent autumn foliage is followed by glorious winter colours, making Anglesey a garden for all seasons.

Over 100 pieces of classical garden statuary nestle against the backdrop of Anglesey's stunning Emperors' Walk, Arboretum, Herbaceous Border and Coronation and Cross Avenues. A true showcase for twentieth century English garden design.

## Fact File

**Opening times:** Gardens open 1 January - 28 February & 1 November - 31 December 10.30 - 4.30 Monday to Sunday. 1 March - 31 October 10.30 - 5.30 Monday to Sunday. House open 3 March - 31 October 11.00 - 5.00 Wednesday - Sunday. Open BH Mons and Good Friday. Closed Christmas Eve, Christmas Day and Boxing Day. Areas of garden open according to Season. *Snowdrop Season* 18 Jan -- 21 Feb 2010 NT Members free. RHS Member free - gardens only

**Admission Rates:** Summer (from 1 Mar 2010) House, Garden & Mill. Adult £10.25, Child £5.15, Family £25.65, Group Adult £8.70, Group Child £4.35
Summer (Gardens & Mill Only), Winter (Garden, Mill & Gallery) Adult £6.10, Child £3.05, Family £15.25, Family, Group Adult £5.20, Group Child £2.55
* Includes a voluntary 10% gift aid donation towards the upkeep and restoration of the property. Standard rates available on request.

**Group Rates:** Minimum Group Size: 15, Admission as above.

**Facilities:** Visitor Centre, restaurant, shop, plant sales, second-hand bookshop

**Disabled Access:** Disabled toilets. Parking. Wheelchairs & PMVs available booking essential. Mill: access to lower floor only, ramp available.

**Parking:** Onsite. Coach parking booking essential

**Length of Visit:** Minimum 2 hours

**Guided Tours:** Yes, booking essential.

**Special Events:** Special events programme, for details see website or Tel. 01223 810080

**Booking Contact:** Administrator, Anglesey Abbey, Gardens & Lode Mill, Quy Rd, Lode, Cambridge CB25 9EJ. Tel No. 01223 810080. Fax No. 01223 810088

**Email:** angleseyabbey@nationaltrust.org.uk

**Website:** www.nationaltrust.org.uk/angleseyabbey

**Location:** 6 miles north-east of Cambridge on B1102. Signed from A14, junc 35.

Please quote this guide when making a booking

# Elgood's Brewery Gardens                    Cambridgeshire

A beautiful 4-acre garden, situated behind Elgood's Brewery, on the banks of the River Nene in Wisbech, in the heart of the Fens.

The garden is famous for its maze and its trees, some over 200 years old, including Ginkgo Biloba, Tulip Tree, and Tree of Heaven.  There is a lake with golden and ghost carp, a pond, which  is home to Great Crested Newts, and a hot-house with many exotic plants.

The Visitor Centre houses a museum with brewery artefacts and pub memorabilia.  A variety of freshly prepared snacks are available in the licensed cafe-bar and there is a well-stocked shop selling quality beers, gifts and plants.

Close by are The Octavia Hill Museum, The Wisbech & Fenland Museum, and the National Trust's Peckover House. These attractions, together with several excellent pubs along the riverbanks, add up to an  enjoyable and interesting visit.

## Fact File

| | |
|---|---|
| **Opening Times:** | 20th April - 30th September 2010 11.30am - 4.30pm. |
| **Admission Rates:** | Garden & Brewery - Adults £6.50, Senior Citizens £6.50, Child (6-16) £4.00<br>We regret that children under 6 are not permitted on Brewery Tours<br>Garden only - Adults £3.00, Senior Citizen £2.50, Child £2.50 |
| **Groups Rates:** | Minimum group size 10<br>Garden & Brewery - £5.50, Garden Only - £2.50 |
| **Facilities:** | Visitor Centre, Gift Shop, Plant Sales, Teas, Licensed bar, Free Parking.<br>No dogs except guide dogs. |
| **Disabled Access:** | Yes.  Toilets and parking for disabled on site.  Wheelchairs on loan. Booking Advisable. |
| **Tours/Events:** | Brewery Tours Tues, Wed, and Thurs 2pm (not suitable for disabled)  Garden show and Craft Fair 9th May & 5th September 10am - 4pm.<br>Christmas open weekend (free entry - free tours) 4th/5th December. |
| **Coach Parking:** | Yes |
| **Length of Visit:** | 1 - 2+ Hours |
| **Booking Contact:** | Kate Pateman<br>North Brink, Wisbech, Cambridge, PE13 1LN<br>Telephone: 01945 583160   Fax: 01945 587711 |
| **Email:** | info@elgoods-brewery.co.uk |
| **Website:** | www.elgoods-brewery.co.uk |
| **Location:** | Wisbech |

Please quote this guide when making a booking

Elton Hall Gardens have been stunningly restored during the last twenty years. The modern design is loosely based on an Edwardian interpretation of the medieval and Victorian gardens. Immaculately kept hedges of hornbeam and yew encompass four different areas.

The main lawn has a mass of topiary and an enchanting sunken lily pond which is surrounded with beds containing a number of specimen plants.

The former rose garden has recently been redesigned and is now a magical flower garden with a modern fountain and wisteria clad arches.

The Millennium was celebrated by the building of an orangery and this is set in a colourful Mediterranean garden with lemon and orange trees.

A small shrubbery area, with such gems as Paulownia Tomentosa, leads the visitor back into the Box Walk to enjoy another view of the house set in these magnificent gardens.

## Fact File

| | |
|---|---|
| **Opening Times:** | 2.00 p.m. – 5.00 p.m.: May Bank Holiday Sunday 30th May and Monday 31st May; Wednesdays in June; Wednesday, Thursday and Sundays in July and August; August Bank Holiday, Monday 30th August. |
| **Admission Rates:** | Adults: £5.50, Senior Citizens: £5.00, Children: Accompanied children under 16 admitted free |
| **Group Rates:** | Minimum Group Size: 20. Adults: £5.50 |
| **Facilities:** | Shop, plant sales, restaurant, teas, toilets. |
| **Disabled Access:** | Yes – to garden |
| **Car Parking on site:** | Yes |
| **Coach Parking:** | Yes |
| **Tours/Events:** | Free flow or guided tours available. Booking required. |
| **Length of Visit:** | 1 hour |
| **Booking Contact:** | The Administrator<br>Elton Hall Gardens, Elton Hall<br>Nr, Peterborough, Cambridgeshire PE8 6SH<br>Booking Telephone No. 01832 280468<br>Booking Fax No. 01832 280584 |
| **Email:** | office@eltonhall.com |
| **Website:** | www.eltonhall.com |
| **Location:** | Elton is located just off the A605 between Peterborough and Oundle. |

Please quote this guide when making a booking

Peckover House is an elegant Georgian merchant's house within the heart of Wisbech, built in 1722. For one hundred and fifty years it was lived in by the Peckover family, a Quaker banking dynasty. The outstanding two-acre garden is a rare gem of surprising size, hidden behind the backs of neighbouring properties. It is regarded as one of the finest walled town gardens in the country, and its "gardenesque" character offers a rambling perambulation through distinct areas, with vistas through gaps and internal walls. The garden contains notable trees, such as Ginko Biloba (Maidenhair tree), Liriodendron tulipiferum (Tulip Tree), and possibly the largest specimen of Cornus mas in the country. The garden also contains three summerhouses, two pool gardens, over 70 species of rose and a croquet lawn. The Victorian glasshouses include an Orangery with 300-year-old orange trees which still fruit prolifically.

## Fact File

| | |
|---|---|
| **Opening times:** | 13th March – 31st October 2010. Saturday, Sunday, Monday, Tuesday, Wednesday 12 – 5pm |
| | Also open Good Friday and 1st and 2nd July for Wisbech Rose Fair |
| **Admission Rates:** | Adults: £6.00, Children: £3.00, Family: £15.00 |
| | National Trust members: Free |
| **Group Rates:** | Minimum Group Size: 15. Adults: £5.00 Booking necessary |
| **Facilities:** | Shop, Plant Sales, Tea Room, Secondhand bookshop |
| **Disabled Access:** | Yes, level access. PMV loan (book in advance) |
| | Toilet on site. No parking on site – drop-off point available. |
| **Tours/Events:** | House and garden tours, day and evening tours available. |
| **Coach Parking:** | No, available nearby |
| **Length of Visit:** | 2+ hours. |
| **Booking Contact:** | Property Secretary |
| | Peckover House and Garden, North Brink, Wisbech, Cambridgeshire PE13 1JR |
| | Tel: 01945 583463 |
| **Email:** | peckover@nationaltrust.org.uk |
| **Website:** | www.nationaltrust.org.uk/peckover |
| **Location:** | Centre of Wisbech, on north bank of River Nene. |

Please quote this guide when making a booking

The award winning gardens, recently voted in the top 50 in Europe and in Britain's top 10, have been lovingly created over 250 years with each generation of the family making its own contribution. The result is a garden of great atmosphere, interest and vitality, which blends strong elements of design from earlier centuries with modern ideas in both planting and design. Arley is, therefore, a wonderful example of the idea that the best gardens are living, changing works of art. Outstanding features are the renowned double herbaceous border (c1846) the Quercus Ilex and pleached Lime Avenues, Victorian rootree, walled gardens, yew hedges and shrub rose collection. The family tradition continues today with the current Viscount Ashbrook, who over the last 30 years has created the less formal Grove and Woodland Walk, where 300 varieties of rhododendron grow amongst a collection of rare trees and shrubs in a delightful tranquil setting.

## Fact File

| | |
|---|---|
| **Opening Times:** | Garden, Chapel & Grove: 11am – 5pm Tuesday - Sunday, 22 March – 27 September, Weekends in October. Gardens open in October 2009 weekend only.<br>The Hall: 12 noon – 5pm, Tuesdays and Sundays plus Bank Holidays*, April through September Sundays only in October. *If your primary reason to visit is to see The Hall, please call The Estate Office on 01565 777353 to confirm opening times. |
| **Admission Rates:** | Gardens: Adults: £6.00, Seniors: £5.50, Children 5-16: £2.00, Family: £14, UNDER 5's free.<br>Hall: Adults: £2.50, Seniors: £2.00, Children 5-16: £1.00.<br>Season Tickets: Adults: £30.00, Joint: £50.00, Children 5-16: £12.00, Family: £70.00 |
| **Group Rates:** | Gardens: £5.00, Seniors: £4.50, Hall & Gardens: £6.50, Seniors: £5.75.<br>Season tickets: Individual £28, Joint: £46, Family: £64. |
| **Facilities:** | Shop, Plant Nursery, Licensed Restaurant, Teas, Picnic & Play Area, Chapel, Estate Walks. |
| **Disabled Access:** | Yes. Toilet and parking on site. Wheelchair available booking (recommended for special events). |
| **Tours/Events:** | Please check website for details. |
| **Coach Parking:** | Yes. |
| **Length of Visit:** | 2 hours |
| **Booking Contact:** | Arley Hall & Gardens, Northwich, Cheshire CW9 6NA<br>Telephone: 01565 777353  Fax: 01565 777465 |
| **Email:** | caroline.fearon@arleyhallandgardens.com |
| **Website:** | www.arleyhallandgardens.com |
| **Location:** | M6 – Junction 19 or 20, M56 Junction 9 or 10. Brown tourist signs from Northwich and Knutsford, both 6 miles approximately. |

Please quote this guide when making a booking

# Cholmondeley Castle Garden Cheshire

Cholmondeley Castle Garden is said by many to be among the most romantically beautiful gardens they have seen. Even the wild orchids, daisies and buttercups take on an aura of glamour in this beautifully landscaped setting. Visitors enter by the deer park mere – one of two strips of water which are home to many types of waterfowl and freshwater fish. Those who take advantage of the picnic site can walk round the lake and enjoy the splendid view of the Gothic Castle which stands so dramatically on the hill surrounded by sweeping lawns and magnificent trees: two enormous cedars of Lebanon and great spreading oaks among sweet chestnut, lime, beech and plane. Whatever the season there is always a wealth of plants and shrubs in flower from the earliest bulbs through many varieties of magnolia, camellia, azalea and rhododendrons. Followed by golden canopied laburnum grove, a very fine davidia involucrate in the glade, and varieties of cornus.
There is also a very pretty rose garden surrounded by mixed borders, containing a large variety of herbaceous plants and shrubs.

## Fact File

**Opening Times:** 2nd April 2010 to 26th September 2010 Wednesday, Thursday, Sundays and all Bank Holidays 1am - 5pm. Autumn tints 10th and 24th October 2010.
Castle only open to groups by prior arrangement.

**Admission Rates:** Adults: £5.00, Children: £2.00 from ages 5 to 16.

**Group Rates:** Minimum Group Size: 25

**Facilities:** Shop, Teas

**Disabled Access:** Yes. Toilet and parking for disabled on site.

**Tours/Events:** Please ring to enquire about special events, plays, concerts

**Car Parking:** Yes.

**Coach Parking:** Yes.

**Length of Visit:** 3 – 4 hours

**Booking Contact:** Cholmondeley Castle, Malpas, Cheshire SY14 8AH
Tel. 01829 720383  Fax. 01829 720877

**Email:** dilys@cholmondeleycastle.co.uk

**Website:** www.cholmondeleycastle.co.uk

**Location:** 7 miles west of Nantwich, 6 miles north of Whitchurch on A49.

Please quote this guide when making a booking

Ness Botanic Gardens celebrate a unique double - winning a Gold Medal and The Best in Show Award for the second year running, at The RHS Tatton Show in July 2009.

The highly imaginative show garden created by Chris Beardshaw, award winning designer and TV presenter has created this unique garden for Ness entitled 'Ness Botanische, Cheshire's Gardens of Distinction – Under the Microscope'. Visitors will have the opportunity to view the garden in spring 2010 which will become a key feature at Ness.

The superb gardens at Ness on the Wirral Peninsular, overlooking the Dee Estuary were founded in 1898 by Arthur Kilpin Bulley, a Liverpool cotton merchant with a passion for gardens and for plant hunting.

Our Visitor Centre provides a warm welcome to the Gardens incorporating the Four Seasons café, gift shop and plant sales. An extensive events programme runs throughout the year including guided walks, Sunday lectures, courses, children's half term activities, see our website for details www.nessgardens.org.uk Much of the garden is accessible for those of limited mobility and both courtesy wheelchairs and motorised buggies are available for advance booking.

## Fact File

**Opening Times:** 1st Feb – 31st Oct: 10 a.m. - 5 p.m.  1st Nov - 31st Jan: 10 a.m. - 4.30 p.m.

**Admission Charges:** Feb - Oct.  £6.50 per adult.  Concession (over 60's)  £5.50.  People with disabilities £5.50 Children (5 - 16 yrs) £3.00.  Family ticket (2 adults + 3 children) £18.00 Groups (up to 20 or more) £5.25.  Guide (up to 30 people) £30
Nov - Jan.  £4.50 per adult.  Concessions  (over 60's) £4.50.  People with disabilities £4.50 Children (5 - 16 yrs) £1.00.  Family ticket (2 adults + 3 children) £10.00 Groups (up to 20 or more) £4.25.  Guide (up to 30 people) £30

**On-Site Facilities:** Visitor Centre, Shop, Plant Sales, Licensed Restaurant, Teas, Lecture Theatre

**Disabled Access:** Yes, partial.  Wheelchair and mobility scooter loan available, booking required.

**Toilets on site:** Yes

**Car Parking on site:** Yes

**Coach Parking:** Yes

**Guided Tours:** Yes, booking required

**Length of Visit:** Approx. 2½ hours

**Special Events:** See www.nessgardens.org.uk

**Booking Contact:** Visitor Services, Ness Botanic Gardens, Ness, Neston, South Wirral, Cheshire CH64 4AY. Booking Tel No. 0151 353 0123  Booking Fax No. 0151 353 1004

**Email:** nessgdns@liv.ac.uk

**Website:** www.nessgardens.org.uk

**Location:** Road: off A540 Chester-Hoylake Road.

Please quote this guide when making a booking

Rode Hall Gardens were created by three notable landscape designers; Humphry Repton drew up the plans for the landscape and Rode Pool in his 'Red Book' of 1790. Between 1800 and 1810 John Webb, a Cheshire landscapist, constructed the Pool, an artificial lake of approximately 40 acres and at the same time he created the terraced rock garden and grotto. This area is covered in snowdrops in February followed by daffodils and bluebells and colour continues with the flowering of many specie and hybrid rhododendrons and azaleas in May.

In 1860 William Nesfield designed the rose garden and terrace where the flowerbeds are now filled with roses and a variety of herbaceous plants.

The two-acre walled kitchen garden dates from 1750 and grows a wide variety of flowers, vegetables and fruit. An Italian garden is being developed in the ruins of the old `Tenants Hall.

There is a fine icehouse and the Hall is open to the public on Wednesdays.

## Fact File

| | |
|---|---|
| **Opening times:** | Snowdrop walks: From 30th January to 7th March – daily except Mondays and Tuesdays 12–4pm. 1 April to 30 September: Tuesdays, Wednesdays, Thursdays and Bank Holidays (not Good Friday): 2 – 5pm. |
| **Admission Rates:** | Adults: £4.00, Senior Citizens £3.00, Children (over 12): £3.00 |
| **Group Rates:** | Minimum Groups Size: 15 |
| **Facilities:** | Shop, plant sales, teas, light lunches for snowdrop walkers in February only. |
| **Disabled Access:** | Limited. Toilet and car parking on site |
| **Tours/Events:** | Guided tours available. |
| **Coach Parking:** | Yes |
| **Length of Visit:** | 1 hour. |
| **Booking Contact:** | Valerie Stretton. Rode Hall Gardens, Rode Hall, Scholar Green, Cheshire ST7 3QN Telephone: 01270 882961 - 873237 Fax: 01270 882962 |
| **Email:** | richard.wilbra@btconnect.com |
| **Website:** | www.rodehall.co.uk |
| **Location:** | 5 miles south of Congleton, between A34 and A50. |

Please quote this guide when making a booking

Stapeley Water Gardens is the perfect destination all year round! The Palms Tropical Oasis is home to beautiful floral displays - from the Mediterranean splendour of the centre palms to the myriad of dazzling and exotic plants in the tropical house.

See aristolochia, beautiful orchids, variegated hibiscus, spectacular bougainvillea and the largest waterlily in the world, the Giant Amazonian Waterlily.

For a breath of fresh air, you can take a stroll outside to the beautiful and tranquil Italian Garden and unwind by the Japanese Koi Carp pool and Waterlily display. For some retail therapy you can take a trip to the enormous garden centre. Here you'll find everything you need for the garden and inspiration from the striking water gardens, with a Collection of Waterlilies in bloom from mid June to September.

## Fact File

| | |
|---|---|
| **Opening Times:** | Garden Centre: 9am–6pm. (summer), 9am – 5pm. (winter), Sundays: 10am– 4pm. |
| | Palms, Tropical Oasis: 10am–6pm. (summer), 10am– 5pm. (winter), Sundays: 10am– 5pm. |
| **Admission Rates:** | (Admission to Palms Tropical Oasis only) |
| | Adults: £4.95, Senior Citizens: £4.45, Children: £2.95, Family tickets (2A, 2C) £12.60. |
| **Group Rates:** | Minimum Groups Size: 15  Adults: £3.95, Senior Citizens: £3.55, Children: £2.35 |
| **Facilities:** | Shop, plant sales, restaurant, teas. Feeding schedule at the Palms Tropical Oasis every Sunday, plus a choice of three group entertainment packages (please request a leaflet). |
| **Disabled Access:** | Yes. Toilet and car parking on site. Wheelchair Loan booking available. |
| **Tours/Events:** | Different events throughout the year. |
| **Coach Parking:** | Yes |
| **Length of Visit:** | Approximately 3 hours. |
| **Booking Contact:** | Palms Reception. Stapeley Water Gardens, London Road, Nantwich, Cheshire. CW5 7LH |
| | Telephone: 01270 628628  Fax: 01270 624188 |
| **Email:** | palms@stapeleywg.com |
| **Website:** | www.stapeleywg.com |
| **Location:** | Signposted from J16, M6. 1 mile south of Nantwich on A51 |

Please quote this guide when making a booking

'*The marvel of the Boconnoc Estate today is that it is a world apart, an island of undulating pasture and mature woodland that abounds in long vistas and panoramas*'.
Marcus Binney, Country Life

Of many delightful gardens in Cornwall there are few which provide the opportunity to see the cornish landscape at its best. The Dorothy Garden, the Shrubbery and the valley garden each provide a contrast with the picturesque park beyond. A Golden Jubilee walk around the lake has been planted with daffodils. Using the original 1853 list the pinetum is being replanted into sections based on the points of the compass: the Americas, Europe and Asia with areas for Chile and New Zealand.

The first major Flower Show of the year, the Cornwall Garden Society Spring Flower Show is held at Boconnoc. The Stable Yard houses the competetive classes of camellias, magnolias, shrubs and daffodils, with nurseries, stands, floral and art exhibitions in the gardens around Boconnoc House.

## Fact File

**Opening Times:** Gardens open Sundays: April 18, 25; May 2, 9, 16, 23, 30 (all Sundays in May) 2 – 5 p.m.
**Admission Rates:** Adults: £4.50, Senior Citizens: £4.50, Children: Under 12 years: FREE
**Group Rates:** Group visits by appointment. Minimum Group Size: 15
Groups priced according to requirements, half day or whole day, coffee, lunch, tea and guided tour of house and garden, pre-booked throughout the year.
**Facilities:** Boconnoc House and stableyard, Catering by appointment.
**Disabled Access:** Yes.
**Toilet On Site:** Yes.
**Tours/Events:** Yes, booking required for tours. Special Events: Cornwall Spring Flower Show, 10, 11 April; Spring Fair 11, 12 May; Music in the Park 25 June; Boconnoc Steam Fair 23 – 25 July
**Coach Parking:** Yes.
**Car Parking:** Yes.
**Length of Visit:** 1½ - 5 hours.
**Booking Contact:** Veryan Barneby
The Estate Office Boconnoc, Lostwithiel, Cornwall PL22 0RG
Booking Telephone No. 01208 872507  Booking Fax No. 01208 873836
**Email:** adgfortescue@btinternet.com
**Website:** www.boconnocenterprises.co.uk
**Location:** Map 1-G8, Ordnance Survey Ref. 148 605.
A38 from Plymouth, Liskeard to Dobwalls roundabout or Bodmin to Dobwalls, then take A390 to Middle Taphouse

Please quote this guide when making a booking

Bosvigo is a 'must see' Cornish Colourist's garden created by owner Wendy Perry; an essential contrast to the grandeur and scale of the great Cornish Spring gardens. Wrapping around the lovely old house are a series of enclosed gardens with dazzling colour displays.

This is a garden both to love and to learn from. A spectacular Spring display of hellebores in the Woodland Garden is followed by breathtaking Summer herbaceous borders and on to the high drama of an Autumn finale of bold hot 'Firework' colours.

Visiting groups are treated to a private tour of the house and to tea in the historic kitchens which have been restored to their original Georgian glory. Bosvigo is a well-loved and lived-in family home, complete with a resident ghost reputed to linger in the Blue bedroom!

## Fact File

| | |
|---|---|
| **Opening times:** | 1 March – 29 September: Wednesday, Thursday & Friday 11 a.m. – 6 p.m. |
| **Admission Rates:** | Adults: £4.50, Senior Citizens: £4.50, Children: Under 5 free, Children 5 – 15 years £2.00 |
| **Group Rates:** | Minimum Group Size: 15. Adults: £4.50, Senior Citizens: £4.50, Children: Under 5 free, Children from 5 – 15 years £2.00 |
| **Facilities:** | Plant Sales, Help-yourself Teas |
| **Disabled Access:** | Yes, but limited |
| **Toilets on site:** | Yes |
| **Car Parking on site:** | Yes |
| **Coach Parking:** | Yes – Lane at side of house, by appointment only. |
| **Guided Tours:** | Yes (of the house only), booking required. |
| **Length of Visit:** | 1 – 2 hours, depending on level of plant interest |
| **Special Events:** | Fantastic Hellebore day, second week in February (look on website for date, or ring) Woodland walk open in aid of local charity, teas/lunches in old kitchens. |
| **Booking Contact:** | Mrs. Wendy Perry Bosvigo, Bosvigo House, Bosvigo Lane, Truro, Cornwall TR1 3NH Booking Tel No.01872 275774. |
| **Email:** | bosvigoplants@talktalk.net |
| **Website:** | www.bosvigo.com |
| **Location:** | OS SW8145 in the western suburbs of Truro by A390. At Highertown, turn down Dobbs Lane by Aldi Store. Bosvigo is 500 yards on the left after the nasty bend! |

Please quote this guide when making a booking

This 30-acre woodland gardens and nursery boasts award-winning displays and flowering features to captivate garden-enthusiasts and horticultural amateurs alike.

Perched on a hilltop, is home to one of the most diverse ranges of plants in the region.  Its sprawling woodland gardens and old flower garden are rich with the likes of camellias, azaleas and rhododendrons, as well as over 20 species of bamboo.

Its vast acreage is packed with prolific blooms all year round and you can take self-guided wanders to appreciate the beauty of the successive seasons.

On a Spring ramble witness the drifts of snowdrops, primroses and wild violets, and later the daffodils and blankets of nodding bluebells.  On a Summer wander it is the hydrangeas that spread their purple-blues and swamp the fading blooms of Spring.  Take an Autumn amble, when more subtle colours and hardy specimens still leave much to be discovered

## Fact File

| | |
|---|---|
| **Opening Times:** | Monday – Saturday: 8.30 – 5 p.m. Sunday 11 a.m. – 5 p.m. |
| **Admission Charges:** | (to gardens only, nursery free):  Adults: £2.00.  Conducted tour £2.50 each |
| **On-Site Facilities:** | Shop, Plant Sales, Teas |
| **Disabled Access:** | Yes |
| **Toilets on site:** | Yes |
| **Car Parking on site:** | Yes |
| **Coach Parking:** | Yes |
| **Length of Visit:** | 1½ - 2 hours |
| **Booking Contact:** | Stephen Dance, Burncoose Nurseries, Gwennap, Redruth, Cornwall TR16 6BJ Telephone No. 01209 860316  Fax No. 01209 860011 |
| **Email:** | info@burncoose.co.uk |
| **Website:** | www.burncoose.co.uk |
| **Location:** | On A393 betweenRedruth and Falmouth approximately half-way between villages of Lanner and Ponsanooth. |

Please quote this guide when making a booking

Lush, lovingly restored and utterly magical, Carwinion Garden lies in a sheltered Cornish valley on the Helford River. Ponds, waterfalls and sheltered pathways are dotted amongst the towering trees, bamboos and well-established plants in this twelve acre family run garden.

The garden contains a plethora of specimen plants, immense tree ferns over a hundred years old, gunnera with leaves spanning over two metres and ferns and Hellebores which flourish in the dappled sunlit woodland. Carwinion has one of the largest collections of bamboos in England; over two hundred different varieties (some exceedingly rare in cultivation) can be found growing throughout the garden and are at their best during the summer months.

The garden is at its pinnacle in Spring-time when the impact of colour, the bluebell carpeted woodland, the fragrance of the Azaleas and the continued blooming of the Camellias provides a sensual experience not to be missed.

## Fact File

| | |
|---|---|
| **Opening Times:** | All Year, every day 10am - 5.30pm |
| **Admission Rates:** | Adults £4.50, Senior Citizens £4.50, Child Free (under 16). |
| **Group Rates:** | Minimum group size: 10 |
| | Adults £4.00, Senior Citizens £4.00. |
| **Facilities:** | Plant Sales, Teas (2 - 5.30pm from May - Sept), Small Gift Shop. |
| **Disabled Access:** | Partial. Toilet and parking for disabled on site. |
| **Tours/Events:** | Occasional Art Exhibits & Theatre displayed in Gardens and House. |
| | We now offer guided tours of the Helford River with Helford River Expeditions by Canoe, Kayak or Boat, please see our website for more details. |
| **Coach Parking:** | yes, by arrangement |
| **Length of Visit:** | 1 - 2 hours |
| **Booking Contact:** | Jane Rogers |
| | Carwinion, Carwinion Road, Mawnan Smith, Nr Falmouth, Cornwall, TR11 5JA |
| | Telephone: 01326 250258 |
| **Email:** | jane@carwinion.co.uk |
| **Website:** | www.carwinion.co.uk |
| **Location:** | Five miles South-West of Falmouth, in the village of Mawnan Smith, North side of the Helford River. |

Please quote this guide when making a booking

Enys is considered to be the oldest garden in Cornwall. Robert de Enys lived there during the reign of Edward 1. The 1709 edition of Camden's Magna Britannia mentioned that Enys was noted for its fine gardens.

One of the main features is the Ladies Garden, later called the Flower Garden. This garden leads in to the Colonel's Garden, named after Colonel Enys (1757 -1818) and is currently being replanted as a scented garden.

J D Enys, an inveterate traveller, greatly enriched Enys with seeds and plants he regularly sent home from New Zealand and Patagonia.

In spring the bluebells in the parkland, known as Parc Lye, are a sight to behold. This area is believed to be undisturbed since ancient times.

Probably the most valuable asset to the garden is its microclimate together with its peaceful and tranquil setting.

## Fact File

| | |
|---|---|
| **Opening Times:** | Tuesdays, Thursdays, and the first Sunday of the month from 2 p.m., 1st April to 30th Sept. |
| **Admission Rates:** | Adults: £4.00, Senior Citizens: £3.00, Children and students: £1.00. |
| **Facilities:** | Teas. |
| **Disabled Access:** | Yes, wheelchair loan available. |
| **Toilets on site:** | Yes. |
| **Tours/Events:** | Guided tours available, booking required. |
| **Coach Parking:** | Yes. |
| **Car Parking on site:** | Yes. |
| **Length of Visit:** | 1-2 hours. |
| **Booking Contact:** | W. H. Ward<br>Enys Gardens, St Gluvias, Penryn, Cornwall<br>Telephone: 01872 274536 or 07770 662849<br>Fax: 01872 223421 |
| **Email:** | whwone@supanet.com |
| **Website:** | www.enystrust.org.uk |
| **Location:** | Off Truro to Falmouth road, A39.<br>From Truro: 2nd left after Norway Inn. Follow signs.<br>From Falmouth: to Penryn (B3292). At Cross Keys pub, right fork into Truro Hill and follow signs. |

Please quote this guide when making a booking

# The Lost Gardens of Heligan Cornwall

Heligan, seat of the Tremayne family for more than 400 years, is one of the most mysterious estates in England. At the end of the nineteenth century its thousand acres were at their zenith; but only a few years after the Great War of 1914, bramble and ivy were already drawing a green veil over this sleeping beauty.

After decades of neglect, the devastating hurricane of 1990 should have consigned the Lost Gardens of Heligan to a footnote in history. Instead, fired by a magnificent obsession to bring these once glorious gardens back to life, a small band of enthusiasts has grown into a large working team with its own vision for Heligan's future.

Today "The Nation's Favourite Garden" offers 200 acres for exploration including restored productive gardens, working buildings and historic glasshouses, atmospheric pleasure grounds and a subtropical "Jungle" valley, surrounded by a sustainably managed estate incorporating a pioneering wildlife project.

## Fact File

**Opening Times:** From 10am daily, all year round. (Except Christmas Eve and Christmas Day).

**Admission Rates:** Adults £10.00, Senior Citizens £9.00, Child £6.00, Family (2 adults and 3 children) £27.00

**Groups Rates:** Minimum group size 20, prior booking is essential.
Adults £8.00, Senior Citizens £7.00, Child £6.00. Pre-booked guided tour additional £1pp.

**Facilities:** Licensed Tea Rooms, Lunchtime Servery, Heligan Shop and Plant Sales, Lobbs Farm Shop. No Dogs April - September incl.

**Disabled Access:** Yes. All facilities and throughout most of the garden restoration and wildlife hide. Wheelchairs are available on a first come first served basis. Contact us for information in various formats.

**Tours/Events:** Please telephone for seasonal details or see our website.

**Coach Parking:** Yes, by prior arrangement.

**Length of Visit:** At least 4 hours

**Booking Contact:** Group Bookings Department.
The Lost Gardens of Heligan, Pentewan, St Austell, Cornwall, PL26 6EN.
Telephone: 01726 845120   Fax: 01726 845101

**Email:** info@heligan.com

**Website:** www.heligan.com

**Location:** From St Austell, take the Mevagissey Road (B3273) and follow the brown tourist signs to "The Lost Gardens of Heligan".

Please quote this guide when making a booking

One of only three Grade 1 listed Cornish Gardens set within the 865 acres of the Country Park overlooking Plymouth Sound. Sir Richard Edgcumbe of Cotehele built a new home in his deer park at Mount Edgcumbe in 1547. Miraculously the walls of this red stone Tudor House survived a direct hit by bombs in 1941 and it was restored by the 6th Earl in 1958. It is now beautifully furnished with family possessions.

The two acre Earl's Garden was created beside the House in the 18th century. Ancient and rare trees are set amidst classical garden houses and an exotic Shell Seat. Colourful flowers and heather grace the re-created Victorian East Lawn terrace. Also formal 18th Century Gardens in Italian, French & English style, modern American & New Zealand sections. There are over 1000 varieties in the National Camellia Collection which received the international award of 'Camellia Garden of Excellence'.

Mount Edgcumbe, RHS Britain in Bloom Public Park Awards 2007.

## Fact File

**Opening Times:** House & Earls Garden open April - September, Sunday to Thursday 11am - 4.30pm; Country Park open all year.

**Admission Rates:** House & Earls Garden - Adults £6.00, Senior Citizen £5.00, Child £3.50, Country Park Free.

**Groups Rates:** Minimum group size: 10 ( April - September) Adults and Senior Citizens £5.00, Child £3.20

**Facilities:** Orangery Restaurant, Stables Tea Room, Plant Centre and Shop (limited opening in winter), Civil Weddings, Conference Facilities.

**Disabled Access:** Yes. Toilet and parking for disabled on site. Wheelchairs on loan, booking necessary.

**Tours/Events:** Guided tours of the gardens available all year. Historic buildings, Camellia Collection in season. Exhibition and events programme. Introductory talk given to booked groups.

**Coach Parking:** Yes

**Length of Visit:** 2 hours

**Booking Contact:** Secretary. Mount Edgcumbe House, Cremyll, Torpoint, Cornwall, PL10 1HZ Telephone : 01752 822236 Fax: 01752 822199

**Email:** mt.edgcumbe@plymouth.gov.uk

**Website:** www.mountedgcumbe.gov.uk

**Location:** From Plymouth Cremyll Foot Ferry, Torpoint Ferry or Saltash Bridge. From Cornwall via Liskeard - to A374, B3247, follow brown signs.

Please quote this guide when making a booking

Pencarrow, the much-loved home of the Molesworth-St Aubyn family for nearly 500 years, is set in 50 acres of Grade II* woodland and garden where dogs and children are most welcome.

Superb specimen conifers from around the world tower over a profusion of azaleas, magnolias and camellias galore, with 700 varieties of rhododendron adding to the blaze of spring colour; blue hydrangeas line the mile-long carriage drive throughout the summer.

Start exploring and you'll find a surprise around every corner – ancient Celtic cross, a 2, 000 year old Iron Age hill fort, Victorian lake and ice house, grotto, restful Italian gardens with fountain and an enormous rockery that was once the largest in the country.

The Georgian house boasts an impressive library with secret door (think of Harry Potter meets Narnia), elegant but "lived in" reception rooms, period bedrooms and collections of family prams, dolls, oriental porcelain, fascinating antique furniture and portraits.

## Fact File

| | |
|---|---|
| **Opening times:** | Gardens: daily 9.30 – 5.30 from March 1st – October 31st.  House, café and shop: Sunday – Thursday inclusive: 11 a.m. – 5 p.m. from 28 March – 30 September (last tour of house at 3 p.m.) |
| **Admission Rates:** | Adults: House: £8.50, Gardens: £4.00, Senior Citizens:  £8.50, Gardens: £4.00, Children: House: £4.00 Gardens: £1.00.  Under 5s: free  Historic Houses Association Members Free |
| **Group Rates:** | Minimum Group Size: 20.  Adults: from £6.00, Senior Citizens: £6.00 Children: Please contact administrator |
| **Facilities:** | Shop, Plant Sales, Teas |
| **Disabled Access:** | Yes (partly).  Wheelchair loan available – booking required |
| **Toilets on site:** | Yes |
| **Car Parking on site:** | Yes |
| **Coach Parking:** | Yes |
| **Guided Tours:** | Yes, booking required on arrival at house. |
| **Length of Visit:** | House: 1 hour; gardens 2+ hours |
| **Special Events:** | Please see website for craft fairs, outdoor theatre etc. |
| **Booking Contact:** | Sally Harvey, Pencarrow, Washaway, Bodmin, Cornwall PL30 3AG Booking Tel No.01208 841369,  Booking Fax No. 01208 841722 |
| **Email:** | info@pencarrow.co.uk |
| **Website:** | www.pencarrow.co.uk |
| **Location:** | 4 miles north of Bodmin on A389 |

# Penjerrick Garden Cornwall

'Few gardens have the wonderful atmosphere of Penjerrick, another creation of the Fox family, the great Cornish master gardeners. Penjerrick has a valley site sloping towards the sea. But here there is a character of wildness which provides exactly the right contrast to some of the more swaggering rhododendrons which are such a striking feature of the garden. Superlative old beeches, copper and ordinary, date from the early 1800s and provide a stately background to more exotic planting.' (Quotation – Patrick Taylor).  Penjerrick is a 15 acre Grade II listed Spring-flowering garden containing rhododendrons, camellias, bamboos, magnolias, azaleas and some magnificent trees.

The lower valley garden, reached by a wooden bridge, contains a network of ponds, giant tree ferns and gunnera in a wild, somewhat primeval woodland setting. It preserves a jungle-like exuberance and visitors, if suitably booted, should enjoy their experience.

## Fact File

| | |
|---|---|
| **Opening Times:** | 1st March – September 30th: Wednesday, Friday and Sunday 1.30 – 4.30 But coach parties any day – mornings preferred |
| **Admission Rates:** | Adults: £3.00, Senior Citizens: £3.00, Children: £1.50 |
| **Group Rates:** | Minimum Group Size: 20, Adults: £2.50 , Senior Citizens: £2.50, Children: £1.50 |
| **Facilities:** | None |
| **Disabled Access:** | No. |
| **Toilet On Site:** | No, but one in house nearby |
| **Tours/Events:** | Occasional guided tours, booking required. |
| **Coach Parking:** | Yes, one at gate 200 yards from garden – prior notice please |
| **Car Parking:** | Yes. |
| **Length of Visit:** | 1½ hours |
| **Booking Contact:** | Mrs. Rachel Morin, Penjerrick Garden, Penjerrick, Budock Water, Falmouth, Cornwall. TR11 5ED Tel. 01872 870105 |
| **Email:** | racheltmorin@tiscali.co.uk |
| **Website:** | www.penjerrickgarden.co.uk |
| **Location:** | Three miles south-west of Falmouth between villages of Budock and Mawnan Smith. Coach access via Budock (not Mabe/Argal as lanes too narrow). |

Please quote this guide when making a booking

A unique and extraordinary maritime garden created in terraces just above the sea, at the foot of a magical castle St. Michael's Mount.

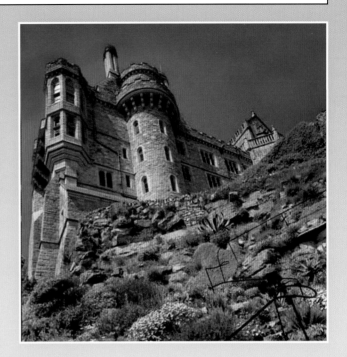

Visitors to St. Michael's Mount are often surprised to find there are gardens here at all, clinging to a granite rock face that is almost vertical, falling some 200 feet from the castle to the sea far below.

The gardens are buffeted by the winter gales and drenched in salt spray, then they become a tranquil oasis during the summer months.  The warm Gulf Stream coupled with the heat retentive granite cliffs and walls enable a wide range of tender and exotic plants to be grown in the south facing gardens.

Access to the island is by motorboat or causeway.

## Fact File

| | |
|---|---|
| **Opening times:** | Garden:  1st May – 30th June, Monday to Friday. |
| | 1st July – 29th October, Thursdays and Friday only. |
| | Castle:  28th March - 31st October - Sunday to Friday. |
| | Combined Castle & Garden ticket also available. |
| | All visits subject to favourable weather conditions |
| **Admission Rates:** | Garden Only, Adults: £3.50, Children: £1.00, NT members Free. |
| | Guided Tour of Gardens with one of Mount Gardeners £5.50 per person. |
| **Group Rates:** | Minimum Group Size: 15 |
| **Facilities:** | National Trust Sail Loft Restaurant and Island Café, shops and plant sales |
| **Disabled Access:** | Bookable Sand wheelchair available for loan. |
| **Tours/Events:** | Guided tours available. Free trail available for younger children. Garden Evenings available - a guided tour of the garden followed by a gourmet buffet at the award-winning Sail Loft restaurant.  Please telephone or check the website for details. |
| **Coach Parking:** | On mainland. |
| **Length of Visit:** | 2 – 3 hours |
| **Booking Contact:** | Clare Sandry, Manor Office, Marazion, Cornwall TR17 0EF |
| | Tel: 01736 710507  Fax: 01736 719930 |
| **Email:** | clare@manor-office.co.uk |
| **Website:** | www.stmichaelsmount.co.uk |
| **Location:** | ½ mile South of A394 at Marazion |

Please quote this guide when making a booking

Discover the magic of 26 acres of sub-tropical paradise falling 200 feet from the 18th century house to a private beach on Helford River.

A stream cascades over waterfalls through ponds full of Koi Carp and exotic water plants, winds through 2 acres of blue and white hydrangeas and spills out over the beach. Huge Australian tree ferns and palms mingle with shrubs of ever changing colours and scent beneath an over-arching canopy of 100 year old rhododendrons and magnolias.

A giant plantation of gunnera and clumps of huge bamboos give the garden a unique and exotic wildness matched by no other garden in the British Isles.

The architecturally dynamic Hibbert Centre houses an award wining cafe, garden and gift shop.  Children love Trebah, as do dogs (welcome on leads).  A garden for all the family and all seasons

## Fact File

| | |
|---|---|
| **Opening Times:** | Open every day of the year from 10.00am. Winter times may vary slightly. |
| **Admission Rates:** | Adults £7.50, Senior Citizen £6.50, Child £2.50. 1st Nov 2009 - 28th Feb 2010, Adults £3.00, Senior Citizen £2.50, Child £1.00. RHS Members Free entry: Nov, Dec, Jan, Feb & March. NT Members Free entry: Nov, Dec, Jan & Feb. |
| **Group Rates:** | Minimum group size: 12 Adults £6.00, Senior Citizen £6.00, Child £2.50. |
| **Facilities:** | Visitor Centre, Shop, Plant Sales, Teas, Restaurant. |
| **Disabled Access:** | Yes, Toilet and parking for disabled on site. Wheelchairs on loan, booking advised. |
| **Tours/Events:** | Free welcome talk on arrival, full guided tour of one and a half hours at an extra £2.00 per head - must be booked in advance. |
| **Coach Parking:** | Yes. |
| **Length of Visit:** | 2 1/2 - 3 hours |
| **Booking Contact:** | V Woodcroft Trebah Garden, Mawnan Smith, Falmouth, Cornwall, TR11 5JZ. Telephone: 01326 252200 Fax: 01326 250781 |
| **Email:** | mail@trebah-garden.co.uk |
| **Website:** | www.trebah-garden.co.uk |
| **Location:** | From north - A39 from Truro to Treliever Cross Roundabout, follow brown and white tourism signs to Trebah. |

Please quote this guide when making a booking

# Trevarno Estate & National Museum of Gardening     Cornwall

A unique and unforgettable garden experience comprising of 70 acres of gardens and grounds, with abundant wildlife and one of Cornwall's largest and most diverse plant collections. Follow the progress of major restoration projects and walk the 2km Estate walk passing the spectacular National Daffodil Collection and visit Santa's reindeer while they holiday in Cornwall.

More formal areas include the Serpentine Yew Tunnel, Italian Garden and Great Lawn. Relax in the Fountain Garden Conservatory and enjoy homemade refreshments. Visit the remarkable National Museum of Gardening, fascinating Soap Museum or nostalgic Vintage Toy Museum, plant sales or shop, which sells our own Organic Skincare products. For the youngsters there is the Woodland Play area to let off steam.

## Fact File

| | |
|---|---|
| **Opening Times:** | 10.30am - 5pm all year except Christmas Day & Boxing Day. |
| **Admission Rates:** | Adults £6.85, Senior Citizens £5.95, Child £2.35, Disabled £3.45. |
| **Group Rates:** | Minimum group size: 12 |
| | Adults £4.75, Senior Citizen £4.25, Child £1.40. |
| **Facilities:** | The National Museum of Gardening, Shop, Plant Sales, Tea Room, Vintage Soap Collection, Craft Workshops, *Vintage Toy Collection (*small additional charge). |
| | National Daffodil Collection Showgarden. |
| **Disabled Access:** | Partial. Toilet and parking for disabled on site. Wheelchairs on loan, booking essential. |
| **Tours/Events:** | Numerous events throughout the year. Please call for details or visit www.trevarno.co.uk. |
| **Coach Parking:** | Yes, for up to 6 coaches. |
| **Length of Visit:** | 4 hours |
| **Booking Contact:** | Garden Co-ordinator |
| | Trevarno Estate, Trevarno Manor, Crowntown, Nr Helston, Cornwall, TR13 ORU |
| | Telephone: 01326 574274  Fax: 01326 574282 |
| **Email:** | enquiry@trevarno.co.uk |
| **Website:** | www.trevarno.co.uk |
| **Location:** | Trevarno is located immediately east of Crowntown village - leave Helston on Penzance Road and follow the brown signs. |

Please quote this guide when making a booking

Trewithen means 'house of the trees' and the name truly describes this fine early Georgian house in its splendid setting of wood and parkland.

Country Life described the house as 'one of the outstanding West Country houses of the 18th century' and Penelope Hobhouse has described the garden as 'perhaps the most beautiful woodland garden in England'.

2004 was the 100th year in which George Johnstone inherited Trewithen and started developing the gardens as we know them today. The great glade on the south side is a masterpiece of landscape gardening and is a monument to the genius of George Johnstone. These gardens covering some thirty acres are renowned for their magnificent collection of camellias, rhododendrons, magnolias and many rare trees and shrubs which are seldom found elsewhere in Britain. The extensive woodland gardens are surrounded by traditional landscaped parkland.

## Fact File

**Opening Times:** Open 1st March to 30th September, 10am to 4.30pm Monday to Saturday. Sundays (March to May only).

**Admission Rates:** Adults £7.50

**Groups Rate:** Minimum group size: 20
Group £5.00

**Facilities:** Trewithen Tea Shop, Plant Sales, Camera Obscura, Viewing Platforms.

**Disabled Access:** Yes. Toilet and Parking for disabled on site. Wheelchairs on loan.

**Tours/Events:** Guided tours available, prior booking is essential. Occasional special events please telephone for details.

**Coach Parking:** Yes

**Length of Visit:** 2 - 2½ hours

**Booking Contact:** Glenys Cates
Trewithen Gardens, Grampound Road, Nr Truro, Cornwall, TR2 4DD
Telephone: 01726 883647  Fax: 01726 882301

**Email:** gardens@trewithen-estate.demon.co.uk

**Website:** www.trewithengardens.co.uk

**Location:** On the A390 between Truro and St Austell.

Brantwood's gardens and estate are like no other. Mature Victorian landscape gardens lead to Ruskin's own experimental landscapes, to ancient woodlands, high Moorland and spectacular views. Completion of the Zig-Zaggy, a garden begun by John Ruskin 130 years ago, and the High Walk, a spectacular Victorian viewing platform, brings a total of eight gardens restored at Brantwood. Expect the unexpected and explore 250 acres of fascinating landscape.

Whichever season you choose to visit you are assured year round interest. Spectacular azaleas in springtime; a collection of ferns, herbs and colourful herbaceous borders in summer; the vibrant colours of autumn; or a winter snowfall can transform the gardens into a winter wonderland.

Stroll the paths, sit and marvel at the magnificent views. Whatever you choose to do, you will take home with you the discovery of John Ruskin's legacy and inspiration.

## Fact File

| | |
|---|---|
| **Opening Times:** | Mid - March to mid - November daily 11am - 5.30pm. |
| | Mid - November to mid - March Wednesday - Sunday 11am - 4.30pm. |
| **Admission Rates:** | Adults £6.95 / £4.95 garden only, Child £1.50 |
| **Groups Rates:** | Minimum group size: 10 |
| | Adults £5.95 / £4.20 garden only, Child £1.50 |
| **Facilities:** | Shop, Plant Sales, Restaurant, Craft Gallery. |
| **Disabled Access:** | Partial. Toilet and parking for disabled on site. Wheelchairs on loan, booking necessary. |
| **Tours/Events:** | A wide variety of events await, please check website for details. |
| **Coach Parking:** | Yes but limited. |
| **Length of Visit:** | 4 - 6 hours |
| **Booking Contact:** | Heather Chislett |
| | Brantwood, Coniston, Cumbria, LA21 8AD |
| | Telephone: 01539 441396   Fax: 01539 441263 |
| **Email:** | heather@brantwood.org.uk |
| **Website:** | www.brantwood.org.uk |
| **Location:** | 2¼ miles east of Coniston. signposted from Coniston. |

Winderwath is a garden of five acres originally laid out at the beginning of the twentieth Century. The mature trees including Wellingtonia, Cut Leaf Beech and Cedar, date from this time. Extensive work has been carried out on the rockeries and herbaceous borders since the 1950s. More recently the pond area has been opened up

There is now a large collection of Alpine and Himalayan plants, including Arisaema and Moconopsis. There are many rare and unusual perennials including a good display of Salvias. We are well known for the display of Aconites and Daffodils in the Spring. There is a working vegetable garden in the Edwardian walled garden with apricots, nectarines and peaches in the greenhouses.

We have a selection of plants grown for sale and also sell second-hand garden tools. There are picnic tables round the pond area where you are welcome to enjoy a quiet lunch.

## Fact File

| | |
|---|---|
| **Opening times:** | 10.00 a.m. – 4.00 p.m. Monday – Friday. Saturday: 9 a.m. – 12 noon |
| **Admission Rates:** | Adults: £3.50. Senior Citizens: £3,50 |
| **Group Rates:** | Minimum Group Size: 12 |
| **Facilities:** | Plant Sales, Second-hand garden tools for sale. Toilets. |
| **Disabled Access:** | Partial |
| **Car Parking on site:** | Yes |
| **Tours/Events:** | Guided tours available. Booking required. |
| **Length of Visit:** | 1½ hours |
| **Booking Contact:** | Jane Pollock |
| | Winderwath Gardens |
| | Winderwath, Nr. Temple Sowerby |
| | Penrith, Cumbria CA10 2AG |
| | Booking Telephone No: 01768 88250 |
| | Booking Fax No: 01786 88250 |
| **Location:** | 5 miles east of Penrith on A66, Take B6412 to Culgaith and Temple Sowerby, from Temple Sowerby bypass, turn left onto old A66, 200 yards on right. |

Renishaw Hall is the home of the Sitwell family, as it has been for 380 years. Its eight-acre Italianate gardens, designed by Sir George Sitwell, were laid out more than 100 years ago, and are among the most beautiful in the country. There are several garden rooms, hedged with sharply-cut yew, and there is always the sound of moving water in the background, often reflected in still pools. On 28 February, we have our Fanfare for Spring, the only opportunity for visitors to see the structure of the garden at its best. There will also be specialist plant nurseries displaying and selling rare winter flowering plants. From 22 April – 9 May Renishaw's bright bluebells are out in the ancient woods, with rhododendrons, camellias and magnolias in the newly-created woodland garden. 1000 roses bloom in June, which is the month the delphinums also reach their peak. The Laburnum Tunnel is bright yellow around the end of May, and later in the summer the herbaceous borders come into their own. Sir George's classical structure remains, but for the past year Head Gardener David Kesteven has been working with internationally-famous designer Anthony Noel, known for his dramatic design and use of colour and shape. Children can work off their energy in the new Fairytale Garden designed especially for them to play in and explore.

## Fact File

**Opening Times:** Gardens open April 1st to September 28th 10.30am - 4.30pm. Thurs to Sun & Bank Holidays.  Hall: every Friday in the season.

**Admission Rates:** Gardens - Adults: £6.00, Concessions: £4.95, Children under 12 Free.  Hall: £11.00

**Facilities:** Café, Shop, The Sitwell Museum, Sir Osbert Sitwell Exhibition, free film: Renishaw Hall and the Sitwells. The Rex Whistler Dinner & Conference Room.  Wedding facilities available.

**Disabled Access:** Partial access. Disabled toilets and car parking.

**Tours/Events:** Group bookings (25+) available for The Hall when closed to public (ring for details – pre booking essential). Guided tours of vineyard and garden available.
Fanfare for Spring - 28 February.  22 April - 9 May: Bluebell Fortnight.
Other events all year (information on website).

**Coach Parking:** Yes

**Length of Visit:** Hall tour – 1½ hours

**Booking Contact:** Administrator
Renishaw Hall Gardens, Renishaw Hall, Renishaw Park, Renishaw, Nr. Sheffield, S21 3WB.
Telephone: 01246 432310  Fax: 01246 430760

**Email:** Info2@renishaw-hall.co.uk

**Website:** www.renishaw-hall.co.uk

**Location:** Junction 30 off the M1. A6135 to Sheffield/Eckington.

Broomhill lies in one of the most glorious valleys in North Devon surrounded by hundreds of acres of woodland and bound by its own stream. The Broomhill Sculpture Park displays one of the largest permanent collections of contemporary art and sculpture in the South West. 300 sculptures by over 60 sculptors are sited in 10 acres of garden that present a wonderful balance between art and nature.  The woodland gardens provide all year round interest and are home to numerous birds and insects. The gardens are full of colour in the Summer, Autumn and are particularly beautiful in the Spring, with successions of Spring flowers including Snowdrops, Daffodils, Primroses, Bluebells and Azaleas.   The award winning Broomhill Kitchen is based around the 'Slow food' philosophy, where respect for authentic produce and local ingredients is paramount to our offering - pure celebration on a plate. Consisting of mainly Mediterranean cuisine using fresh, organic, fair trade produce from neighbouring farms and the coast, the menu affords splendid choice and excellent value.  Group lunches and cream teas are available, served in our intimate restaurant or outside on the sun-warmed terrace.  Special offer for groups of Ten and over: Mediterranean one-course lunch and garden ticket, £10pp (booking is essential). If you fancy making an all-day trip to the area, the stunning Marwood Hill Gardens is only 10 minutes away from Broomhill.

## Fact File

**Opening times:** Sculpture Gardens: Open all year (Mon-Sun) 11:00 until 16:00. Art Gallery: Open all year (Wed-Sun) 11:00 until 16:00.  (Occasionally the gallery will be closed for short periods for re-hanging or for other reasons.)  Restaurant: Lunch - Wed, Thu, Fri & Sun, Dinner -  Fri & Sat  (Occasionally the restaurant will be closed for functions.) Hotel:  Open all year Mon - Sun.   Please note: We are closed between 20 Dec and 15 Jan.

**Admission Rates:** Adults: £4.50, Senior Citizens: £3.50, Children: £1.50, (15 and under,) Family ticket: £10.00 (2 adults + 2 under 15)

**Group Rates:** Minimum Group Size: 10.  Adults: £3.50, Senior Citizens: £2.50, Children: £1.50

**Facilities:** Restaurant / Café, Sculpture Park & Gallery, Hotel Accommodation, Conference / Meeting Rooms, Event Venue, Wedding Receptions and Ceremonies.  Available for purchase at Broomhill: Sculptures, gallery art-work, gift vouchers, postcards and art T-shirts.

**Disabled Access:** Yes, but limited.   The restaurant, gallery, & terrace is accessible by wheelchair, the accommodation and garden is not.  Disabled parking is available.

**Toilets on site:** Yes

**Parking:** Yes, car and coach parking for up to 2 coaches.

**Tours/Events:** Booking required for tours, Broomhill hosts a variety of exciting events throughout the year, exhibitions, workshops, monthly Jazz concerts, lectures and food events. The Broomhill Art & Sculpture Foundation's National Sculpture Prize Exhibition opens in June 2010 (please visit our website for details).

**Length of Visit:** 2 – 3 hours

**Booking Contact:** Broomhill Art Hotel, Muddiford Rd, Barnstaple, Devon, EX31 4EX. Telephone. 01271 850262

**Email/Website:** info@broomhillart.co.uk  -  www.broomhillart.co.uk

**Location:** From Barnstaple, A39 towards Lynton, left onto the B3230 towards Ilfracombe.  Broomhill is signposted 2 miles after the NDD Hospital

Please quote this guide when making a booking

# Castle Hill Gardens Devon

Situated in the rolling hills of Devon, Castle Hill Gardens provides a tranquil and spectacular setting for the elegant Palladian house built in 1730 by the Earl of Fortescue. Stroll through the 18th century landscaped garden with mystical temples, follies, statues and ponds and enjoy the Millenium Garden designed by Xa Tollemache with its striking water feature. The path then leads you across the formal terraces in front of the house where the eye is drawn to the distant Triumphal Arch. Wander through the woodland gardens, planted with rhododendrons, azaleas, camellias, magnolias and many fine shrubs and trees and finally down to the river at Ugley Bridge and the magical Satyr's Temple. The splendid castle perched on top of the hill has panoramic views to Exmoor, Dartmoor and Lundy Island. Finish your visit with a look round the recently planted walled garden.

## Fact File

**Opening Times:** 2nd April 2010 - 30th September 2010, Every day except Saturdays 11.00am - 5.00pm Last admission 4.30pm. Autumn colour walks every sunday in October 11.00am - 4.00pm.

**Admission Rates:** Adults - £4, Senior Citizens £3.50, Children under 14 free.

**Group Rates:** Minimum size 20+, Adults £3.50.National Trust members not free, RHS members not free.

**Facilities:** Teas and refreshments available, Groups and coach parties must pre order lunches and teas in the West Wing.

**Disabled Access:** Yes but there are gravel paths and some areas are only accessible by steep paths.

**Tours/Events:** Yes, booking required, time required - minimum 1 hour.

**Events:** Primrose Sunday and Monday - Sunday 2nd and Monday 3rd May.
One of the most beautiful times of the year in the gardens. Enjoy a wander through the woodland gardens where carpets of primroses stretch down to the river. Cream teas and refreshments available. Easter Bunny Hunt - Sunday 4th April. Filleigh Fun Day 21st August More events on website. Booking Tel. 01598 760336 x 1. Booking Fax. 01598 760457

**Car/Coach Parking:** Yes.

**Toilets On Site:** Yes.

**Length of Visit:** 3 – 4 hours

**Booking Contact:** Clare Agertoft, Castle Hill Gardens, Filleigh, Barnstaple, Devon EX32 0RQ.

**Email:** gardens@castlehill-devon.com

**Website:** www.castlehilldevon.co.uk

**Location:** See website - Leave A361 (north devon link road) at roundabout signed South Molton onto B3226. Take second turning right signed 'Stags Head and Filleigh'. Shortly after passing through Stags Head look out for yellow lodge on right.

This inspirational garden blends seamlessly into a timeless Devon landscape, and offers magnificent views in all directions. Today, the garden extends to 8 acres and is several gardens in one, using over 6,000 varieties of plants to great effect in both traditional and naturalistic planting styles.

In spring – admire magnificent collections of camellias, magnolias and rhododendrons. Enjoy the Bulb Meadow with its masses of woodland plants such as erythroniums, anemones, cyclamen and bluebells.

In summer – experience the delights of the famous Walled Garden built around medieval ruins, wisteria bridges, the exotic South African Garden as well as the romantic Cottage Garden and Wild Flower Meadow.

In autumn – over 50 Japanese maples provide a kaleidoscope of autumnal colour.

Plant Sales has an excellent range of plants, including many of the beautiful ones grown in the garden.

The Garden Tearooms are situated in the 18th century former vicarage and serve delicious homemade cakes, Devon cream teas and light lunches.

## Fact File

**Opening times:** 10.30 a.m. – 5.00 p.m. daily 27 February – 31 October 2010.
Weekends only in February (Snowdrops and early spring bulbs).
**Admission Rates:** Adults: £6.00, Children: £2.50 (5 – 16 years)
**Group Rates:** Minimum Group Size: 15. Standard Rate: £5.50
**Facilities:** Plant Sales, tearooms serving lunches and teas
**Disabled Access:** Limited disabled access. Not all areas are flat.
**Toilets on site:** Yes
**Car Parking on site:** Yes
**Coach Parking:** Yes
**Guided Tours:** Yes, booking required.
**Length of Visit:** 2 hours
**Special Events:** A full event programme throughout the year. Please telephone for details or see our website.
**Booking Contact:** Rachel Young, Administrator, The Garden House, Buckland Monachorum,
Yelverton, Devon, PL20 7LQ
Booking Tel No. 01822 854769.
**Email:** office@thegardenhouse.org.uk
**Website:** www.thegardenhouse.org.uk
**Location:** 10 miles north of Plymouth. Signed off A386 at Yelverton.

Please quote this guide when making a booking

Created by Dr. Jimmy Smart – a fine plantsman. Marwood Hill has 20 acres of beautiful gardens and three small lakes set in a sheltered valley setting. A haven for trees and shrubs from around the world as well as herbaceous and alpine plants giving all year round interest and colour. The gardens are well known for the extensive collection of Camellias and National Collections of Astilbe, Japanese Iris and Tulbaghia. There are many areas where the visitor can rest, experience the tranquillity and enjoy the many inspiring aspects of the gardens.

The walled garden plant centre sells a wide range of plants, most of which have been grown and propagated in the gardens. Knowledgeable staff are usually available to help and advise.

The Garden Tearoom overlooking the garden offers a selection of light lunches, home baked cakes and Devon cream teas.

You could also visit Broomhall Art & Sculpture Garden nearby all in one day.

## Fact File

| | |
|---|---|
| **Opening Times:** | Open Daily 1st March – 31st October. Gardens and the Garden Tea Room: 10am – 5pm. Plant Centre: 11am – 5pm. Special openings in winter please contact us for information or check our website for details. |
| **Admission Rates:** | Adult £5.50, Children (under 12) Free, Children 12-16 £2.50. |
| **Group Rates:** | Group 10+ £5.00 Includes an introductory talk by Head Gardener. By appointment only. |
| **Facilities:** | Visitor Information, Plant Centre, the Garden Tea Room |
| **Disabled Access:** | Yes but limited. Ramped access to Plant Centre and The Garden Tea Room. Please contact us for more information. |
| **Tours/Events:** | Guided tours available. Events held. Contact the booking office for details. |
| **Coach Parking:** | Yes |
| **Length of Visit:** | 3 hours – all day. |
| **Booking Contact:** | Mrs Patricia Stout<br>Marwood Hill Gardens, Marwood, Barnstaple. North Devon EX31 4EB<br>Telephone 01271 342528. |
| **Email:** | info@marwoodhillgarden.co.uk |
| **Website:** | www.marwoodhillgarden.co.uk |
| **Location:** | 4 miles north of Barnstaple (Google map link on our website) |

Please quote this guide when making a booking

The 80 acre gardens of Paignton Zoo consist of mature shrubberies and newer areas developed over the past 10 years. The plantings are designed to create the feeling of a natural habitat by using geographic and educationally themed displays. New garden areas include a Mediterranean climate garden, an economic plant garden and a medicinal garden.

There are three glasshouses, which contain tender and tropical plants from around the world. The newest is Crocodile Swamp which opened last year and displays wetland tropical plants.

The warm climate in the South West allows the Zoo to grow many tender plants outside as part of the exhibits as well as some of the rarest plants in the world. Palms, bananas and citrus are amongst the plants that contribute to the tropical feel. The Zoo is also home to the NCCPG National Collection of species Buddleja.

## Fact File

| | |
|---|---|
| **Opening Times:** | Open daily from 10 a.m. Closing times vary according to the season. |
| **Admission Rates:** | Adults: £13.60*, Senior Citizens: £10.30*, Children: £8.80* |
| | *Includes a 10% voluntary donation (These are 2009 prices, 2010 will change). |
| **Group Rates:** | Minimum Group Size: 15. Adults: £9.40, Senior Citizens: £7.70, Children: £6.30. |
| **Facilities:** | Visitor Center Shop, Restaurant, Teas. |
| **Disabled Access:** | Yes. Bookable wheelchair loan available. |
| **Toilets on site:** | Yes. |
| **Tours/Events:** | Guided tours available.  Booking required. Extra charge. |
| **Coach Parking:** | Yes - free. |
| **Car Parking on site:** | Yes - free. |
| **Length of Visit:** | 4-5 hours. |
| **Booking Contact:** | John Rea |
| | Paignton Zoological & Botanical Gardens, Totnes Road, Paignton, Devon TQ4 7EU |
| | Telephone: 01803 697515 |
| | Fax: 01803 523457 |
| **Email:** | groupvisits@paigntonzoo.org.uk |
| **Website:** | www.paigntonzoo.org.uk |
| **Location:** | We are located on the A3022 Totnes Road, 1 mile from Paignton town centre. |

Please quote this guide when making a booking

Come and see this enchanting 65-acre garden set in the beautiful Torridge Valley. Whatever the season, Rosemoor is a unique place that people return to time and again for ideas, inspiration or simply to enjoy a relaxing day out.

From Lady Anne's original garden to rose gardens (with over 200 varieties), formal and informal gardens, the fruit and vegetable garden, the arboretum, stunning lake and cottage garden, as well as woodland walks, there is something for everyone to enjoy.

Over 80 exciting events are also held at Rosemoor throughout the year, such as art exhibitions and workshops, horticultural lectures and walks, family events, craft fairs, and musical events. For information, please ring 01805 624067 for a FREE brochure.

Licensed Restaurant, Tea Room, Plant Centre and Shop also on site and free parking.

## Fact File

| | |
|---|---|
| **Opening times:** | April - September 10am - 6pm, October - March 10am - 5pm, open every day except Christmas Day.  Visitor Centre Closed noon Christmas eve and re-opens 10am 27th Dec. |
| **Admission Rates:** | Adults £7.00, Senior Citizen £7.00, Child (6-16yrs) £2.50, (under 6yrs Free), RHS Members + 1 Guest Free |
| **Group Rates:** | Minimum group size: 10. £6.00 per person RHS members + 1 guest, Free, Carers for diabled people Free. |
| **Facilities:** | Visitor Centre, Shop, Restaurant, Wisteria Tea Room, Plant Centre. |
| **Disabled Access:** | Yes. Toilet and Parking for disabled on site.  Wheelchairs on loan, booking necessary. |
| **Tours/Events:** | Full programme of events throughout the year. |
| **Coach Parking:** | Yes |
| **Length of Visit:** | Half to full day |
| **Booking Contact:** | Admin Department RHS Garden Rosemoor, Great Torrington, North Devon, EX38 8PH Telephone 01805 624067 Fax: 01805 624717 |
| **Email:** | rosemooradmin@rhs.org.uk |
| **Website:** | www.rhs.org.uk/rosemoor |
| **Location:** | 1 mile south of Torrington on the A3124 (formerly B3220) |

Please quote this guide when making a booking

Established in 1765 by the first Countess of Ilchester. Developed since then into a 30-acre grade 1 listed magnificent woodland valley garden. world famous for it's Camellia Groves, Magnolias, Rhododendron and Hydrangea collections. In summer it is awash with colour.

Since the restoration after the great storm of 1990 many new and exotic plants have been introduced. The garden is now a mixture of formal and informal, with a charming walled garden and spectacular woodland valley views.

Facilities include a Colonial Restaurant for lunches, snacks and drinks, a Plant Centre and quality Gift Shop. Events and concerts are presented during the year.
The Floodlighting of the Garden at the end of October (Oct 13th - 31st Oct 2010) should not be missed.

## Fact File

**Opening Times:** Summer: 10am - 6pm last entry at 5pm.
Winter (November - February) - 10.00am - 4pm or dusk, last entry 1 hour before.

**Admission Rates:** Adults £9.50, Senior Citizen £9.00, Child £6.50

**Groups Rates:** Minimum group size 10
Adults £7.00, Senior Citizen £6.50, Child £4.50

**Facilities:** Colonial Restaurant, Gift Shop, Plant Centre.

**Disabled Access:** Yes. 50% of garden accessible. Toilet and parking for disabled on site. Wheelchairs F.O.C.

**Tours/Events:** £1 per person (minimum charge £20) on top of the group rate (minimum 10 people). Special events see web site.

**Coach Parking:** Yes

**Length of Visit:** 2 hours

**Booking Contact:** Jessica Lambert. Abbotsbury Sub Tropical Garden, Bullers Way, Abbotsbury, (Nr Weymouth),
Dorset, DT3 4LA. Telephone: 01305 871130  Fax: 01305 871092

**Email:** info@abbotsbury-tourism.co.uk

**Website:** www.abbotsburygardens.co.uk & www.abbotsburyplantsales.co.uk

**Location:** On the B3157 between Weymouth and Bridport in Dorset. come off the A35 near Dorchester at Winterborne Abbas.

Ⓡ SEPT 10

The 8 acres of gardens here hold National & International Plant Collections of Water Lilies, flowering from late spring to autumn, creating one of the most outstanding displays of water lilies in Britain with a Monet style Japanese Bridge as a centrepiece.

Many of the original lilies planted here by the Bennett family in 1959 came from the same nursery in France that supplied Claude Monet's garden in Giverny. These same varieties that Monet painted are among the collections on display.

Grass pathways lead you through the series of lakes surrounded by wetland plants, native trees, palms, wild plants and flowers. The gardens are a 'Site of Nature Conservation Interest' and home to abundant wildlife.

The Museum contains local history including Chesil Beach & Fleet lagoon, plus the fascinating story of this site from Brickworks & Clay Pits in 1859 through to the gardens today.

## Fact File

| | |
|---|---|
| **Opening times:** | Mid-March to Mid-October: 10 a.m. – 5 p.m. daily except Saturdays |
| **Admission Rates:** | Adults: £6.95, Senior Citizens: £6.25, Children: £3.95 (5 – 16 years) |
| **Group Rates:** | Minimum Group Size: 15.  Adults: £4.75, Senior Citizens: £4.75, Children: £3.25 |
| **Facilities:** | Visitor Centre, Shop, Plant Sales, Restaurant, Teas |
| **Disabled Access:** | Yes |
| **Toilets on site:** | Yes |
| **Coach Parking:** | Yes |
| **Car Parking on site:** | Yes |
| **Guided Tours:** | Yes, booking required |
| **Special Events:** | Please see website |
| **Length of Visit:** | 2 hours+ |
| **Booking Contact:** | Angie or James Bennett, Bennetts Water Gardens, Putton Lane, Chickerell, Weymouth, Dorset DT3 4AF |
| | Booking Telephone No. 01305 785150.  Booking Fax No. 01305 781619 |
| **Email:** | info@waterlily.co.uk |
| **Website:** | www.waterlily.co.uk |
| **Location:** | 2 miles west of Weymouth on the B3157 – follow brown signs for Water Gardens from the A354 at Weymouth |

Please quote this guide when making a booking

Forde Abbey is a treasure in an area already known for its outstanding beauty. More than 900 years of history are encapsulated in this elegant former Cistercian monastery and its 30 acres of award winning gardens. In the peaceful solitude of its secluded position it is possible to imagine just how it looked to many of its previous owners: monks going about their daily round of work and prayer, prosperous parliamentary gentlemen discussing the cavalier threat, gifted philosophers debating the imponderable, elegant Victorian ladies fanning themselves by the fireside and country gentlemen going about their work on the estate.

The architectural beauty of the house, with its striking interior, and the varied garden, including a mature arboretum, rockery, bog garden and working walled kitchen garden makes Forde Abbey a delightful destination. The cascade of lakes provides a wonderful setting for the Centenary Fountain, the highest powered fountain in England.

However, Forde Abbey is first and foremost a family home giving it an atmosphere of warmth and ease not often found in stately homes. The fruits of the garden and farm can be sampled in the Undercroft restaurant with a wide selection of delicious homemade lunches and cakes. A gift shop, plant centre and pottery exhibition add to the day.

Enjoy England Awards for Excellence, Silver winner 2008

## Fact File

| | |
|---|---|
| **Opening times:** | Gardens open daily throughout the year from 10am (last admission 4.30pm). House open, 1st April to end of October, 12noon-4pm on Tue -Fri, Sundays & Bank Holiday Mondays. |
| **Admission Rates:** | Tel: 01460 221290 |
| **Groups Rates:** | Minimum group size 15, Tel: 01460 220231. |
| **Facilities:** | Shop, Plant Sales, Teas, Restaurant and Pottery Exhibition. |
| **Disabled Access:** | Yes. (house not suitable for wheelchairs) Toilet and parking for disabled on site. Wheelchair and Battery Car on loan, booking necessary. To book 01460 221699. |
| **Tours:** | Tours for pre-arranged groups only. |
| **Coach Parking:** | Yes |
| **Length of Visit:** | 3 hours |
| **Booking Contact:** | Mrs Carolyn Clay Forde Abbey, Chard, TA20 4LU Telephone: 01460 220231  Fax: 01460 220296 |
| **Email:** | info@fordeabbey.co.uk |
| **Website:** | www.fordeabbey.co.uk |
| **Location:** | Signposted from A30 Chard to Crewkerne & from A358 Chard to Axminster. 4 miles south east of Chard. |

Please quote this guide when making a booking

Laid out by successive members of the Bankes family over the last three centuries, the grounds of this extensive estate are presented by the National Trust in their Edwardian splendour. Most recent of the restoration projects is the Japanese Gardens of Henrietta Bankes, the formal Tea Gardens of which were opened in 2005, set in seven acres of the southern shelter-belt and include an Acer Glade, a Quarry Garden, an Evergreen Garden and a Cherry Garden. Closer to the magnificent Mansion are the Sunk Garden and the Parterre, both of which remain true to their early twentieth century planting patterns throughout the year. The Fernery, with over thirty-five varieties, is also the home of the National Collection of Anemone nemorosa, while the surrounding three hundred-acre Parkland reflects the Bankes' passion for specimen trees whether as single examples or as groups and avenues.

## Fact File

**Opening Times:** 13th March – 31st October, Daily 10.30 a.m. – 6 p.m.
1st November – 23rd December: Daily 10.30 a.m. – 4 p.m.

**Admission Rates:** Gardens Only: Adults: £6.00, Children: £3.00. Includes a voluntary donation but visitors can choose to pay the standard prices displayed at the property and on the website.

**Group Rates:** Minimum Groups Size: 15
Group rates for House and Gardens only: Adults: £10.00, Children: £5.00.

**Facilities:** Woodland Walks, Children's play areas.

**Disabled Access:** Yes – gardens only. Lavatory and car parking on site. Wheelchair Loan booking available.

**Tours/Events:** Guided tours available. Events leaflet available.

**Coach Parking:** Yes – booking essential.

**Length of Visit:** 2 hours +

**Booking Contact:** Carol Dougherty, Property Administrator, Kingston Lacy, Wimborne Minster, Dorset BH21 4EA
Telephone: 01202 883402  Fax: 01202 882402

**Email:** kingstonlacy@nationaltrust.org.uk

**Website:** www.nationaltrust.org.uk

**Location:** 1½ miles west of Wimborne Minster, on B3082.

Set in idyllic surroundings Kingston Maurward Gardens are one of Dorset's best kept secrets. A tranquil, and peaceful spot, the gardens are situated in undulating Dorset countryside, with a large ornamental lake, broad sweeping and formal gardens.

The gardens were laid out in the "Jardin Anglais" style popularised by Capability Brown in the 18th Century. The formal gardens consist of a matrix of small gardens each with its own theme. The Rainbow beds and beautiful herbaceous borders compliment the Croquet lawn and an extensive display of tender perennials. The charming Japanese style garden lies adjacent to the north shore of the lake, with stately Chusan Palms, Bamboos and Japanese Maples. There are also tree trails, lakeside walks and a delightful walled garden.

The Animal Park has an interesting collection of animals, including Rabbits, Guinea Pigs, Sheep, Goats, Shetland ponies, Alpacas and lots more. There is plenty of space for picnics and the Visitor Centre has a wide variety of plants and gifts for sale.

## Fact File

| | |
|---|---|
| **Opening times:** | 4th January 2010 to 22nd December 2010, 10am - 5.30pm. |
| **Admission Rates:** | Adults £5.00, Senior Citizen £4.50, Child £3.00, Family £15.50. |
| **Group Rates:** | Minimum group size: 10 |
| | Adults £4.50, Senior Citizen £4.50, Child £3.00. |
| **Facilities:** | Visitor Centre, Shop, Tea Room, Plant Sales, Picnic Area |
| | Children's Play Area, Animal Park. |
| **Disabled Access:** | Yes. Toilet & parking for disabled on site. Wheelchairs on loan, booking necessary. |
| **Tours/Events:** | Guided walks are available if booked in advance. |
| | Special events take place throughout the year, telephone for details. |
| **Coach Parking:** | Yes |
| **Length of Visit:** | Minimum 2 hours |
| **Booking Contact:** | Ginny Rolls |
| | Kingston Maurward, Dorchester, Dorset, DT2 8PY |
| | Telephone 01305 215003 Fax: 01305 215001 |
| **Email:** | events@kmc.ac.uk |
| **Website:** | www.kmc.ac.uk/gardens |
| **Location:** | Signposted from the roundabout at the eastern end of the Dorchester by-pass A35. |

Please quote this guide when making a booking

# Minterne Gardens Dorset

Home of the Churchill and Digby families for 350 years, Minterne, described by Simon Jenkins as 'a corner of paradise', was landscaped after the manner of Capability Brown in the 18th century with small lakes and cascades. The first Arboreum Rhododendrons were planted in the 1850's, many more from Himalayan expeditions by George Forrest, Wilson and Rock around 1905, and from Kingdon Ward's expedition in 1924.

Wander peacefully through 20 wild woodland acres of hidden gardens laid out in a horseshoe over a mile round; March sees the Magnolias, and early Rhododendrons. April and May, Japanese cherries and a profusion of rhododendrons and azaleas. Late May and June many fine specimens of Davidia Involucrata (the Pocket Handkerchief Tree) are a particular feature. Eucryphias, Hydrangeas, water plants and water lilies provide a new vista at each turn. The autumn colouring is quite sensational.

## Fact File

| | |
|---|---|
| **Opening times:** | 10 a.m. – 6 p.m. daily, 1st March – 9th November. |
| **Admission Rates:** | Adults: £5.00, Senior Citizens: £5.00, Children under 12 FOC if accompanied. |
| **Disabled Access:** | Not suitable for wheelchairs. |
| **Toilets on site:** | Yes. |
| **Tours/Events:** | See website events page. |
| **Coach Parking:** | Yes. |
| **Car Parking on site:** | Yes. Free car park with picnic facilities. |
| **Length of Visit:** | 1-2 hours. |
| **Booking Contact:** | Minterne Gardens<br>Minterne Magna, Dorchester, Dorset DT2 7AU<br>Telephone: 01300 341370<br>Fax: 01300 341747 |
| **Email:** | enquiries@minterne.co.uk |
| **Website:** | www.minterne.co.uk |
| **Location:** | Situated in the village of Minterne Magna on the A352 Dorchester/Sherborne road, 2 miles north of Cerne Abbas. |

There is much to see in over 100 acres of gardens and arboretum throughout the year.

In the Walled Garden the five individual gardens and the longest double herbaceous border in East Anglia are a unique blend of traditional and contemporary, combining unusual landscaping and creative and colourful planting. The garden is at its best from early summer through to autumn but on the opposite lake bank there is the Millennium Walk, designed to be at its best on the shortest days of the year. Here stems of dogwood, rubus and birch reflect in the lake and the scent of Hamamelis lingers.

Each year new plantings mature, surprise and delight.

## Fact File

| | |
|---|---|
| **Opening Times:** | 1st April-31st October Tuesday to Sunday & Bank Holidays 10.30am - 5pm.<br>1 November-31st March Fridays, Saturdays & Sundays 10.30am to dusk. |
| **Admission Rates:** | £4.00 Adult, Child £1.00 (5 to 16, under 5's Free), £3.50 Concessions. |
| **Groups Rates:** | Minimum group size 12<br>£3.00 per person |
| **Facilities:** | Visitor Centre, Shop, Plant Sales, Tea Room. |
| **Disabled Access:** | Yes.  Toilet and parking for disabled on site.  Wheelchairs and buggy on loan. |
| **Tours/Events:** | Please telephone for details. |
| **Coach Parking:** | Yes |
| **Length of Visit:** | 2-3 hours |
| **Booking Contact:** | Visitor Centre Manager<br>Marks Hall, Coggeshall, Essex, CO6 1TG<br>Tel: 01376 563796 Fax: 01376 563132 |
| **Email:** | enquiries@markshall.org.uk |
| **Website:** | www.markshall.org.uk |
| **Location:** | Signed from A120 Coggeshall by-pass. |

Please quote this guide when making a booking

# Batsford Arboretum & Wild Garden      Gloucestershire

Batsford Arboretum & Wild Garden - The Cotswolds Secret Garden and former home of the Mitford family.

One of the largest private collection of trees in Great Britain. See spring flowers as they cascade down the hillside. Many wild orchids and fritillaries adorn the arboretum. In autumn the many rare and unusual trees explode into their magnificent reds, golds and purples.

Follow the stream through pools and waterfalls to its source, make a wish with the giant Buddha. find the Foo Dog hidden amongst the trees, then negotiate the waterfall without getting too wet. See if you can find Algernon and Clemantine on the lake, then rest awhile and view the deer in the Deer Park. Fifty acres of peace, traquillity - pure Cotswold magic!

## Fact File

**Opening Times:** Open every day 9am - 5pm. (May close Wednesdays in December and January - Check before travelling long distances).
Also open Boxing day & New Years Day.

**Admission Rates:** Adults £6.00, Senior Citizen £5.00, Child £2.00.

**Groups Rates:** Minimum group size 20. Admission Rates less 10%

**Facilities:** Visitor Centre, Shop, Plant Sales, Teas, Restaurant, Garden Centre and Falconry Centre.

**Disabled Access:** Partial. Toilet and parking for disabled on site, wheelchairs on loan, booking necessary.

**Tours/Events:** Tours by arrangement. Events to be arranged.

**Coach Parking:** Yes.

**Length of Visit:** 2 Hours

**Booking Contact:** Mr Chris Pilling
Batsford Arboretum, Batsford Park, Moreton in Marsh, Glos GL56 9AB.
Telephone: 01386 701441 Fax: 01386 701829

**Email:** arboretum@batsfordfoundation.co.uk

**Website:** www.batsarb.co.uk

**Location:** 1 mile west of Moreton in Marsh on A44 road.

Please quote this guide when making a booking

Berkeley Castle is England's oldest inhabited castle and most historic home. Over 24 generations of Berkeley's have transformed a savage Norman fortress into a stately home full of treasures.

Successive generations softened the stern aspect of the Castle walls with flowers, until finally the present planting of the terraces was carried out with the help of Gertrude Jekyll at the turn of the last century. The gardens specialise in scent and the roses are a delight in June. Rare plants, shrubs and trees are to be enjoyed and a butterfly house.

From the Lily Pond, first built as a swimming pool during the time of the last Earl, sweeping curved steps lead down to the Great Lawn on which the remaining Culloden pine stands, said to have been brought back as a pine cone from the Battle of Culloden by the 4th Earl of Berkeley.

Today, the castle landscape remains largely as it was in the mid 20th century, but retains a sense of 'slumbering peacefulness' as described by Jekyll. This mellow old age is part of the castle's beauty and, visitors can ramble freely through the castle gardens and grounds, getting a sense of its long and eventful life.

## Fact File

**Opening Times:** 28th March – 31st October 2010. 11:00am – 5:30pm
Easter Holidays 28th March – 18th April Sunday – Thursday & Easter Weekend
April & May Sundays, Thursdays & Bank Holiday Mondays
May Half Term onwards 30th May – 5th September Sunday – Thursday
September & October Sundays & Thursdays
October Half Term 24th – 31st October Sunday - Thursday

**Admission Rates:** Adults: £7.50, Senior Citizens: £6.00, Children: £4.50

**Group Rates:** Minimum Group Size 25
Adults: £7.00, Senior Citizens: £5.50, Children: £3.50

**Facilities:** Visitor Centre, Shop, Teas

**Disabled Access:** Partial access only.

**Tours/Events:** Yes, see website for details

**Coach Parking:** Yes.

**Length of Visit:** 1.5 hours gardens. 1.5 hours castle

**Booking Contact:** David Exworth
Berkeley Castle, Berkeley, Gloucestershire GL13 9BQ
Tel: 01453 810332  Fax: 01453 512995

**Email:** info@berkeley-castle.com

**Website:** www.berkeley-castle.com

**Location:** Just off the A38, midway between Bristol and Gloucester.
10 minutes from Junctions 13 or 14, M5

Please quote this guide when making a booking

Cerney House Gardens are a romantic, secret step back into the past. Set amongst parkland, this family-run estate bulges with old-fashioned splendour. The central walled garden boasts a working kitchen garden complemented with generous herbaceous borders and roses of every description. A quieter knot garden plays host to the annual 'Floral Fireworks' tulip festival. There is a well-labelled herb garden that leads to the woodland, which is carpeted in the spring with snowdrops followed by bluebells. The avenue beds lead to genera borders that map out plant connections and end in turn amongst the ever-growing arboretum. There are plant collections throughout, including the national collection of Tradescantia. The air is full of scents and nature's sounds. But this is still essentially a family garden where your guide will often be one of the many resident pets.

## Fact File

| | |
|---|---|
| **Opening Times:** | Open from Mid January for Snowdrops until the end of July or by appointment. Open: Tuesday, Wednesday, Friday, Sunday. |
| **Admission Rates:** | Adults: £4.00, Children: £1.00. |
| **Group Rates:** | Adults: £4.00, organiser entrance free, Children: £1.00 |
| **Facilities:** | Shop, Plant Sales, Teas, Pottery. |
| **Disabled Access:** | Yes. Toilet and car parking on site. Wheelchair loan available please book. |
| **Tours/Events:** | Guided tours available. Annual Tulip Festival. |
| **Coach Parking:** | By arrangement. |
| **Length of Visit:** | 1 1/2 hours |
| **Booking Contact:** | Barbara McPherson Cerney House Gardens, North Cerney, Cirencester, Gloucestershire GL7 7BX Telephone 01285 831300/831205  Fax: 01285 831421 |
| **Email:** | barbara@cerneygardens.com |
| **Website:** | www.cerneygardens.com |
| **Location:** | On the A435 at North Cerney. Turn up behind village church, 400 metres from main road. |

Hidcote Manor Garden is one of England's great Arts and Craft gardens. Created by the American horticulturist Major Lawrence Johnston in 1907, Hidcote is famous for its rare trees and shrubs, outstanding herbaceous borders and unusual plants from all over the world.

The garden is divided by tall hedges and walls to create a series of outdoor 'rooms' each with its own special and unique character. From the formal splendour of the White Garden and Bathing Pool to the informality and beauty of the Old Garden, visitors are assured of a surprise around every corner.

The numerous outdoor rooms reach their height at different times of the year, making a visit to Hidcote Manor Garden enjoyable whatever the season.

## Fact File

| | |
|---|---|
| **Opening Times:** | 13 March - 31 October: Monday, Tuesday, Wednesday, Saturday & Sunday 10am - 6pm (last admission 5pm). From October last admission 4pm. Also open Thursdays & Fridays in July & August. Please call the property for further seasonal openings. |
| **Admission Rates:** | Adults £9.50, Senior Citizen £9.50, Child £4.75. (National Trust members free) |
| **Groups Rates:** | Minimum group size: 15 Adults £8.20, Senior Citizen £8.20, Child £4.10 (National Trust members free) |
| **Facilities:** | Shop, Plant Centre, Teas & Restaurant. |
| **Disabled Access:** | Partial. Toilet and parking for disabled on site. Wheelchairs on loan. |
| **Tours/Events:** | Please contact the property for a list of special events. |
| **Coach Parking:** | Yes. Groups must book in advanced. |
| **Length of Visit:** | 2 hours |
| **Booking Contact:** | Lisa Edinborough, Hidcote Manor Garden, Hidcote Bartrim, Chipping Campden, Gloucestershire, GL55 6LR Telephone: 01386 438333 Fax: 01386 438817 |
| **Email:** | hidcote@nationaltrust.org.uk |
| **Website:** | www.nationaltrust.org.uk |
| **Location:** | 4 miles north east of Chipping Campden; 8 miles south of Stratford Upon Avon & signposted from B4632 Stratford/Broadway road, close to the village of Mickleton. |

Please quote this guide when making a booking

# Kiftsgate Court Garden Gloucestershire

Kiftsgate is a glorious garden to visit throughout the seasons with spectacular views to the Malvern Hills and beyond. Three generations of women gardeners have designed, planted and sustained this garden.

The upper gardens around the house are planted to give harmonious colour schemes, whilst the sheltered lower gardens recreate the atmosphere of warmer countries. The latest addition is a modern water garden which provides an oasis of tranquillity and contrast to the exuberance of the flower gardens.

On open days plants grown from the garden are for sale. A wide and interesting selection are always available. The tearoom in the house offers delicous home made cream teas and light lunches in May, June and July.

"Winner of the HHA/Christies Garden of the Year award 2003"

## Fact File

**Opening times:** May, June & July - Saturday to Wednesday 12noon - 6pm.
August - Saturday to Wednesday 2pm - 6pm.
April & September - Sunday, Monday & Wednesday, 2pm - 6pm.
**Admission Rates:** £6.50 Adults, £2.00 Children.
**Groups Rates:** Coaches by appointment, 20 adults or more £5.50 per person
**Facilities:** Plants for Sale, Tea Room, Gift Shop.
**Disabled Access:** Limited
**Tours/Events:** None
**Coach Parking:** Yes.
**Length of Visit:** 1 ½ hours
**Booking Contact:** Mrs Anne Chambers
Kiftsgate Court Garden, Chipping Campden, Gloucestershire, GL55 6LN
Telephone: 01386 438777   Fax: 01386 438777
**Email:** anne@kiftsgate.co.uk
**Website:** www.kiftsgate.co.uk
**Location:** 3 miles north east of Chipping Campden.  Follow signs towards Mickleton, then follow brown tourist signs to Kiftsgate Court Gardens.

A place of tranquil beauty amidst fine formal gardens, Lydney Park is home to Viscount Bledisloe, and is steeped in history from Iron Age to the present day. In early season, the visitor to Lydney Park drives between a resplendent display of daffodils and narcissi, and beyond the car park are the Spring Gardens, a secret wooded valley with lakes, providing a profusion of Rhododendrons, Azaleas and other flowering shrubs. Discover an important Roman Temple Site and the site of a Normal Castle. Picnic in the Deer Park amongst some magnificent trees, and visit our museums, which includes a New Zealand Museum. Home made teas in Dining Room of House. Dogs welcome on leads.

## Fact File

**Opening times:** 10am - 5pm Sundays, Wednesdays and Bank Holiday Mondays from 28th March until 6th June

**Admission Rates:** Adults £4.00, Children 50p.

**Groups Rate:** Minimum group size: 25 - Phone for group rates.

**Facilities:** Tea Rooms, Roman Temple Site, Museums, Gift Shop, Plant Sales.

**Disabled Access:** Not Suitable.

**Tours/Events:** Tour of Garden can be made available.

**Coach Parking:** Yes

**Length of Visit:** 1 - 2 hours

**Booking Contact:** Sally James
Lydney Park Gardens, Lydney Park, Estate Office, Old Park, Lydney, Gloucestershire, GL15 6BU.
Telephone: 01594 842844 or 01594 842922  Fax: 01594 842027

**Email:** mrjames@phonecoop.coop or tracey_lydneype@btconnect.com

**Website:** www.lydneyparkestate.co.uk

**Location:** Situated off A48 between Chepstow and Gloucester.

Please quote this guide when making a booking

# Misarden Park                                    Gloucestershire

This lovely, timeless garden, with spectacular views over both deer park and rolling Cotswold hills beyond, was created in the 17th Century and still retains a wonderful sense of peace and quietness. There are extensive yew hedges, including a notable yew walk, a Lutyens loggia hung with wisteria and a wide York stone terrace over-looked by a fine specimen of Magnolia soulangeana. Beneath the terrace splendid grass steps, fringed with campanula, lead to the South Lawn and an ancient mulberry tree, believed planted in 1620. West of the house, a rill with fountain and a stone summerhouse are recent garden additions to commemorate the Millennium. Beyond the rill a large walled garden boasts extensive double borders which have undergone a total re-plant over the last two years and now contain a wide range of roses, clematis, shrubs and herbaceous, all arranged in individual colour sections and planted to provide flower and interest from spring to autumn. A noteable year walk.

## Fact File

| | |
|---|---|
| **Opening Times:** | 10am - 5pm, Tuesday, Wednesday & Thursday, 1st April - 30th September. |
| **Admission Rates:** | Adults £4.00, Senior Citizen £4.00, Child Free |
| **Group Rates:** | Minimum group size: 20 |
| | Adults £3.60, Senior Citizen £3.60, Child Free |
| **Facilities:** | Nurseries Adjacent. |
| **Disabled Access:** | Yes. Parking for disabled on site. |
| **Tours/Events:** | None. |
| **Coach Parking:** | Yes |
| **Length of Visit:** | 1 1/2 hours |
| **Booking Contact:** | Estate Office |
| | Misarden Park, Miserden, Stroud, Glos, GL6 7JA |
| | Telephone 01285 821303 Fax: 01285 821530 |
| **Email:** | estate.office@miserdenestate.co.uk |
| **Website:** | www.misardenpark.co.uk |
| **Location:** | Follow signs to Miserden from A417 or from B4070. |

Please quote this guide when making a booking

Painswick Rococo Garden is a fascinating insight into 18th century English garden design. The only complete Rococo garden in England, it dates from a brief period (1720-1760) when English gardens where changing from the formal to the informal. These Rococo gardens combined formal vists with winding woodland walks and more natural planting. However Rococo gardens were so much more, their creators showed off their wealth and included features that were both flamboyant and frivolous. The gardens featured buldings of unusual architectural styles, to be used as both eye catchers and view points. These gardens became regency playrooms, an extension of the house to be enjoyed by the owner and his guests.

We are restoring the Garden back to how it was shown in a painting dated 1748. We have contemporary buidings, woodland walks, herbaceous borders, and a large kitchen garden all hidden away in a charming Cotswold valley with splendid views of the surrounding countryside. Visit our Anniversary Maze, or come in early spring to see our stunning snowdrop display.

## Fact File

| | |
|---|---|
| **Opening times:** | 10th January - 31st October. Daily 11am - 5pm. |
| **Admission Rates:** | Adults £6.00, Senior Citizen £5.00, Child £3.00 |
| **Groups Rates:** | Minimum group size: 20 (includes free introductory talk) Adults £5.00. |
| **Facilities:** | Visitor Centre, Shop, Plant Sales, Teas, Restaurant. |
| **Disabled Access:** | No. Toilet for disabled on site. |
| **Tours/Events:** | Several day courses - see website for details. |
| **Coach Parking:** | Yes. |
| **Length of Visit:** | 2 hours |
| **Booking Contact:** | Paul Moir Painswick Rococo Garden, Gloucestershire, GL6 6TH Telephone: 01452 813204   Fax: 01452 814888 |
| **Email:** | info@rococogarden.org.uk |
| **Website:** | www.rococogarden.org.uk |
| **Location:** | ½ mile outside Painswick on B4073 |

Please quote this guide when making a booking

## Rodmarton Manor        Gloucestershire

Rodmarton Manor is the supreme example of the Cotswold Arts and Crafts Movement. The garden was laid out as the house was being built (1909-1929) as a series of outdoor rooms covering about 8 acres. Each garden room has a different character and is bounded by either walls or hedges. One "garden room" has 26 separate beds with a wide variety of planting dominated by yellow shrubs and roses. There is a collection of stone troughs with alpines as well a rockery with bigger alpines. Topiary is a feature of the garden with extensive yew, box beech and holly hedges and clipped features including some new topiary. The herbaceous borders are magnificent from May but peaking late June but with plenty flowering into September. Many different types of roses flourish in the garden including old fashioned well-scented ones. There is a walled Kitchen Garden which has other plants besides vegetables including trained apples and pears. There is a big snowdrop collection. Most people who visit Rodmarton see the house which has specially made furniture as well as seeing the garden.

### Fact File

| | |
|---|---|
| **Opening times:** | 1st, 8th, 12th, 15th February from 1.30pm, (Garden only for snowdrops). House and Garden Easter Monday 2pm - 5pm. Wednesdays, Saturdays, Bank Holidays May - September 2pm - 5pm. Private coach bookings also at other times. |
| **Admission Rates:** | House and Garden £8.00 (5-15yrs £4.00). Garden only £5.00 (5 - 15yrs £1.00) (no dogs) |
| **Facilities:** | Teas |
| **Disabled Access:** | Yes. Most of garden and ground floor of house. |
| **Tours/Events:** | Guided tours of house and garden available. |
| **Coach Parking:** | Yes |
| **Length of Visit:** | 2 hours for house and garden |
| **Booking Contact:** | Sarah Pope, Rodmarton Manor, Cirencester, GL7 6PF. Telephone 01285 841253 |
| **Email:** | sarahpoperodmarton@yahoo.co.uk |
| **Website:** | www.rodmarton-manor.co.uk |
| **Location:** | Off A433 between Cirencester and Tetbury. |

Please quote this guide when making a booking

14 acres of glorious, organically managed gardens. Bold areas of planting such as those surrounding the 15th century Tithe Barn ruins contrast with intricate detail as seen in the Tudor Knot Garden. Topiary features strongly throughout and the famous Queens Garden, full of English roses, is furnished on two sides by magnificent double yew hedges planted in 1860. A Victorian Kitchen Garden links with the HDRA to help preserve rare and endangered vegetables. More recent additions include the East Garden, its arbour and beds planted with white wisterias, oriental clematis and tree peonies, and a landscaped Pheasantry area.

## Fact File

**Opening Times:**  Open 29th March to 31st October 2010. Daily; 10.30am - 5.00pm.
Please ensure you telephone or visit our website for updated information before visiting.

**Admission Rates:**  Adults £7.20, Concessions £6.20, Children £4.20. Family (2 adults and 2 children) £20.80.

**Group Rates:**  Group rates available.

**Facilities:**  Visitor Centre, Plant Sales, Coffee Shop, Picnic Area and Children's Play Area.

**Disabled Access:**  Limited - garden only. Toilet and Parking for disabled on site.

**Tours/Events:**  Group guided tours available - must be pre-booked. Special events programme, please call for details. (Information may be subject to change, please call or check website).

**Coach Parking:**  Yes

**Length of Visit:**  3 hours

**Booking Contact:**  Group Bookings
Sudeley Castle, Winchcombe, Cheltenham, Gloucestershire, GL54 5JD
Telephone: 01242 602308  Fax: 01242 602959

**Email:**  enquiries@sudeley.org.uk

**Website:**  www.sudeleycastle.co.uk

**Location:**  On B4632, 8 miles north east of Cheltenham.

Please quote this guide when making a booking

Tortworth Court is a Grade Two listed property built by Lord Ducie in the Victorian Gothic style and set in 32 acres of recently restored grounds. The grounds are split in two main areas. There is a formal garden with a parterre, which has now been replanted with over six hundred roses and then the arboretum which has around one thousand trees many of which are rare and some of the first of their kind in the country.

In its day Tortworth Court rivalled Westonbirt the famous arboretum nearby. Today the arboretum is still extremely important and is recognised as one of the finest of its type in the British Isles. One of our most famous trees is the original Corkscrew Hazel made famous by Sir Harry Lauder as his twisted walking stick.

## Fact File

| | |
|---|---|
| **Opening Times:** | N/A |
| **Admission Charges:** | Adults: N/A, Senior Citizens: N/A, Children: N/A |
| **On-Site Facilities:** | Restaurant, Teas, Bar |
| **Disabled Access:** | Yes. Toilet and parking on site. Wheelchair loan available – booking advisable. |
| **Toilets on site:** | Yes |
| **Car Parking on site:** | Yes |
| **Coach Parking:** | Yes – 200 yards away |
| **Guided Tours:** | Yes (must be booked in advance) |
| **Length of Visit:** | 2 hours |
| **Booking Contact:** | Clive Smith, Tortworth Court Four Pillars Hotel, Wotton Under Edge, South Glos. GL12 8HH Booking Tel No. 01454 263000 Booking Fax No. 01454 263001 |
| **Email:** | tortworth@four-pillars.co.uk |
| **Website:** | www.tortworth-court-hotel.co.uk |
| **Location:** | From the north: leave the M5 at junction 14. Follow the B4509 towards Wotton. On the hill and take the first right into Tortworth Road. After half a mile, the hotel is on the right up a long drive. From the south: leave M5 at junction 14, signposted to Dursley. At the T Junction turn right on the B4509 and follow directions above. |

# Westonbirt The National Arboretum

## Gloucestershire

Westonbirt, The National Arboretum, situated in the glorious Cotswolds, is one of the outstanding tree collections in the world covering an area of 600 acres. Westonbirt is noted for its vast range of stunning mature specimen trees. A short walk from the original arboretum is Silkwood, with collections of native Asian and American species that in spring are carpeted with primroses, wood anemones and bluebells. There are in excess of 17,000 numbered trees, including an exceptional National Collection of Japanese maples, extended in 2006 by the newly planted Rotary Glade. Colour is best in May (rhododendrons, magnolias, etc.) and October (Japanese maples, Persian ironwoods, Katsuras etc.). The plant centre offers some rare, interesting shrubs and trees, especially Japanese maples, conifers and specimen trees. Westonbirt arboretum is an inspiring place to relax, get back to nature and indulge your senses. You will want to return to explore time and time again …

## Fact File

**Opening times:** 9 a.m. – 5 p.m.

**Admission Rates:** Adults: £6.00 - £8.00 (subject to seasonal variation), Senior Citizens: Concessions available Children: £2 - £4 for children aged 5-18, Under 5 – Free. Annual mebership from £29.00 RHS members free at certain times

**Group Rates:** Minimum Group Size: 10, Adults: £6.00, Senior Citizens: £5.00, Children: £2.00

**Facilities:** Visitor Centre, Shop, Plant Sales, Restaurant, Teas, play areas for under 5s, play zones for up to age 10

**Disabled Access:** Yes. Wheelchair loan available – booking required.

**Toilets on site:** Yes **Car Parking on site:** Yes **Coach Parking:** Yes

**Guided Tours:** Yes, weekend tours April - October. Booking required for groups

**Length of Visit:** 3 hours plus

**Special Events:** Main Events: Festival of the Tree August, Enchanted Christmas: December. Dog Days, February, Summer concerts, June/July, Many more smaller events all through the year.

**Booking Contact:** Helen Daniels, Westonbirt The National Arboretum, Westonbirt, Tetbury, Gloucestershire GL7 2RW
Booking Tel No.01666 881200 Booking Fax No. 01666 880559

**Email:** helen.daniels@forestry.gsi.gov.uk **Website:** www.forestry.gov.uk/westonbirt

**Location:** From the southwest, Wales and London – we are 15 minutes north of Junction 18 of the M4 (Bath junction) on A433
From Cheltenham, the North and Oxfordshire – go to Tetbury via Cirencester and follow the brown signs south on the A433.

Please quote this guide when making a booking

Capability Brown designed more parks and gardens in England than any other man before or since. The Cadland gardens are unique in that they are his smallest surviving pleasure ground and were designed in 1775 for a thatched cottage, a Fishing Cottage, on the Solent shore overlooking the Isle of Wight.  Gravel walks wind among the shrubberies  with peeps out over the water; the evergreens or  'shining greens' were a favourite of the period, often overlaid with roses and under planted with wild flowers.

More parkland and two walled gardens were added later, one has a glorious run of fruit houses, a tool shed with a collection of old tools  and a plantsmen's parterre, a series of gravel gardens with rare, low-growing plants; the second contains the plant collection.  For those with time and energy, there is a woodland walk with a collection of oaks.

A visit to Cadland and Exbury Gardens and Steam Railway (page 66), just 35 minutes by coach away, makes a perfect day out.

## Fact File

| | |
|---|---|
| **Opening Times:** | Not open to the public except for group visits by appointment only. Weekdays  4th May to 30th July: 13th September to 18th October.  10.30-5pm. |
| **Group Rates:** | Minimum Group Size: 20, £5.00 per person, Children free. |
| **Facilities:** | Visits hosted by the owner and Head Gardener; home made cakes, teas or morning coffee by arrangement;  wheelchair access to most of the gardens: free garden leaflets; dogs on leads.  House also open by special arrangement only. |
| **Disabled Access:** | Yes. |
| **Toilet On Site:** | Yes. |
| **Tours/Events:** | Guided tours available. |
| **Car/Coach Parking:** | Free. Directions sent. |
| **Length of Visit:** | 2-3 hours. |
| **Booking Contact:** | Mrs Gilly Drummond. Stanswood Farm House, Fawely, Southampton, Hampshire SO45 1AB Tel. 023 8089 2039 or 07760 296922  Fax. 023 8089 3040 |
| **Email:** | gd@cadland.org.uk |
| **Website:** | N/A |
| **Location:** | 16 miles South East of Southampton on Solent shore via A 326/B 3053 |

Please quote this guide when making a booking

Natural beauty is in abundance at Exbury Gardens, a 200 acre woodland garden on the east bank of the Beaulieu River in the New Forest National Park. Created by Lionel de Rothschild in the 1920's the Gardens are a stunning vision of his inspiration. Spring displays of rhododendrons, azaleas, camellias and magnolias are world famous. The daffodil meadow, rock, exotic, iris and herbaceous and grasses gardens ensure year round interest. Summer is a favoured time for cool and shady walks, whilst the River Walk offers magnificent views over the Solent to the Isle of Wight. Autumn sees spectacular colours from acers, sweet gums and dogwoods and magnificent displays from *Nyssa* and *Oxydendrum*, two of Exbury's National Plant Collections. Visitors can enjoy over 20 miles of pathways, or "let the train take the strain" with a 20 min journey around part of the Yard Wood, with magnificent vistas over the Rock Garden and features which include a bridge, viaduct and tunnel. Chauffeur driven buggy tours ensure access for all. A visit to Exbury and Cadland on page 65 makes for a perfect day out'.

Copyright Colin Roberts

## Fact File

**Opening Times:** Opening times: 13 March – 7 November daily, 10 a.m. – 5 p.m. last admission. Gates close 6 p.m. or dusk if earlier. Please call for winter opening dates/Exbury Santa Steam Specials in December

**Admission Rates:** Adults: £8.50, Senior Citizens: £8.00, Children (3-15): £1.50, under 3s free Family (2 adults & 3 children 3-15): £19.00. Railway + £3.50 (includes tour of Engine Shed) Rover ticket (unlimited daily travel) + £4.50. Buggy tours (30/45 minutes) + £3.50/£4.00 'Exbury Experience ticket' £13.50 – inclusive of entry, railway journey, buggy tour and Tree Trail leaflet, and discounts based on a minimum spend in restaurant and gift shop. Available from early June onwards

**Groups Rates:** Minimum Group Size: 15, Adults/Senior Citizens: £7.50 Group organiser free entrance to Gardens and Steam Train. Coach driver incentives

**Facilities:** Gift Shop; Plant Sales; Teas; restaurant; Buggy Tours.

**Disabled Access:** Yes. Toilet and parking for disabled on site. Wheelchairs available on free loan. Accessible carriages on train. Carers admitted free of charge on 1:1 basis to gardens.

**Tours/Events:** Guided tours of Gardens (including specialist interest)and "Meet & Greets" are available.

**Coach Parking:** Yes, free. We endeavour to meet groups on arrival in main season, April / May.

**Length of Visit:** 2½ - 3½ hours min, but between 4-6 hours in main flowering season, April / May.

**Booking Contact:** Reception, Exbury Gardens, Estate Office, Exbury, Southampton, Hants SO45 1AZ. Telephone: 023 80 891203  Fax: 023 80 899940

**Email:** nigel.philpott@aol.com

**Website:** www.exbury.co.uk

**Location:** Junction 2 west of M27, just follow A326 to Fawley, off B3054, 3 miles Beaulieu, in New Forest National Park. B&W signposted.

Please quote this guide when making a booking

# Sir Harold Hillier Gardens

Sir Harold Hillier Gardens is one of the most important modern plant collections in the world. Established in 1953 by the distinguished plantsman Sir Harold Hillier, the magnificent collection of over 42,000 plants from temperate regions around the world grows in a variety of superb themed landscapes set over 180-acres of rolling Hampshire countryside.

Open throughout the year, the Gardens offer four seasons of beauty, inspiration and discovery and includes 11 National Plant Collections, over 250 Champion Trees and the largest winter Garden in Europe.

A £3.5 million Visitor & Education Pavilion offers fine views of the collection and surrounding countryside and features; a stylish licensed restaurant for home-cooked meals, light refreshments and afternoon teas, open-air terrace, gift shop, events, exhibitions, concerts and workshops for all ages and interests all year round.

## Fact File

**Opening Times:** Open all year except Christmas Day and Boxing Day, daily: 10am - 6pm or dusk if earlier, open until 8pm every thursday in June, July and August.

**Admission Rates:** Adults £8.25, Concession £7.15, (seniors, jobseekers, full-time students and people with disabilities) Under 16 years - free of charge.

**Group Rates:** Minimum group size 10, £6.60 per person.

**Facilities:** £3.5 million Visitor & Education Pavilion, Open-air terrace and restaurant, Gift Shop, Plant Centre.

**Disabled Access:** Yes. Toilet and parking for disabled on site. Wheelchairs on loan and Mobility Scooters for hire, booking advised.

**Tours/Events:** Pre-booked guided tour with Curator, Botanist, Head Gardener and Horticultural staff available by arrangement. Please telephone for details about Special Events.

**Coach Parking:** Yes (Free)

**Length of Visit:** 2 - 4 hours

**Booking Contact:** Group Bookings. Sir Harold Hillier Gardens, Jermyns Lane, Romsey, Hampshire, SO51 0QA Telephone: 01794 369317/318 Fax: 01794 368027

SEPT 10

**Email:** info@hilliergardens.org.uk

**Website:** www.hilliergardens.org.uk

**Location:** The Gardens are situated, 2 miles north-east of Romsey. M3/M27 (West) to Romsey town centre. At Romsey follow brown heritage signs to the Hillier Gardens off the A3090. Alternatively, the Gardens can be approached from the A3057 Andover direction.

Please quote this guide when making a booking

Nestling in a woodland corner of Hampshire is this ravishingly attractive 1720's manor house, where busts of gods, emperors and dukes look down from the walls onto two major gardens.  The inner gardens, enclosed by eighteenth century walls, are all devoted to parterres. One is filled with water lilles, another of classical design with box topiary and a third enacts the whimsy of Alice in Wonderland with the story's characters in ivy and box topiary surrounded by roses of red and white.  The main walled garden is planted in subtle hues of mauve, plum and blue, contained in beds that have been faithfully restored to their original outlines.  A decorative potager is centred around berry-filled fruit cages where herbs, flowers and unusual vegetables are designed into colourful patterns. All this is surrounded by a second garden, a remarkable neo-classical park studded with follies, birdcages and monuments. A Paradise water garden. A Red Paeony Dragon Garden now join the Garden of the Five Bridges opening in 2009.  West Green House was the first garden to have a whole `Gardeners World' programme dedicated to itself.

## Fact File

**Opening Times:** Saturday 3rd, Sunday 4th April then every Wed, Sat, Sun until Sept 19th (except July 24, 25 & 31, Aug 1, 7 & 8)

**Admission Rates:** Adults £8.00, Children £4.00.

**Group Rates:** Groups by arangement please telephone for details. 4th April to 19th September 2009.

**Facilities:** Tea Rooms, Nursery, Garden Shop.

**Disabled Access:** Parking for disabled on site.

**Tours/Events:** Opera July 24, 25 & 31, Aug 1, 7 & 8, check website for details.

**Coach Parking:** Yes

**Length of Visit:** 2 hours approximately.

**Booking Contact:** West Green House, Thackhams Lane, West Green, Hartley Wintney, Hants RG27 8JB Telephone: 01252 845582 Fax: 01252 844611

**Email:** pip@westgreenhouse.co.uk

**Website:** www.westgreenhouse.co.uk

**Location:** 10 miles north east of Basingstoke, 1 mile west of Hartley Wintney, 1 mile north of A30.

# Hampton Court Castle Gardens Herefordshire

One of England's best kept secrets, Hampton Court Castle's Gardens are genuinely some of the most romantic. Set in the shadow of the medieval Castle, the gardens were recently rescued from neglect. The gardens open to a spectacular display of tulips but even in winter, the water canals and island pavilions provide a magical and tranquil backdrop that is reminiscent of the Alhambra with its tinkling waters.

At the heart of the gardens, the now fully mature maze with its gothic tower and secret tunnel lead to a hidden grotto garden and waterfall delighting visitors of all ages.

The gardens also have a charming Kitchen Garden whose organic produce is available in both the Orangery Café (in the historic Joseph Paxton Conservatory) and also in the Bothy Shop.

## Fact File

**Opening Times:** 11am-5pm 23 March 2010 – 31 October 2010.  Closed on Mondays March, April, May, Sept, and Oct except Bank Holidays.  Open for 7 days June, July and August.
Open until 7pm every Friday and Saturday throughout the Summer.
Last entry, one hour before closing time.

**Admission Charges:** Adults £6, Concessions £5, Children £3, Under 5's free, Family (2+3) £15. Prices may vary for special events. Membership £35 per person per annum allows unlimited visits.

**Group Rates:** Minimum Group Size 20 Adults £5, Concessions £4.50, Children £2.50

**On-Site Facilities:** The Castle is open to the public for tours at a supplementary charge. For times and prices, please call the booking office. Gift, Flower and Plant Shop, Café, Private Dining Room available for Groups. Afternoon teas a speciality.

**Disabled Access:** Yes, wheelchair loan available.  Booking required.

**Toilets on site:** Yes

**Car Parking on site:** Yes

**Coach Parking:** Yes

**Length of Visit:** not restricted

**Booking Contact:** Ticket Office, Hampton Court Castle & Gardens, Hampton Court Castle, Nr Hope-under-Dinmore, Leominster, Herefordshire, HR6 0PN
Telephone 01568 797777

**Email:** office@hamptoncourt.org.uk

**Website:** www.hamptoncourt.org.uk

**Location:** Situated on the A417 near to its junction with the A49 between Hereford and Leominster.

Please quote this guide when making a booking

Enjoy the mystery of leaving the beaten track to visit this hidden jewel of Herefordshire.

An enchanting and unique 7-acre organic garden overlooking the beautiful Kyre Valley and brimming with trees, shrubs, flowers and bulbs from around the world, it would tax even the most avid plantaholic trying to identify some of the many rarely seen species. It has been created by the same family over 50 years and includes an outstanding grass garden, fernery, herbaceous beds and borders, cottage-style gardens, herb garden and kitchen garden. It comprises of a little 'formal', through a lot of 'ordered chaos', to 'bring your own machete'; with secretive shrubberies and meandering paths there is something to surprise and fascinate at all times of year.

It is a garden full of inspiration and ideas with many intriguing features, seats and sculptures throughout the garden, and pools and ponds help to encourage myriad wildlife.

## Fact File

| | |
|---|---|
| **Opening times:** | Friday - Tuesday 11.00 a.m. – 5.00 p.m.<br>25th March – 7th September. If you would like to visit any other time, please ring. |
| **Admission Rates:** | Adults: £4.00, Senior Citizens: £4.00, Children: £1.00 |
| **Group Rates:** | Minimum Group Size: 10. Adults: £4.00, Senior Citizens: £4.00, Children: £1.00<br>(Includes free introductory talk) |
| **Facilities:** | Plant Sales. All the plants in the nursery are propagated from the garden.<br>Artist blacksmith on some days. Picnics welcome. |
| **Disabled Access:** | Yes – very limited wheelchair access |
| **Toilets on site:** | Yes |
| **Car Parking on site:** | Yes |
| **Coach Parking:** | Yes, by prior arrangement |
| **Guided Tours:** | Yes, booking required. Guided tours conducted by the Head Gardener, subject to availability. |
| **Length of Visit:** | 2 hours + |
| **Booking Contact:** | Ros Bissell, Moors Meadow Garden & Nursery, Collington, Bromyard, Herefordshire, HR7 4LZ<br>Booking Tel No.01885 410318 |
| **Email:** | moorsmeadow@hotmail.co.uk |
| **Website:** | www.moorsmeadow.co.uk |
| **Location:** | 4 miles North Bromyard, 6 miles South Tenbury Wells on B4214,<br>half mile up lane – follow yellow arrows |

Please quote this guide when making a booking

Broadview Gardens is a wonderful place in which to spend a couple of hours. Set in the peaceful picturesque Kent countryside it comprises 10 acres of beautifully manicured gardens each one of which is divided into smaller themed areas. You will be able to experience the wonders of a traditional Italian garden, wander around the Oriental garden as well as explore the sensory and water gardens. It is guaranteed to provide inspiration for both the amateur and professional.

Holding the National Collection of Hellebores and Japanese anemones we host a wide range of events throughout the year and, because each area is seasonally planted, there is always something interesting to see. Our spectacular dogwoods create a living flame effect during the winter which, combined with the peeling bark of birches and vibrant eranthis, iris reticula and other early flowering bulbs, means that there is a variety of colour on offer.

## Fact File

| | |
|---|---|
| **Opening times:** | Monday – Saturday: 9 a.m. – 5 p.m.  Sunday: 10 a.m. – 4 p.m. |
| **Admission Rates:** | Free admission |
| **Group Rates:** | Minimum Group Size 20 |
| **Facilities:** | Shop, Plant Sales, Restaurant, Teas, Garden Centre, Fresh Produce Shop |
| **Disabled Access:** | Yes |
| **Toilets on site:** | Yes |
| **Car Parking on site:** | Yes |
| **Coach Parking:** | Yes |
| **Wheelchair Loan:** | Yes, booking required |
| **Guided Tours:** | Yes, booking required |
| **Length of Visit:** | 1 – 2 hours |
| **Special Events:** | Hellebore weekends – your chance to visit the National Collection of Hellebores, Feb 2009 |
| **Booking Contact:** | Louise Yearwood, Broadview Gardens, Hadlow College, Tonbridge Road, Hadlow, Kent, TN11 0AL |
| | Booking Tel No. 01732 853227.  Booking Fax No. 01732 853207 |
| **Email:** | enquiries@hadlow.co.uk |
| **Website:** | www.broadviewgardens.co.uk |
| **Location:** | 4 miles north of Tonbridge on the A26, just outside the village of Hadlow |

Please quote this guide when making a booking

Situated in the heart of the rolling Kent countryside, Great Comp is an exceptionally beautiful 7-acre garden surrounding an early 17th century manor. The skilful design of sweeping lawns, winding woodland paths and formal areas near the house entices the visitor to explore around the next corner.

Romantic ruins combine with luxuriant planting to great effect, allowing panoramic views of the garden whilst creating the perfect microclimate for the extensive range of exotic plants collected by the Curator over the past 15 years.

In Spring the garden erupts into bloom with numerous Magnolias, Azaleas and Rhododendrons, under-planted with large drifts of Hellebores and bulbs whilst Summer brings warmth and extravagance from the rich and fiery colours of Salvias, Dahlias, Kniphofias, Crocosmias and Fuchsias; these are punctuated with ornamental grasses in great variety.

Also on offer at Great Comp are delicious homemade teas and lunches in the Old Dairy and an eclectic range of choice and unusual plants from the award-winning Dyson's Nursery.

## Fact File

**Opening Times:** April 1st – October 31st 11 a.m. – 5 p.m. daily
**Admission Rates:** Adults: £5.50, OAP/Disabled: £5.00, Children (6-16): £1.00
**Group Rates:** £5.00 Minimum 20 persons.
Season Ticket, Adults: £15.00, Senior Citizens: £10.00, Family: £25.00
**Facilities:** Tearoom/restaurant, gift shop, nursery for plant sales
**Disabled Access:** Yes, wheelchair loan available (booking required)
**Toilet On Site:** Yes.
**Tours/Events:** Annual garden show 7th and 8th August
**Coach Parking:** Yes.
**Car Parking:** Yes.
**Length of Visit:** 1-2 hours
**Booking Contact:** Karen Dyson,
Great Comp Garden, Comp Lane, Platt, Nr. Sevenoaks, Kent TN15 8QS
Booking Telephone No. 01732 886154
**Email:** greatcompgarden@aol.com
**Website:** www.greatcompgarden.co.uk
**Location:** Great Comp is about 2 miles from Borough Green. Follow the brown signposts on the A20 near Wrotham Heath and along the B2016 and Comp Lane.

Please quote this guide when making a booking

# Groombridge Place Gardens & Enchanted Forest — Kent

WINNER - Best Tourism Experience of the Year 2005 - Tourism Excellence Awards.

There's magic and mystery, history and romance at this enchanting award-winning venue - which provides such an unusual combination of a traditional heritage garden with the contemporary landscaping of the ancient woodland.

First laid out in 1674 on a gentle, south-facing slope, the formal walled gardens are set against the romantic backdrop of a medieval moat house (not open to the public). They include herbaceous borders, an exquisite white rose garden with over 20 varieties of roses, a secret garden, knot garden, nut walk, paradise walk and oriental garden plus the drunken garden with its crazy topiary, and there's wonderful seasonal colour throught spring, summer and autumn.

In complete contrast, in the ancient woodland of the 'Enchanted Forest" there are quirky and mysterious gardens developed by innovative designer, Ivan Hicks.

## Fact File

**Opening times:** Open daily 28th March to 7th November (2009), 10am to 5.30pm (or dusk if earlier)

**Admission Rates:** Please see our website for 2010 date and admission price information www.groombridge.co.uk or call the Estate Office on 01892 861444.

**Group Rates:** Minimum group size: 12
Adults £7.25, Senior Citizens £5.50 (off peak) and £6.25 (July and August - Peak)
Students £6.25, and Children (3-12yrs) £5.50.

**Facilities:** Gift Shop, Licensed Restaurant, Plant Sales.

**Disabled Access:** Yes. Toilet & limited parking for disabled on site. Wheelchairs on loan.

**Tours/Events:** Guided tours for groups - pre booked only, £30 per guide. Packed programme of Special Events throughout the season.

**Coach Parking:** Yes

**Length of Visit:** 3 - 4 hours

**Booking Contact:** Carrie Goodhew
Groombridge Place, Groombridge, Tunbridge, Wells, Kent TN3 9QG
Telephone 01892 861444  Fax: 01892 863996

**Email:** office@groombridge.co.uk

**Website:** www.groombridge.co.uk

**Location:** 4 miles south west of Tunbridge Wells on B2110, just off the A264 between Tunbridge Wells and East Grinstead.

Managed by Bexley Heritage Trust, Hall Place is a fine Grade I listed country house built in 1537 for Sir John Champneys, a wealthy merchant and former Lord Mayor of London. Surrounding the house are award-winning formal gardens with magnificent topiary, enclosed gardens and inspirational herbaceous borders. In the walled gardens there is a nursery selling plants grown in the Hall Place gardens, and a sub-tropical glasshouse where you can see ripening bananas in mid-winter.

The house, which boasts a panelled Great Hall with Minstrel's Gallery, ornate 17th century plaster ceilings and various other furnished historic rooms, has recently undergone extensive restoration and was fully open to the public for the first time in 2009. There are new displays including an introduction to the house's history and exhibits from Bexley's extensive museum collection. The new visitor centre in the grounds offers a riverside tearoom and a gift shop as well as tourist information.

## Fact File

**Opening times:** Gardens open 9 a.m. – sunset throughout the year. Please telephone 01322 526574 for seasonal house, visitor centre and tearoom opening hours.

**Admission Rates:** Free (except on special event days)

**Group Rates:** Charges apply for guided tours and special events.

**Facilities:** Free parking, Gift Shop, Plant Sales, Tearoom, Visitor Centre

**Disabled Access:** Partial. Designated disabled toilet and parking on site.

**Toilets on site:** Yes

**Car Parking on site:** Yes

**Coach Parking:** Yes

**Guided Tours:** Pre-booked guided tours of the house and/or gardens available.

**Special Events:** Extensive programme of events – please telephone 01322 526574 to request a leaflet.

**Length of Visit:** 3 – 4 hours

**Booking Contact:** Sue Pothecary, Bourne Road, Bexley Kent, DA5 1PQ
Booking Tel No.020 8298 6951. Booking Fax No. 020 8303 6641

**Email:** info@hallplace.org.uk

**Website:** www.hallplace.org.uk

**Location:** Black Prince Interchange of the A2, 3 miles from junction 2 of the M25, towards London. Nearest rail connection: Bexley. Buses 229. 492, B12, 132 to the foot of Gravel Hill

Please quote this guide when making a booking

## Hever Castle & Gardens

Discover 700 years of history at this romantic double-moated 13th century castle, once the childhood home of Anne Boleyn and set in award-winning gardens.

The spectacular gardens are the masterpiece of William Waldorf Astor who between 1904 and 1908 created a garden paradise. Visitors can view the stunning topiary, wander through pergolas of roses, climbing shrubs and perennial planting in the magnificent Italian gardens. Absorb the breathtaking scent of over 3000 roses in the walled rose garden and tapestries of colour in the 110-metre herbaceous border or take a peaceful stroll through Sunday Walk in this quintessential garden.

Enjoy the yew and water mazes, grottoes, cascades and fountains, 38-acre boating lake or walk around Hever Lake Walk with splendid mature trees, splashes, waterfalls.

A garden for all seasons and perfect for weddings, conferences and special occasions.

### Fact File

| | |
|---|---|
| **Opening Times:** | March - December 2010, Gardens open at 10.30am, Castle opens at 12 noon. |
| | Main Season, 3 - 31 March (Wed-Sun), Last admission 4pm, Final exit 5pm. |
| | 1 April - 31 October daily, Last admission 5pm, Final exit 6pm, (31 October exit 5pm) |
| | Winter Season (Thurs-Sun) 1 November - 19 December, (see website for opening times) |
| | Closed from 20 December. |
| **Admission Charges:** | Adults: £13.00, Senior Citizens: £11.00, Child: £7.00, Family: £33.00 |
| | Gardens Only:  Adult: £10.50, Senior Citizens: £9.00, Child: £6.50, Family: £27.50 |
| **On-Site Facilities:** | Restaurants, Picnic Areas, Shops, Plant Sales, Audio Tours |
| **Disabled Access:** | Partial.  Toilet and parking for disabled and a limited number of wheelchairs |
| **Toilets on site:** | Yes |
| **Car Parking on site:** | Yes |
| **Coach Parking:** | Yes |
| **Guided Tours:** | Pre-booked guided tours available of castle and gardens.  Full calendar of special events. |
| **Length of Visit:** | 4 hours |
| **Booking Contact:** | Nicky Rees, Hever Castle, Hever TN8 7NG |
| | Telephone No. 01732 861701  Information Tel. No. 01732 865224 |
| **Email:** | mail@hevercastle.co.uk |
| **Website:** | www.hevercastle.co.uk |
| **Location:** | 30 miles from Central London.  3 miles SE of Edenbridge. |
| | Exit M25 junctions 5 or 6. |

Please quote this guide when making a booking

Situated in the High Weald on the Kent and Sussex borders, Hole Park Garden is one of the Garden of England's best-kept secrets.

Spread over 15 acres is a garden for all seasons, set in the heart of the English countryside. Hole Park is located on the edge of the picturesque Weald village of Rolvenden. Hole Park has been owned by the Barham family for the past four generations. This outstandingly beautiful country house garden reflects the care and long-term planning that is unique to family-owned estates.

Formal, walled, meadow and woodland gardens are a feature and Hole Park is perhaps best noted for the extensive topiary, fine lawns and specimen trees and an amazing display of spring colour from the bluebells and rhododendrons.

Many visitors combine their visit to Hole Park Gardens with a trip to the historic Cinque Port of Tenterden, Sissinghurst Gardens or Great Dixter, only 6 miles distant.

## Fact File

| | |
|---|---|
| **Opening Times:** | 2pm – 6pm, Wednesdays and Thursdays from beginning of April to end of October. Sundays April to end of June. Bank Holiday Mondays 5th April, 3rd & 24th May. Autumn Sundays, 3rd, 10th, 17th and 24th October. Or by arrangement. |
| **Admission Rates:** | Adults: £5.00, Children: £0.50 |
| **Group Rates:** | Group rates, including conducted tours available, please telephone for details. |
| **Facilities:** | Toilets, Plant Stall, Tea Room |
| **Disabled Access:** | Yes. |
| **Tours/Events:** | Tours, including all catering, to your requirements. Bluebell & Spring Spectacular, from 11th April to 9th May inclusive. Meet the Gardener 17th & 24th October (2.30 prompt) |
| **Coach Parking:** | Yes. |
| **Length of Visit:** | 1½ - 2 hours. |
| **Booking Contact:** | Edward Barham, Hole Park Estate, Rolvenden, Cranbrook, Kent TN17 4JA Tel: 01580 241344  Fax: 01580 241386 |
| **Email:** | info@holepark.com |
| **Website:** | www.holepark.com |
| **Location:** | 4 miles south west of Tenterden, mid-way between villages of Rolvenden and Benenden on B2086 |

Please quote this guide when making a booking

Ightham Mote's 14-acre garden nestles in a sunken valley and surrounds the beautiful medieval moated manor house.

The North Lake Pleasure ground and ornamental pond were created in the early 19th century and are currently being restored to their former glory. Pleasurable views to the house show off its romantic setting. The sweet pea and lavender walk is a delight in late June /July. The Orchard, Enclosed Garden, Fountain Garden and Vegetable & Cutting Garden all contribute to the garden's sense of tranquillity for which it is famed.

The garden has "sat quietly" as a backdrop during the 15 year conservation project on the house.  Now emerging out of the shadows for its moment of real glory, it is an exciting time to visit as the garden becomes an attraction in its own right. Changes will be interpreted for our visitors as they occur.

## Fact File

| | |
|---|---|
| **Opening Times:** | 13th March – 31st October 2010. 10.30am – 5.00pm (last entry at 4.30pm) every day except Tuesday and Wednesday. For winter opening times please visit our website. |
| **Admission Rates:** | Adults: £11.00, Senior Citizens: N/A, Children: £5.50 |
| **Group Rates:** | Minimum Group Size: 15 Adults: £9.40, Senior Citizens: N/A, Children: £4.70 |
| **Facilities:** | Visitor Centre, Shop, Plant Sales, Restaurant, Teas |
| **Disabled Access:** | Yes, wheelchair loan available. Toilet and parking on site. |
| **Tours:** | Pre-booked only. |
| **Coach Parking:** | Yes. |
| **Length of Visit:** | 2 hours approximately. |
| **Booking Contact:** | Pamela Westaway, Ightham Mote, Mote Road, Ivy Hatch, Sevenoaks, Kent TN15 0NT Telephone: 01732-810378 Ext 100, Fax: 01732-811029 |
| **Email:** | ighthammote@nationaltrust.org.uk |
| **Website:** | www.nationaltrust.org.uk/ighthammote |
| **Location:** | Between Sevenoaks and Borough Green, 11/2 miles south of A25 |

Please quote this guide when making a booking

Winner of the UK's Best New Tourism Project Award in 2005. Set within 120 acres of beautiful Kent countryside, Lullingstone Castle is one of England's oldest family estates. The manor house and gatehouse – which overlook a stunning 15-acre lake – were built in 1497 and have been home to the same family ever since. In 2005, Tom Hart Dyke – 20th generation of Hart Dykes to live at Lullingstone – created within the Castle grounds a unique and inspiring 'World Garden' and filled it with thousands of rare, unusual and beautiful plants collected from all over the world (Tom came up with the idea for the garden whilst being held hostage at gunpoint in the Colombian jungle in 2000!) By the 2010 season these plants, some 8000 different types, will have established and begun to fill the borders, Tom would now like to offer your group a chance to join him on a unique and personal tour of the 'World Garden'. You will also have the opportunity to view inside his home – Lullingstone Castle.

## Fact File

**Opening times:** April through September; Garden open Fridays and Saturdays 12-5pm (except Good Friday) Sundays and Bank Holidays 2-6pm. House open bank holidays! Special events 11-5pm. Pre-booked guided groups for House, Church and Garden on Wednesdays and Thursdays by arrangement.

**Admission Rates:** Adults £6.00, Senior Citizen £5.50, Child £3.00, Family £15.00.

**Group Rates:** Minimum group size: 20
Adults £8.00 per person plus £40.00 per group for Tom or a dedicated guide.

**Facilities:** Toilets, book and plant sales on site. Refreshments available at nearby Visitor Centre (10 minutes walk), or why not bring a picnic?

**Disabled Access:** Yes. Toilet and parking for disabled on site. Wheelchairs available upon request.

**Tours/Events:** April 10/11 Plant Hunter Weekend. May 9 Plant Fair. June 6 Florist Day. June 13 National Gardens Scheme. August 14/15 Dahlia Weekend. September 12 Hardy Plant Society. For more details See website.

**Coach Parking:** Yes.

**Length of Visit:** Guided tour of House, Church and Garden lasts approximately 3 hours.

**Booking Contact:** Mr and Mrs G Hart Dyke. Lullingstone Castle, Eynsford, Kent DA4 0JA. Tel: 01322 862114 Fax: 01322 862115

**Email:** hartdyke@btinternet.com

**Website:** www.lullingstonecastle.co.uk

**Location:** Off the A225 near the village of Eynsford and just 10 minutes drive from Junction 3 of M25.

Please quote this guide when making a booking

Ancestral home of the Sidney family since 1552, with a history going back six and half centuries, Penshurst Place has been described as "the grandest and most perfectly preserved example of a fortified manor house in all England".

See the awe-inspiring Baron's Hall with its 60ft high steeply angled roof and the State Rooms filled with fine tapestries, furniture, portraits and armour. The 11 acres of Gardens are as old as the original house - the walls and terraces were added in the Elizabethan era - and are divided into a series of self-contained garden rooms. Each garden room offers an abundance of variety in form, foliage and bloom and ensures a continuous display from Spring to Autumn. Victorian Herbaceous border restoration project taking place 2009-11

With Penshurst Place at its centre, there is the village of Penshurst to explore, ancient Parkland (walks leaflets available), Garden Tea Room serving hot lunches as well as lighter meals and refreshments, Gift Shop, Plant Centre and a Woodland Trail with a traditional Venture Playground for Children

## Fact File

| | |
|---|---|
| **Opening Times:** | 6th March - 28th March open weekends and then daily from 29th March - Sunday 31st October 2010. |
| **Admission Rates:** | To Gardens: Adults £7.50, Child (5-16) £5.50, Family Ticket (2+2) £22.00 Cyclists family £18.00 (or £1 off normal admission prices per person). |
| **Groups Rates:** | Freeflow (non guided) House & Gardens Adults £7.50, School Children £4.50. Garden or House tours for groups (15+) includes entrance to house & grounds. House Tours Adults £9.50, Children £5.00. Garden Tours Adults £9.50, Children £6.00. Combined House & Garden tours: Adults £15.00, Children £9.00 |
| **Facilities:** | Gift Shop, Garden Tea Room & Garden History Exhibition in Garden Tower. |
| **Disabled Access:** | Garden Yes, House DVD of state rooms in Baron's Hall Toilet and parking for disabled on site, wheelchairs on loan, booking necessary. |
| **Tours/Events:** | Special joint entrance with other nearby attractions. Penshurst cream tea offer and high tea for groups if pre-booked. Events programme. |
| **Coach Parking:** | Yes. |
| **Length of Visit:** | 2 - 3 hours |
| **Booking Contact:** | Head of Visitor Services. Penshurst Place, Penshurst, Nr Tonbridge, Kent TN11 8DG Telephone: 01892 870307  Fax: 01892 870866 |
| **Email:** | groups@penshurstplace.com |
| **Website:** | www.penshurstplace.com |
| **Location:** | M25 junction 5, follow A21 to Hastings.  Exit at Hildenborough then follow brown tourists signs. |

The Secret Gardens are 3.5 acres of stunning Lutyens and Jekyll designed grounds surrounding the The Salutation, a Lutyens manor house in the heart of Sandwich, East Kent. Neglected for 25 years, an extensive restoration and re-planting programme has now returned the Gardens to their former glory.

Some original features have been revived whilst contemporary and traditional planting styles mix harmoniously to create a garden that has evolved and yet still captures the spirit of its heritage. The Gardens include a Tropical Border and Spring, Vegetable, Kitchen, White and Yellow Gardens which create a many "roomed" effect and provide something new to look at around every hedge.

After a stroll in the Gardens visit the Tea Rooms for a reviving cup of tea and a slice of homemade cake, indulge in a cream tea or linger longer for a spot of lunch and a glass of wine.

## Fact File

| | |
|---|---|
| **Opening Times:** | 5th Jan – 10th April, 10-4pm.  11th April - 30th Sept, 10-5pm.  1st Oct – 17th Dec, 10-4pm |
| **Admission Rates:** | Adults £6.00, Senior Citizens £5.50, Children (6-16) £3.00, Under 6 FREE, Family £16.00 (2 adults and up to 3 children).  Season £25.00,  Golden (1+1) £38.00. |
| **Group Rates:** | Minimum group size 10. Prices on application. |
| **Facilities:** | Licensed Tea Room with outdoor terrace built specifically for groups, space must be pre-booked. Plant Sales and personal Audio Tours. |
| **Disabled Access:** | Yes throughout the gardens and into the Tea Room. Parking and toilet facilities on site. |
| **Tours/Events:** | Guided tours available if pre-booked.  June - Solstice Garden Tours. August - Candlelit Dusk Tours. Please see website for further details and other events. |
| **Car Parking:** | Yes. |
| **Coach Parking:** | Available in the public car park adjacent to the gardens. |
| **Length of Visit:** | 2-3 hours |
| **Booking Contact:** | Dominic Parker.  Tel. 01304 619 919 |
| **Email:** | info@the-secretgardens.co.uk |
| **Website:** | www.the-secretgardens.co.uk |
| **Location:** | In the centre of Sandwich town. Follow signs to Quayside carpark; the entrance to the gardens is located at the top right corner of the car park. |

Please quote this guide when making a booking

When Elizabeth (the 5th Duchess) commissioned James Wyatt to build the Castle in 1799 she undertook the design and landscaping of the gardens park and grounds herself. She saw the entire Vale of Belvoir as her garden and was merely framing the views with her valley gardens.

Elizabeth's design and the feel of the individual gardens have many overtures brought back from the Grand Tour of an Italian terraced garden. The gardens facing Belvoir are a natural amphitheatre left by the moraines of two glaciers; she used this to her advantage. She designed and built a series of 'root houses' (summer houses), one of which can be seen today in the Duchess's Garden.

As part of the ongoing restoration, there is a new woodland path that leads down to the Duchess's Gardens. These magical woodland gardens, set in a natural amphitheatre with fresh water springs, are carefully planned to ensure plants bloom all year round.

The Duchess is also working on bringing together collections of specialist plants and roses in different areas of the garden so keen gardeners can come and smell the Best Beale rose and the most exquisite peony and such like.

## Fact File

| | |
|---|---|
| **Opening Times:** | March – October (14th March – 3rd October) |
| **Admission Rates:** | Adults: £5.00, Senior Citizens: £4.00, Children: £3.00 |
| **Group Rates:** | Minimum Group Size: 15. Adults: £9.00, Senior Citizens: £8.00. Schools: £5.00 |
| | RHS Members Free, Yes, on specified days April and July, see website |
| **Facilities:** | Visitor Centre, Shop, Restaurant, Teas |
| **Disabled Access:** | Partial. One bookable wheelchair available, please phone for details. |
| **Toilets:** | Yes. |
| **Tours/Events:** | Yes, See website |
| **Car Parking:** | Yes. |
| **Coach Parking:** | Yes. |
| **Length of Visit:** | Up to 3 hours |
| **Booking Contact:** | Mary McKinlay, Belvoir Castle, Nr. Grantham, Leics. NG32 1PE |
| | Tel. 01476 871004 |
| **Email:** | mmckinlay@belvoircastle.com |
| **Website:** | www.belvoircastle.com |
| **Location:** | East access by car and signposted from A1, A607, A52 |

Please quote this guide when making a booking

Set in 300 acres of woodland and pleasure grounds, the Victorian walled garden is a unique experience. The garden has been carefully restored to its late Victorian heyday and grows fruit, flowers and vegetables dating from 1901 or earlier. Trained fruit, vegetable beds and cut flower borders are complemented by a range of glasshouses including a peach case, vinery, display house and fernery.

The huge herbaceous borders in the Secret Garden boast a colourful selection of unusual plants, whilst the Sunken Garden near the Hall is planted in pastel shades. There is also a parterre and rose beds, A 400ft long bog garden has been created in the base of the old ha-ha and a Victorian woodland garden is under development.

## Fact File

**Opening Times:** Park open all year, 9am - dusk.
Walled Garden open 10.30am - 5pm in summer, 10.30am - 4pm in winter.

**Admission Rates:** Adults £5.00, Senior Citizens (over 60's) £4.50, Child £2.50 (2009 prices).
Season Ticket admits 2 Adults & Children all year for £19.00. (2009 prices) or ticket for two admits two people all year round for £11 (2009 prices) under 5's go free.

**Group Rates:** Minimum group size: 15. Freedom visit: Adults £4.40, Senior Citizens £4.20, Child £2.20.
Visit with tour: Adults £7.00, Senior Citizens £6.30, Child £2.20 (includes admission to all areas).

**Facilities:** Visitor Centre, Shop, Tea Room, Restaurant, Plant Sales.

**Disabled Access:** Yes. Toilet & parking on site. Wheelchairs & motorised scooters on loan, booking necessary.

**Tours/Events:** Guided tours of walled Garden & Hall available - approx 1 1/2 hours.
Special gardening events throughout the year.

**Coach Parking:** Yes

**Length of Visit:** 3 - 4 hours

**Booking Contact:** Stuart Campbell
Normanby Hall Country Park, Normanby, Scunthorpe, DN15 9HU
Telephone: 01724 720588 Fax: 01724 721248

**Email:** normanbyhall@northlincs.gov.uk

**Website:** www.northlincs.gov.uk/normanby

**Location:** 4 miles north of Scunthorpe off the B1430.

Please quote this guide when making a booking

London's oldest botanic garden is a beautiful oasis of living history in the heart of the capital, home to a unique collection of medicinal and rare plants. Used as a place to teach people about plants and the environment for more than 300 years, today it exists as a self-supporting charity with two main goals: to help children understand more about the environment, and to conserve a 'living history' of medicinal herbs and plant introductions.

This four-acre walled garden is a haven for rare and tender plants, and also has several glasshouses, the largest fruiting olive tree grown outside in Britain and the oldest rock garden in Europe made from rubble from the tower of London. Particularly successful has been the Fortune Tank Pond, installed more than a hundred years ago by the famous collector of Chinese plants, Robert Fortune.

## Fact File

| | |
|---|---|
| **Opening Times:** | 1st Apr - 31st Oct: Wednesdays - Fridays 12 - 5 p.m., Sundays & Bank Holiday Mondays 12 - 6 p.m. Last entry 30 minutes prior to closing. Late Openings until 10pm on Wednesdays in July and August with last entry at 8.30 p.m. |
| **Admission Charges:** | Adults: £8.00, Senior Citizens: £8.00, Children & Students: £5.00 |
| **Group Rates:** | £25 per guide + entrance fee. Minimum Group Size: No minimum Adults: £8.00, Senior Citizens: £8.00, Children: £5.00 |
| **On-Site Facilities:** | Shop, Plant Sales, Licensed Cafe, Teas |
| **Disabled Access:** | Yes. Wheelchair loan available - booking required. |
| **Toilets on site:** | Yes |
| **Car Parking on site:** | No |
| **Coach Parking:** | No |
| **Guided Tours:** | Yes, subject to availability. Booking required for groups of eight or more |
| **Length of Visit:** | 1 - 2 hours |
| **Special Events:** | Christmas Fair, Summer Lectures and Winter Openings - check our website for more details. |
| **Booking Contact:** | Group Visits, Chelsea Physic Garden, 66 Royal Hospital Road, London SW3 4HS Telephone No. 0207 352 5646 Extension 221  Fax No. 0207 376 3910 |
| **Email:** | enquiries@chelseaphysicgarden.co.uk |
| **Website:** | www.chelseaphysicgarden.co.uk |
| **Location:** | No. 170 bus from Victoria or Clapham Junction stations to Flood Street stop. Circle/District line to Sloane Square then 10 mins' walk; 20 mins' walk from Imperial Wharf or Battersea Park stations. |

Please quote this guide when making a booking

Capel Manor gardens and estate surround a Georgian Manor House and Victorian Stables. The gardens are broadly divided into five zones:

Historic landscape – includes a walled garden, magnolia border, holly walk, Italianate maze and seventeenth century gardens.

Model gardens – a range of domestic gardens including Sunflower Street (relocated from The Chelsea Flower Show), a garden designed by Kim Wilde and gardens dedicated to the late Queen Mother and Princess of Wales.

Trials garden – experimental and thought-provoking gardens, sponsored by Gardening Which?

Theme gardens

Wilderness and woodland gardens – best in Spring for daffodils, bluebells and azaleas.

All of this together with animal stock including Clydesdale horses, make the gardens an excellent family day out.

Visitors see behind the scenes of greater London's specialist college of Horticulture, Floristry, Garden Design, Animal Care, Arboriculture and Countryside Studies.

## Fact File

| | |
|---|---|
| **Opening Times:** | Summer Opening: March to October, open daily 10am - 6pm (last ticket 4.30pm). Winter Opening: November to February, open weekdays only 10am - 5pm (last ticket at 3.30pm) Closed Xmas eve to 2nd January. Please telephone to check times. |
| **Admission Rates:** | Adults £5.50, Senior Citizens £4.50, Child £2.50, Family Ticket £13.50 (from April 2009). |
| **Group Rates:** | Minimum group size: 20 Adults: £5.00. Concessions: £4.00 (Senior citizens, disable, students, UB40 holders). Children: £2.00 (5s and under go free) |
| **Facilities:** | Visitor Centre, Shop, Restaurant, Dogs allowed entry on lead. |
| **Disabled Access:** | Yes. Parking for disabled on site. Wheelchairs on loan, booking necessary. |
| **Tours/Events:** | Please telephone for details of tours and events programme. |
| **Coach Parking:** | Yes |
| **Length of Visit:** | 2 - 3 hours |
| **Booking Contact:** | Julie Ryan Capel Manor Gardens, Bullsmoor Lane, Enfield, Middx, EN1 4RQ Telephone: 08456 122 122 Fax: 01992 717544 |
| **Email:** | cservices@capel.ac.uk |
| **Website:** | www.capelmanorgardens.co.uk |
| **Location:** | Near junction 25 of M25 |

Please quote this guide when making a booking

# Myddelton House Gardens

The Gardens at Myddelton House are the creation of Edward Augustus Bowles (1865 – 1954), a gifted botanist, author, artist, philanthropist and Fellow of the Royal Horticultural Society. The gardens were taken over and are being beautifully restored by Lee Valley Regional Park since 1984.

Within the gardens is the National Collection of award winning iris, thousands of  naturalised Crocus and Snowdrops. The gardens feature many of Bowles original plantings, carpets of spring bulbs, box edged beds and scented shrubs. There are historical artefacts collected by E.A. Bowles located in the grounds as well as a Victorian conservatory, summer house and a pergola garden. Visit the "Lunatic Asylum", as Bowles lovingly called it because it was home to unusual plants, Tom Tiddler's Ground (a collection of variegated plants) and the Tulip Terrace. Seats beside the attractive carp lake offer beautiful views for visitors who want to relax and take a break. A visit to this hidden garden is a must at any time of the year.

London Development Agency

## Fact File

**Opening Times:** Open every day except Christmas week. April to September 10.00 – 16.30, October – March 10.00 – 15.00. National Garden Scheme days 12.00 – 16.00.

**Admission Rates:** Adults: £3.10 Concessions £2.60 (prices change April 1 2010)

**Facilities:** Plant Sales, Teas

**Disabled Access:** Yes. Toilet and car parking on site (most, but not all, paths accessible). Wheelchair loan available (bookable).

**Tours/Events:** Guided tours available. National Garden Scheme days plus other events throughout the year.

**Coach Parking:** Yes.

**Length of Visit:** 2 hours

**Booking Contact:** Head Gardener, Myddleton House, Bulls Cross, Enfield, Middlesex EN2 9HG. Tel: 08456 770 600, fax: 01992 719 937

**Email:** info@leevalleypark.org.uk

**Website:** www.leevalleypark.org.uk

**Location:** The Gardens are located close to J25 of the M25 off the A10 near Enfield. Turkey Street station is within walking distance.

Please quote this guide when making a booking

Tony Marshall

There have been gardens at Syon since the 15th century when a Brigettine abbey occupied the site of the present house. Recent archaeological excavations have revealed the remains of the 17th century formal gardens created around the house which were swept away by "Capability" Brown when he landscaped the park for the 1st Duke of Northumberland.

The centrepiece of the gardens is the spectacular Great Conservatory, built by the 3rd Duke in the 1820's by Charles Fowler.

The 40 acres of gardens open to visitors are renowned for their extensive collection of rare trees. Brown's lake is overlooked by a Doric column bearing Flora, Goddess of flowers. The vistas across the Thames-side water meadows, still grazed by cattle, give Syon a unique rural landscape so close to the heart of London.

## Fact File

**Opening Times:** Gardens: Mar – Oct daily (closed Dec 25th and 26th) – 10.30 – 17.00. Nov – Feb, weekends & New Year's Day only: 10.30 – 16.00. Last admission 1 hour before closing.
House open: 17th Mar to 31st Oct 2010 Weds, Thurs, Sundays & Bank Holiday Mondays.

**Admission Rates:** House & Gardens. Adults: £9.00, Concessions: £8.00, Child: £4.00, Family £20.00
Gardens Only. Adults: £4.50, Concessions: £3.50, Child: £2.50, Family £10.00

**Group Rates:** Available on request.

**Facilities:** Garden centre, shops & Refectory cafe.

**Disabled Access:** Disabled access to the gardens. Limited access to the house. Toilet and car parking on site.

**Tours/Events:** Guided tours + audio available for the house only.

**Length of Visit:** 1 hour house, 1 hour gardens.

**Booking Contact:** Emma Hadleigh-Sparks.
Syon House Gardens & Park, Syon Park, Brentford, Middlesex, TW8 8JF.
Tel: 020 8560 0882, Fax: 020 8568 0936

**Email:** info:syonpark.co.uk

**Website:** www.syonpark.co.uk

**Location:** Location map on website. By rail from Waterloo to Kew Bridge then bus as below or North London line to Gunnersbury then bus 237 or 267 to Brentlea Bus stop. Pedestrian entrance 50 yards. Free car park.
Vehicle entrance Park Road, Isleworth, TW8 8JF
Sat Nav Ref: TW7 6AZ

Please quote this guide when making a booking

# The Birmingham Botanical Gardens & Glasshouses    W Midlands

Opened in 1832, the Gardens are a 15 acre 'Oasis of Delight' with over 200 trees and the finest collection of plants in the Midlands.  The Tropical House, full of rainforest vegetation, includes many economic plants and a 24ft lily pond.  Palms, tree ferns and orchids are displayed in the Subtropical House.  The Mediterranean House features citrus fruits and conservatory plants while the Arid House conveys a desert scene.  There is colourful bedding on the Terrace plus Rhododendrons, Rose, Rock, Herb and Cottage Gardens, Trials Ground and Historic Gardens.  The Gardens are notably home to the National Bonsai Collection.

Other attractions include a Children's Playground, Children's Discovery Garden, exotic birds in indoor and outdoor aviaries, an art gallery and Sculpture Trail.  Bands play on summer Sunday afternoons and Bank  Holidays.

## Fact File

| | |
|---|---|
| **Opening times:** | Open daily from 9am (10am Sundays) |
| | Closing: April to September - 7pm, October to March - 5pm (or dusk). |
| **Admission Rates:** | Adults £7.50, Senior Citizen £4.75, Child £4.75 |
| **Groups Rates:** | Minimum group size: 10 |
| | Adults £6.50, Senior Citizen £4.50, Child £4.50 |
| **Facilities:** | Shop, Tea Room, Plant Sales, Children's Discovery Garden, Sculpture Trail, Aviaries, Organic Garden and many Themed Gardens. |
| **Disabled Access:** | Yes.  Toilet and parking for disabled on site.  Wheelchairs on loan, booking necessary. |
| **Tours/Events:** | Tours by appointment.  Please telephone for details of Special Events programme. |
| **Coach Parking:** | Yes by appointment. |
| **Length of Visit:** | 2 - 4 hours |
| **Booking Contact:** | Tony Cartwright |
| | The Birmingham Botanical Gardens, Westborne Road, Edgbaston, Birmingham, B15 3TR |
| | Telephone: 0121 454 1860   Fax: 0121 454 7835 |
| **Email:** | admin@birminghambotanicalgardens.org.uk |
| **Website:** | www.birminghambotanicalgardens.org.uk |
| **Location:** | Access from M5 junction 3 and M6.  follow the signs for Edgbaston then brown tourist signs to Botanical Gardens. |

Please quote this
guide when
making a booking

An exceptional plant-lover's garden for all seasons. The house and garden walls are covered with unusual shrubs, climbers and fruit. The flower gardens are formally designed and richly planted within beautiful yew hedges: formal rose gardens, a paved garden, and herbaceous and shrub borders. The arboretum has a remarkable collection of trees – more than 800 different species, many of them rare or very rare. All are labelled. The walled kitchen gardens are traditionally managed, with vegetables, cut flowers, mixed borders, and two glasshouses. In spring, the parkland and arboretum are filled with daffodils – massed plantings of more that 90 carefully chosen and graded cultivars. A delight and an education.

## Fact File

| | |
|---|---|
| **Opening times:** | 2.00 – 5.30 p.m. 3rd Sunday April and 2nd and 4th Sundays, June – September. Groups at other times by appointment |
| **Admission Rates:** | Adults: £4.00, Senior Citizens: £4.00, Children: FOC |
| **Group Rates:** | On application. |
| **Facilities:** | Teas, toilets. |
| **Disabled Access:** | Yes. |
| **Car Parking on site:** | Yes. |
| **Tours/Events:** | Guided tours available. Booking required. |
| **Length of Visit:** | 2 – 3 hours |
| **Booking Contact:** | Chris Allhusen Bradenham Hall Gardens, Bradenham, Thetford Norfolk IP25 7QP Booking Telephone No. 01362 687279/243 Booking Fax No. 01362 687669 E-mail. info@bradenhamhall.co.uk |
| **Location:** | A47, 2 miles West of Dereham, Junction of Dale Road, then south to Bradenham, 2 miles on right. |

Please quote this guide when making a booking

Those who haven't visited the Bressingham Gardens lately are certainly missing a treat, for there have been important additions and changes to make this a gardener's paradise.

The late Alan Bloom's Dell Garden created from 1953 with over 50 immaculate Island Beds of more than 4500 varieties of perennials, and Adrian Bloom's spectacular Foggy Bottom garden with views and vistas of year round colour are worth a visit on their own. But both now are linked with new gardens, in total covering 16 acres. Follow the Foggy Bottom Trail from the Summer Garden with its National Collection of Miscanthus, through the Dell Garden and the latest development of the Fragrant Garden, to Adrian's Wood, planted with a wide range of plants of North American origin to the final destination of the delightfully peaceful Foggy Bottom garden, famous too for its use of conifers.

New Winter Garden open from November to March 11-4. Groups Welcome.

## Fact File

| | |
|---|---|
| **Opening Times:** | Normal opening daily 30th March - 1st November, Winter garden open November - March |
| **Admission Rates:** | Adults: £7.00, Senior Citizens: £6.00, Children: £4.00 |
| | Winter garden, November – March only: £3.50 |
| **Group Rates:** | Minimum Group Size: 12. |
| | Adults: £6.00, Children: £4.50 |
| **Facilities:** | Visitor Centre, Shop, Plant Sales, Restaurant, Teas, Steam Museum |
| **Disabled Access:** | Yes, bookable wheelchair loan available. Toilet and car parking on site |
| **Tours/Events:** | Guided tours available.  Special events: see website www.bressingham.co.uk |
| **Coach Parking:** | Yes. |
| **Length of Visit:** | 2½ - 5 hours, (2 hours in Winter including Garden Centre). |
| **Booking Contact:** | Sue Warwick |
| | The Bressingham Gardens, Bressingham, Nr. Diss, Norfolk IP22 2AB |
| | Tol: 01379 686900  Fax: 01379 686907 |
| **Email:** | info@bressingham.co.uk |
| **Website:** | www.bressingham.co.uk & for plant, garden details, www.bressinghamgardens.com |
| **Location:** | On A1066 Thetford – Diss road, 3 miles west of Diss, Norfolk. |

Please quote this guide when making a booking

**A haven of peace and tranquillity…..**
Set in the heart of the Norfolk Broads, Fairhaven Woodland and Water Garden is one of the county's best kept secrets. Boasting the UK's finest naturalised collection of Candelabra primulas, a 950 year old Oak Tree (home to a family of ducks), and 130 acres of natural Woodland and Water Garden. The Garden was developed by the late 2nd Lord Fairhaven Major Henry Broughton, who bought South Walsham Estate in 1946. The garden was planted with shade and water loving plants including Primulas, Gunnera, Camellias and Rhododendrons.

**A garden for all seasons…**
Whether you choose to visit in the height of Summer, or in the depths of Winter there is always something to see. Spring highlights include carpets of Wild Primroses and Wood Anemones (April), numerous nesting waterfowl and the famed Candelabra primulas (last two weeks in May). During the Summer you can enjoy Sunday afternoon concerts in the Glade, or take a relaxing trip on the private Broad where you have the chance to see Kingfishers, Otters and masses of Dragonflies. October and November bring stunning Autumn colours as the ancient Beech and Oak trees loose their leaves. The Winter months at Fairhaven bring forth an abundance of migrating birds which over-Winter on the private Broad.

## Fact File

**Opening times:** Open daily 10am—5pm (10am-4pm Winter, closed Christmas Day)   Evening opening May-August on Wednesday and Thursday evenings (10am—9pm)

**Admission Rates:** Adult £5.00, Concession £4.50, Child £2.50, under 5's free, Dogs 25p
Annual membership: Family £45.00 Single £18.50, Dog £2.50

**Groups Rates:** Adult £4.75, Concession £4.25, Child £2.25

**Facilities:** Visitor Centre, Gift Shop, Tearoom, Plant sales, Boat trips (April to end of October), Sensory garden and Winter garden.

**Disabled Access:** The garden is easily accessible by wheelchair, and if you book in advance you can hire a mobility buggy if you require one. Throughout the garden we have Braille information points. The Tearoom, Gift Shop and Boat have hearing loops installed for those with hearing aids.

**Tours/Events:** Events throughout the year. Please telephone (quoting this guide) for a brochure, or visit our website for a full list of events.

**Coach Parking:** Yes.

**Length of Visit:** Minimum of 2 hours for garden visit. Also available as a Tea/Coffee stop – no entrance fee for Tearoom, Gift Shop and Plant Sales.

**Booking Contact:** Louise Rout, Fairhaven Woodland and Water Garden, School Road, South Walsham, Norwich, Norfolk, NR13 6DZ. Tel. 01603 270449 / 270683

**Email:** enquiries@fairhavengarden.co.uk

**Website:** www.fairhavengarden.co.uk

**Location:** Nine miles East of Norwich at School Road, South Walsham, Norwich, Norfolk, NR13 6DZ. Brown signs from A47 / B1140 junction.

Please quote this guide when making a booking

Most people long for tranquillity, a garden they are happy to be in ; such is Gooderstone Water Gardens.

Billy Knights, with no training but great enthusiasm began his garden in 1970, according to his own taste; his likes and dislikes were not dictated by fashion. When he died aged 93 in 1994 he left behind an entrancing 6-acre garden that sits comfortably in the Norfolk countryside. From the natural stream he created ponds and flowing waterways spanned by thirteen bridges. With its additional 8-acre Nature Trail and Kingfisher Hide it's truly a haven for people and wildlife.

Combining native and cultivated plants in informal beds, his daughter Coral is endeavouring to further enhance this atmospheric garden. From well-placed seats visitors can enjoy enchanting vistas and the changing moods of the sky reflected in the clear spring water. And the homemade cakes are delicious!

## Fact File

**Opening times:** 10 a.m. – 5.30 p.m. (dusk in winter)
**Admission Rates:** Adults: £4.75, Senior Citizens: £4.25, Children: £1.50
**Group Rates:** Minimum Group Size: 15. Adults: £4.00, Senior Citizens: £4.00, Children: £1.25
**Facilities:** Plant Sales, Teas
**Disabled Access:** Yes
**Toilets on site:** Yes
**Car Parking on site:** Yes
**Coach Parking:** Yes
**Length of Visit:** 2 – 3 hours
**Special Events:** A wonderful show of astilbe first two weeks July.
**Booking Contact:** Gooderstone Water Gardens, c/o Sunny Cottage, Lingwood, NR13 4HG
Booking Tel No. 01603 712913/07730 551945
**Email:**
**Website:** www.gooderstonewatergardens.co.uk
**Location:** In west Norfolk, 6 miles SW of Swaffham between Cockley Cley and Oxburgh Hall (N.T.). Brown signed from Swaffham and Oxborough. Swaffham is on A47.

# Hoveton Hall Gardens Norfolk

Set in the Norfolk Broads area, the gardens offer an exceptional range of plants, design features, landscape and inspiration throughout the season for garden and plant lovers. In early spring masses of narcissi, including many rare and unusual varieties collected during the 20th century, flower in drifts by the lakes and streams in the woodland areas. From late April to end of May the fragrance of the azaleas and rhododendrons is spectacular on the woodland walks; the lake and Water Garden area has beautiful displays of candelabra primulas and other moisture loving plants. During summer, hydrangeas from deep blue to pale pink and purple flank the sides of the main drive whilst the herbaceous borders and Clematis Walk are at their height of displays.

With lakes, streams and wetland areas meandering through the estate together with a large wood, the gardens are also home to extensive birdlife, both migratory and native species.

## Fact File

**Opening times:** March: Sunday 14th, 21st and 28th. April: Easter Weekend - Friday 2nd, Saturday 3rd, Sunday 4th and Monday 5th then Sunday 11th, 18th and 25th, Wednesday 28th, Thursday 29th and Friday 30th. May and June: Open every Wednesday, Thursday, Friday, Saturday, Sunday and Bank Holiday Monday. July & August: Open every Wednesday, Thursday, Friday, Saturday, Sunday and Bank Holiday Monday. 10.30am to 5.00pm (Last orders in the tea room 4.15pm) Group bookings are welcome throughout the open season and in September.

**Admission Rates:** Adults: £5.00, Children: £2.50 (5-14 years), Wheelchair users & Carers: £3.00, Single Season Ticket: £15.00, Family Season Ticket: £25.00.

**Group Rates:** (25 or more) booking and paying in advance £4.50 per head on open days, Evening Visits £6.00 per head, Non Open Days 10.30am to 5.00pm £6.00 per head by arrangement.

**Facilities:** Plant Sales, Teas

**Disabled Access:** Partial.

**Tours/Events:** Yes

**Coach Parking:** Yes.

**Length of Visit:** 2 - 3 hours

**Booking Contact:** Barbara Buxton, Hoveton Hall Gardens, Norwich, Norfolk NR12 8RJ Telephone: 01603 782798  Fax: 01603 784564

**Email:** info@hovetonhallgardens.co.uk

**Website:** www.hovetonhallgardens.co.uk

**Location:** Follow brown and white signs off the A1151 just north of Wroxham

Set in the beautiful Wensum Valley in North Norfolk, Pensthorpe, home of BBC Springwatch in 2009 is an award winning attraction for all those who love nature, wildlife and the outdoors.

Enjoy the inspirational Millennium Garden designed by Piet Oudolf, with swathes of perennials and grasses. Discover the striking lances of Astilbe chinensis var.taquetii 'Purpulanze' which are married perfectly with the spun gold Deschampsia cespitosa 'Goldtau'. The Garden builds dramatically to its peak in August, then settles into a stunning new aspect with thousands of seed heads in autumn.

The Wave Garden opened in 2006 and has year-round structure and interest, with Luzula dipping under the crests of yew and meandering through the resident trees in this lakeside garden. Thousands of bulbs and flowering fruit trees bring splashes of colour in winter and spring to this wooded lakeside garden. The Garden designed by Julie Toll works with nature using calm and naturalistic planting.

## Fact File

| | |
|---|---|
| **Opening times:** | 10 a.m. – 4 p.m. (January – March) |
| | 10 a.m. – 5 p.m. (April – December) |
| **Admission Rates:** | Please call or visit our website for prices. |
| **Group Rates:** | Minimum Group Size: 15. |
| | Please call or visit our website for prices. |
| **Facilities:** | Visitor Centre, Shop, Plant Sales, Restaurant, Teas. |
| **Disabled Access:** | Yes. Bookable wheelchair loan available. |
| **Toilets on site:** | Yes. |
| **Tours/Events:** | Guided tours available. Booking required. |
| **Coach Parking:** | Yes. |
| **Car Parking on site:** | Yes. |
| **Length of Visit:** | 4-6 hours. |
| **Booking Contact:** | Kirsty Willingham |
| | Pensthorpe Nature Reserve, Norwich Road, Fakenham, Norfolk NR21 0LN |
| | Telephone: 01328 851465 |
| | Fax: 01328 855905 |
| **Email:** | info@pensthorpe.com |
| **Website:** | www.pensthorpe.com |
| **Location:** | 1 mile from Fakenham on the A1067 to Norwich. |

Please quote this guide when making a booking

Peter Beales Roses are world leaders in Classic Roses. In glorious full bloom, the inspirational rose gardens of Peter Beales are a must for any enthusiast, with over three acres of RHS Chelsea Flower Show gold medal winning varieties, the National Collection of Rosa species and many interesting and colourful companion plants and shrubs. The garden has many points of interest in its room-like layout including an attractive pond with koi carp, pergolas, arbours and archways. Visitors are free to wander and enjoy the beautiful flowers and sensuous perfumes.

There is also an excellent licensed Bistro and Garden Centre on site where you can enjoy a meal and a glass of wine or stock up on gardening essentials, luxury gifts and, of course, lots of roses too. There are hundreds of container roses as well as other plants available during the summer or you can choose to order for winter delivery.

## Fact File

**Opening Times:** Daily 9 a.m. – 5 p.m. Sundays and Bank Holidays: 10 a.m. – 4 p.m.

**Admission Rates:** Adults: Free, Senior Citizens: Free, Children: Free.

**Group Rates:** Minimum Group Size: 15. Please contact us for further information.

**Facilities:** Garden Centre, Gift Shop, Bistro, Gardens. Marquee available for hire.

**Disabled Access:** Yes. Bookable wheelchair loan available.

**Toilets on site:** Yes.

**Tours/Events:** Guided tours available. Booking required.
Pruning and Planting in the Peter Beales Rose Gardens. A full day of instruction with lunch included to help you get the most from your roses, please enquire.

**Coach Parking:** Yes.

**Car Parking on site:** Yes.

**Length of Visit:** 2 hours.

**Booking Contact:** Peter Beales Roses, London Road, Attleborough, Norfolk NR17 1AY
Telephone: 0845 481 0277  Fax: 01953 456845

**Email:** events@peterbealesroses.com

**Website:** www.peterbealesroses.com

**Location:** Approaching from the south – leave the A11 at the Breckland Lodge roundabout. The nursery is approximately 1/2 mile north on the old London Road. Approaching from Norwich, bypass Attleborough and turn left at the roundabout.

Please quote this guide when making a booking

# Sandringham

A visit to Sandringham's sixty-acre gardens is a delight at any time of year.  Woodland walks, lakes and streams are planted to provide year-round colour and interest; sheets of spring - flowering bulbs, avenues of rhododendrons and azaleas, beds of lavender and roses, dazzling autumn colour - there is always something to see.  Other highlights include the formal North Garden, Queen Alexandra's summerhouse beside its own cascading stream, sixteen species of oak and many commemorative trees.  Guided garden walks offered regularly.

Open Easter to mid-July and early August to end October, 10.30am to 5pm daily (4pm in October).

## Fact File

| | |
|---|---|
| **Opening times:** | Easter - mid July and early August - end October |
| **Admission Rates:** | Adults £7.00, Senior Citizen £6.00, Child £3.50. |
| **Groups Rates:** | Minimum group size: 20, Group discounts available. |
| **Facilities:** | Visitor Centre, Gift Shop, Plant Sales, Teas, Restaurant, Sandringham Museum (inc in ticket) Sandringham House (Extra Charge). |
| **Disabled Access:** | Yes. Toilet and parking for disabled on site, Wheelchairs on loan. |
| **Tours/Events:** | Guided garden walks offered regularly. |
| **Coach Parking:** | Yes |
| **Length of Visit:** | 2 hours. (for Garden only, longer for House and Museum). |
| **Booking Contact:** | Mrs N Colman |
| | Sandringham, Norfolk. PE35 6EN. |
| | Tel: 01553 612908 Fax: 01485 541571 |
| **Email:** | visits@sandringhamestate.co.uk |
| **Website:** | www.sandringhamestate.co.uk |
| **Location:** | 8 miles northeast of Kings Lynn on A149. |

Please quote this guide when making a booking

The Park is listed Grade One in the Register of Parks and Gardens of Special Historic Interest and originates from the 18th Century when Ralph, first Duke of Montagu created an ornamental and intricate landscape, inspired by the ones he had seen at Versailles whilst serving there as English Ambassador to Louis XIV. The River Ise was canalised and lakes, waterways, fountains, ornamental plantings and statuary were added by him and his son John, the Second Duke of Montagu. Avenues of trees created a network of rides stretching out for over seventy miles.

The benign neglect into which the House fell for the remainder of the 18th and 19th centuries was equally beneficial for the landscape. The bones survived, albeit hidden and now the landscape is being restored, inspired by the original plans of 1746. Waterways are being cleared and realigned to the original scheme, whilst many features and avenues are being re-created.

The Orpheus project (pictured left) was commissioned by the 10th Duke of Buccleuch who wished to create a new feature, the first for nearly 300 years, on the empty space opposite the mount. The space is intended for quiet contemplation and music, whilst echoing existing features of the park. An inverted grass pyramid descends, ensuring that the new design is invisible until one draws near.

## Fact File

| | |
|---|---|
| **Opening Times:** | (2009) Grounds opening May 1st - July 31st, every day except Saturday, August 1st - September 1st every day, noon - 5pm. |
| **Admission Rates:** | (2010) Adults £6.00, Children (5-16 years old) £2.00, Family Ticket £14.00 (2+2). |
| **Group Rates:** | Please enquire. |
| **Facilities:** | Shop, Plant Sales, Toilets. |
| **Disabled Access:** | Yes. No charge for wheelchair borne visitors. |
| **Coach Parking:** | Yes. |
| **Booking Contact:** | Charles Lister, House Manager |
| | The Living Landscape Trust |
| | Boughton House |
| | Kettering |
| | Northamptonshire |
| | NN14 1BJ |
| | Booking Tel Number. 01563 515731 Booking Fax Number. 01536 417255 |
| **Email:** | llt@boughtonhouse.org.uk |
| **Website:** | www.boughtonhouse.org.uk |
| **Location:** | Boughton House is situated off the A43, 3 miles north of Kettering and the A14, through the village of Geddingdon. |

Please quote this guide when making a booking

Castle Ashby House is the ancestral home of the 7th Marquess of Northampton. The house is set amidst a 10,000 acre working estate with an extensive 25 acres of gardens which are open to the public 365 days a year.

Castle Ashby Gardens are a mixture of many different styles including a beautiful butterfly garden, picturesque rainbow border, colourful fuschia house, large arboretum including a nature trail and the formal Italian gardens.

A children's farmyard with a wide selection of rare breed animals can also be found within the gardens and new attractions now also include a tea room and gift shop.

## Fact File

**Opening Times:** 10am – 5;30 pm 1st April to 30th September
10am - 4;30 pm 1st October to 31st March
**Admission Rates:** Adults: £5.00, OAP/ children over 10 £4.50, Children under 10 free.
**Group Rates:** Minimum Group Size: 15
**Facilities:** Shop, plant sales, restaurant/teas, toilets.
**Disabled Access:** Yes.
**Car Parking on site:** Yes
**Coach Parking:** Yes
**Tours/Events:** Guided tours available.  Booking required.
**Length of Visit:** 2 – 3 hours.
**Special Events:** TBC
**Booking Contact:** Mark Brooks  - Head Gardener, Peter Cox - Assistant Head Gardener
Castle Ashby Gardens, Castle Ashby
Northampton NN7 1LQ
Booking Telephone No. 01604 695200 Booking Fax No. 01604 696516
**Email:** sales@castleashbygardens.co.uk
**Website:** www.castleashbygardens.co.uk
**Location:** Castle Ashby is situated off the A428 between Northampton and Bedford, and is also accessible from the A45.

Please quote this guide when making a booking

Coton Manor lies in peaceful Northamptonshire countryside providing an ideal setting for the ten-acre garden.
Originally laid out in the 1920s by the grandparents of the current owner, it comprises a number of smaller gardens, providing variety and interest throughout the season.
The 17th century manor house acts as a central focus for the garden, with the walls supporting unusual climbing roses, clematis and shrubs, while the surrounding York stone terraces are populated by numerous pots and containers overflowing with pelargoniums, verbenas, heliotropes, salvias and agapanthus.

The rest of the garden slopes down from the house and is landscaped on different levels, lending a natural informality. Old yew and holly hedges complement the many luxuriant borders packed with unusual plants (mostly available in the specialist nursery) and displaying inspirational colour schemes throughout the season.
Water is abundant with natural flowing streams, ponds and fountains everywhere.
Beyond the confines of the garden there is a magnificent bluebell wood (early May) and established wildflower meadow (mid-June to mid-July).

## Fact File

| | |
|---|---|
| **Opening times:** | Thursday 1st April – Saturday 2nd October 2010 – Tuesday to Saturday and Bank Holiday weekends (also Sundays in April and May): 12 noon – 5.30 p.m. |
| **Admission Rates:** | Adults £5.00, Senior Citizens £4.50, Child £2.00. |
| **Group Rates:** | Adults £4.50 |
| **Facilities:** | Restaurant available for group bookings. Cafe serving light lunches and teas, Extensive nursery with many unusual plants mostly grown from the garden.  Shop. |
| **Disabled Access:** | Yes (difficult in places) Toilet and parking for disabled on site. |
| **Tours/Events:** | Tours by appointment (Wednesdays), Hellebore weekends (Mid Feb), Bluebell Wood (late April/early May), Roses (late June). |
| **Coach Parking:** | Yes. |
| **Length of Visit:** | 2 - 2 ½ hours |
| **Booking Contact:** | Sarah Ball, Coton Manor Garden, Nr Guilsborough, Northampton NN6 8RQ. Telephone: 01604 740219 Fax: 01604 740838 |
| **Email:** | pasleytyler@cotonmanor.co.uk |
| **Website:** | www.cotonmanor.co.uk |
| **Location:** | 9 miles NW of Northampton, between A5199 (formerly A50) and A428. |

The award winning formal gardens are a series of individually planted rooms which open up before you and surround the Hall. The Magnificent re-designed 65 metre long double herbaceous borders, pools and lily ponds and on the south front a formal parterre frames the amazing vista towards the famous 7th century church at Brixworth. There are also pergolas, statues and rose borders and the visitor can enjoy a treasured view from May through to September.

The magical Wild Garden is a short walk across the Park and is planted along the course of a stream with its small cascades and arched bridges. Here are the wonderful colours of acers and rhododendrons, with bamboos and gunneras.

A number of distinguished landscape designers have been involved with gardens at Cottesbrooke including, Robert Weir Schultz, Sir Geoffrey Jellicoe, Dame Sylvia Crowe and more recently, James Alexander-Sinclair.

## Fact File

| | |
|---|---|
| **Opening Times:** | May 3rd to the end of September. May & June: Wed & Thurs 2pm - 5.30pm, July, Aug & Sept: Thurs 2pm - 5.30pm, Plus Bank Hol Mondays (May-Sept) 2pm - 5.30pm |
| **Admission Rates:** | House & Gardens: Adults £8.00, Child £3.50. (5 - 14yrs), Concession £6.50 Gardens only: Adults £5.50, Child £2.50 (5 - 14yrs), Concession £4.50 |
| **Group Rates:** | Group and private visit rates on application. |
| **Facilities:** | Tearoom, Free car park. |
| **Disabled Access:** | Yes (Gardens only), Toilet and parking for disabled on site. (Please contact administrator regarding disabled access) |
| **Tours/Events:** | Guided tour of the house (45 mins), Garden tours by arrangement, groups welcome - please pre book. The Cottesbrooke Hall Plant Finders Fair - 25th, 26th and 27th June 2010. See website for more event details. |
| **Coach Parking:** | Yes. |
| **Length of Visit:** | 1 1/2 hours (Garden) 45 mins (House). |
| **Booking Contact:** | Via the Administrator on 01604 505 808 or Fax on 01604 505 619 or email enquiries@cottesbrooke.co.uk |
| **Email:** | enquiries@cottesbrooke.co.uk |
| **Website:** | www.cottesbrookehall.co.uk |
| **Location:** | Cottesbrooke is situated 10 miles north of Northampton off the A5199. Easily accessible from the A14 (junction 1 - A5199) and M1/M6. |

Please quote this guide when making a booking

The original grounds laid out in 1655 now consist of a mellow and attractive combination of lawns and fine extensive herbaceous borders with the original wisteria. In the mid 19th century the famous rockery was built to house the first garden gnomes and a small Italian garden with a shell fountain added. There is also a box bower, stately Irish yews and a Cedar of Lebanon. Opening in 2010 is a large walled cutting garden containing mainly tall, unusual herbaceous plants, many sourced from Piet Oudolf's Dutch nursery, bringing the total garden size to approximately 5 acres.

The tea room is located in the Victorian dining room within the house. Guided tours of The Hall are also available at 2.15 and 3p.m on Wednesdays and Thursdays and non-guided tours on most Bank Holidays and fair days. Live events also take place in the garden, see website for details.

## Fact File

**Opening Times:** From Easter Sunday to October 10th, Wednesday and Thursday 2 p.m. – 5 p.m. from April 7th – October 7th, plus BH Sundays/Mondays & some event days – see website for details. Groups at other times by arrangement

**Admission Rates:** Adults: £4.00 gardens only; £7.50 house & Gardens, Senior Citizens: £3.50 gardens only; £7.00 house & Gardens, Children: (11-16) £2.00 gardens only; £2.50 house & Gardens.

**Group Rates:** For private visits, pre-booked, minimum £100 garden only and £200 house and garden

**Facilities:** Tearoom, fixed menu for groups, teas only at present for public.

**Disabled Access:** Yes.

**Toilet On Site:** Yes.

**Tours:** Yes, house only, not garden at present. Booking required.

**Events:** See website.

**Coach Parking:** Yes.

**Car Parking:** Yes.

**Length of Visit:** House & Garden 2-3 hours.

**Booking Contact:** Mrs. Carole Almond
Lamport Hall & Gardens, Lamport, Northamptonshire NN6 9HD
Telephone No. 01604 686272.  Fax No. 01604 686224

**Email:** admin@lamporthall.co.uk

**Website:** www.lamporthall.co.uk

**Location:** On A508 midway between Northampton and Market Harborough.

Please quote this guide when making a booking

The Alnwick Garden is one of the great wonders of the contemporary gardening world. The centrepiece is the Grand Cascade, a magnificent tumbling mass of water, ending in an eruption of fountains sending 350 litres of water into the air every second. A computer system synchronises four sensational displays that offer not only a visual treat but also an interactive experience for children who can play in the water jets.

Beyond this lies the Ornamental Garden, a symmetrical, structured garden with a strong European influence containing 16,500 plants. Nestled in a corner of The Garden is the Rose Garden, with pergola lined paths covered in climbing and shrub roses mixed with glorious honeysuckle and clematis. The Garden is also home to one of the largest wooden tree houses in the world with rope bridges and walkways in the sky. There's the Serpent Garden, with a wonderful array of water features and topiary, the Bamboo Labyrinth, the intriguing Poison Garden and the Cherry Orchard, planted with hundreds of the wonderful great white cherry, Tai Haku.

Designed by the renowned Belgian father and son company, Wirtz international, The Garden is the vision of the Duchess of Northumberland.

## Fact File

**Opening Times:** Open from 10am daily except Christmas Day, closing at 6pm in Summer and 4pm in Winter.

**Admission Rates:** Adults £10.00, Senior Citizen £7.50, Children 1p (up to 4 children per adult). Prices include an optional donation to The Alnwick Garden Trust. Prices valid until 31st March 2010, see www.alnwickgarden.com for current information.

**Groups Rates:** Minimum group size: 14. Adults £6.25, Children 1p (up to 4 children per adult). Prices valid until 31st March 2010, see www.alnwickgarden.com for current information.

**Facilities:** Treehouse restaurant and bar, Pavilion Café, Courtyard Coffee Shop, Gift Shop & Plant Sales.

**Disabled Access:** Yes. Toilet and parking for disabled on site.

**Tours/Events:** Please tel 01665 511350 or visit www.alnwickgarden.com for details of tours & special events.

**Coach Parking:** Yes

**Length of Visit:** At least 2.5 hours

**Booking Contact:** The Alnwick Garden, Alnwick, Northumberland, NE66 1YU Telephone: 01665 511350 Fax: 01665 511351

**Email:** info@alnwickgarden.com

**Website:** www.alnwickgarden.com

**Location:** Leave the A1 North of the town at the junction signposted by the tourist information sign for The Alnwick Garden. The Garden is clearly signposted, approx 1 mile from the A1 junction.

Please quote this guide when making a booking

The award winning gardens of Blenheim Palace.
On passing through the triumphal arch at Woodstock gate entrance to Blenheim Palace, it is clear to see why Lord Randolph Churchill proclaimed 'This is the finest view in England'

The Park was landscaped in the 1760's by 'Capability' Brown and is hailed as one of his greatest achievements. It is one of the main reasons that the Palace and Park was created a World Heritage site in 1987. The 2,100 acres of sweeping parkland and 100 acres of formal gardens provide an awe-inspiring setting for Britain's Greatest Palace.

The stunning Formal Gardens have so much to offer, whether for a group or individuals a new Audio Garden Tour is now available throughout the season, with commentary from the Palace experts offering visitors the opportunity to take in the wonders of the Gardens at their own pace. From the ornate fountains in the Water Terraces and Lakeside Walks to the elegant Rose Garden and recently restored Secret Garden, there is something for anyone with a love of gardens.

## Fact File

**Opening Times:** Opening Dates: Saturday 13 February to Sunday 12 December 2010
Saturday 13 February to Sunday 31 October 2010 open daily
Wednesday, 3 November to Sunday 12 December open Wed to Sunday

**Opening Times:** Palace open daily from 10.30am; Formal Gardens from 10am
(last admission 4.45pm) areas to be vacated by 6pm.
Park open daily from 9am to 6pm (last admission 4.45pm) except Christmas Day
all areas to be vacated by 6pm.

**Admission Rates:** Palace, Park & Gardens: Adult £18.00 Concession £14.50 Child £10.00 Family £48.00
Park & Gardens: Adult £10.30 Concession £7.70 Child £5.00 Family £26.00

**Group Rates:** Palace, Park & Gardens Ticket: Adult £12.30 Concession £10.80 Child £6.75 Family N/a

**Facilities:** Shop, Restaurant, Hampers, Afternoon Teas, Sunday Lunches

**Disabled Access:** Yes, toilet on site. Buggies, wheelchairs & Mobility Scooters available.

**Coach Parking:** Yes

**Length of Visit:** At least 2 hours

**Booking Contact:** Cathy Tuckey, Blenheim Palace, Woodstock, Oxfordshire OX20 1PP
Telephone: 01993 811091 Freephone: 0800 849 6500 (24hr recorded message)
Fax: 01993 810570

**Email:** operations@blenheimpalace.com

**Website:** www.blenheimpalace.com

**Location:** situated in Woodstock eight miles north west of Oxford on A44

Please quote this guide when making a booking

Buscot Park was laid out in the late eighteenth century in the English Landscape style to provide a naturalistic setting for the Palladian style house built between 1780 and 1783.

The famous water garden was added in 1904 by Alexander Henderson, later the first Lord Faringdon, who commissioned the architect and garden designer Harold Peto to create a link between the eighteenth century house and the great lake. Peto was the leading exponent of formal Italianate garden design of his day and this water garden is widely regarded as one of his finest works. It consists essentially of a series of stairways, formal lawns, pools and basins interlinked by a descending canal complete with rills, miniature cascades and a bridge all flanked by box hedges sheltering statuary and stone seats.

The present Lord Faringdon continues to enhance the grounds and has transformed the former eighteenth-century kitchen garden into a beautifully structured ornamental garden.

*'I consider Buscot Park to be one of England's most unsung country estates' - Tony Russell, Country Gardener Magazine.*

*Photo of Peto Water Garden by David Dixon*

## Fact File

**Opening Times:**    1st April – 30 September
House, Grounds and Tearoom*: Wed-Fri, 2-6pm (last entry to House 5pm).
Also open Good Friday, Bank Holiday Mondays and the following weekends: 3/4, 17/18 April; 1/2, 15/16, 29/30 May; 12/13, 26/27 June; 10/11, 24/25, July; 14/15, 28/29 August; 11/12, 25/26 September. (*Tearoom open 2.30-5.30pm)
Grounds only: Mon – Tue, 2-6pm

**Admission Rates:**    Adults: £8.00 (House & Gardens), £5.00 (Gardens only)
Children (aged 5-16): £4.00 (House and Gardens), £2.50 (Gardens only)

**Facilities:**    Picnic Area, Homemade Teas, Occasional plant sales.

**Disabled Access:**    Partial. Adapted Lavatory. Ramps to tearoom, marquee and garden. Two single seater powered mobility vehicles for use in the grounds can be booked in advance.

**Coach Parking:**    Up to two coaches. Groups **must** book in advance.

**Length of Visit:**    3 hours

**Booking Contact:**    Estate Office
Buscot Park, Faringdon, Oxfordshire, SN7 8BU.
Telephone: 01367 240786 Fax: 01367 241794

**Email:**    estbuscot@aol.com

**Website:**    www.buscotpark.com

**Information Line:**    0845 345 3387

**Location:**    Buscot Park is situated on the south side of the A417 between Lechlade and Faringdon

Always a family favourite with animal lovers the Park has, in more recent times, become an unexpected attraction to gardeners surprised at the rich diversity of plants and planting styles throughout the 160 acre parkland surrounding a Listed Regency Gothic Manor House.

Herbaceous borders and formal parterres are a link with the past whereas the original walled kitchen garden is now adorned with exuberant exotic displays including unique arid borders of cacti; dramatic foliage displays of bananas and cannas and giant water lilies in the open air. The calling of kookaburras and macaws further enhance the exotic atmosphere.

Planting in and around the 270 animal species has become an important feature with particular highlights being the Madagascar exhibit, where you can walk with lemurs, and the Tropical House which combines exotic plants, birds and sloths.

Extensive plantings of ornamental grasses and perennials give a flavour of the savannah around the white rhino paddock. Flowering shrubs, magnificent specimen trees, mixed borders and flower meadows provide year round interest. Elsewhere spring and summer bedding and container displays provide riots of colour well into the autumn

## Fact File

| | |
|---|---|
| **Opening Times:** | Everyday (except Christmas Day). 10am. (last admission 3.30pm October - February). |
| **Admission Rates:** | Adults £11.50, Senior Citizens (over 65) £8.00, Children £8.00, (age 3-16yrs). |
| **Group Rates:** | Minimum group size: 20 Adults £10.00, Senior Citizens (over 65) £7.00, Children £6.50 (age 3-16 yrs). |
| **Facilities:** | Shop, Teas, Restaurant. (Restaurant available for booked lunches and teas, waitress service in Orangery). |
| **Disabled Access:** | Yes. Parking for disabled on site. Wheelchairs on loan, booking necessary. |
| **Tours/Events:** | Gardens Special for inclusive charge, talk by Head Gardener or his Deputy in the Drawing room of the Manor House and Cotswold Cream Teas in the Orangery. |
| **Coach Parking:** | Yes |
| **Length of Visit:** | 2 ½ - 3 hours |
| **Booking Contact:** | General Office. Cotswold Wildlife Park, Burford, Oxfordshire, OX18 4JP Telephone: 01993 823006 Fax: 01993 823807 |
| **Email:** | feedback@cotswoldwildlifepark.co.uk |
| **Website:** | www.cotswoldwildlifepark.co.uk |
| **Location:** | On A361 2.5 miles south of A40 at Burford. |

Please quote this guide when making a booking

ROUSHAM and its landscape garden should be a place of pilgrimage for students of the work of William Kent (1685 - 1748).

Rousham represents the first phase of English landscape design and remains almost as Kent left it, one of the few gardens of this date to have escaped alteration, with many features which delighted eighteenth century visitors to Rousham still in situ.

The house, built in 1635 by Sir Robert Dormer, is still in the ownership of the same family. Kent added the wings and the stable block. Don't miss the walled garden with their herbaceous borders, small parterre, pigeon house and espalier trees. A fine herd of rare Long-Horn cattle are to be seen in the park.

Rousham is uncommercial and unspoilt with no tea room and no shop. Bring a picnic, wear comfortable shoes and its yours for the day.

## Fact File

| | |
|---|---|
| **Opening times:** | Every Day All Year |
| **Admission Rates:** | Adults £5.00, Senior Citizen £5.00, No Children under 15. |
| **Groups Rates:** | None |
| **Facilities:** | None |
| **Disabled Access:** | Partial, parking for disabled on site. |
| **Tours/Events:** | None |
| **Coach Parking:** | Yes |
| **Length of Visit:** | 1 - 2 hours. |
| **Booking Contact:** | C Cottrell - Dormer |
| | Rousham, Nr Steeple Aston, Bicester, Oxon, OX25 4QX. |
| | Tel: 01869 347110 Fax: 01869 347110 |
| **Email:** | ccd@rousham.org |
| **Website:** | www.rousham.org |
| **Location:** | South of B4030, East of A4260. |

Please quote this guide when making a booking

Situated in a beautiful Chiltern Valley, the walled garden rises up behind the ancient house built and lived in by the Stonor family since the twelfth century. The garden today features swathes of daffodils in April. A field of Narcissi "Pheasant Eye" can be seen through iron gates at the top of the garden, while irises bloom inside the walls in May. Old fashioned roses, peonies and lavenders bloom on the seventeenth century terraces in June, flanked by ancient yew trees and clipped box hedges by the lily ponds. Climbing the terrace stages one finds a long mixed border, ending with a Japanese garden house built by the 5th Lord Camoys after his visit to Kyoto in 1906. The jasmine and rose bower offers spectacular views of the house and deer park. This area was the old kitchen garden now converted by Lady Camoys in the 1980's into a pleasure garden. It is divided into six plots as shown in the seventeenth century painting of the house, which can be seen in the drawing room. Irish yews box hedging and old fruit trees delineate the design.

## Fact File

**Opening times:** Open in 2009 on Sundays (Easter to mid September inclusive), Bank Holiday Mondays and Wednesdays (July and August only)

**Admission Rates:** House and Gardens: Adult: £8.00, first child (5-16) £4.00, additional children, under 5's free
Gardens only: Adult £4.00, first child (5-16) £2.00, additional children, under 5's free.

**Group Rates:** Minimum Group Size: 20  A private guided tour is available at £9.00 per person on Tuesday to Thursday, April to September by prior arrangement.

**Facilities:** House, Chapel, Gardens, Shop, Old Hall Tea Room

**Disabled Access:** Unsuitable for physically disabled.

**Tours:** The house, tea room and shop open at 2.00pm - last entry 4.30pm.
Gardens are open on each of the above days between 1.00pm and 5.30pm.

**Events:** VW Rally (Sunday 6 June 2010), Classic Concert (Saturday 7 August), Chilterns Craft Fair (Friday 27 August - Monday 30 August)

**Coach Parking:** Yes.

**Length of Visit:** 1 – 4.5 hours.

**Booking Contact:** Administrator, Stonor Park, Henley-on-Thames, Oxon RG9 6HF
Tel: 01491 638587  Fax: 01491 639348

**Email:** administrator@stonor.com

**Website:** www.stonor.com

**Location:** Five miles north of Henley-on-Thames, on the B480
Henley-on-Thames – Watlington Road.

Please quote this guide when making a booking

Discover 32 acres of magnificent gardens set in unspoilt countryside on the Warwickshire-Oxfordshire border. Created from two spring-fed valleys on the Edge Hill plateau, the gardens have been in use since the 12th Century, but were largely transformed by Kitty Lloyd-Jones in the 1930's, with the creation of cascading terraces on the valley sides, extensive herbaceous borders, and a rare Bog Garden on the site of medieval fish ponds. The gardens provide today's visitors with a variety of experiences, including large lawns, terraced borders, elegant stone staircases, rose garden, orchards, and a rare kitchen display garden.

A highlight is the National Collection of Aster amellus, Aster cordifolius, and Aster ericoïdes, providing sumptuous colour in early autumn. Also recognised as one of the National Trust's Top 10 gardens for butterflies.

At the heart of the site is the 17th century mansion, extended and remodelled in the 1930s for the 2nd Viscount Bearsted as a weekend retreat, and as a gallery for his incredible art collection, regarded as one of the nation's most important private collections of the 20th century.

## Fact File

| | |
|---|---|
| **Opening Times:** | Spring: 13th Feb - 10th Mar, Sat - Wed 11-5pm, House by tour only.<br>Summer: 13th Mar - 31st Oct, Fri - Wed, 11-5pm, House by tour 11-1pm.<br>Winter: 1st Nov - 3rd Jan 2011, Sat - Wed 12-4pm, House (ground floor), weekends only until Christmas. |
| **Admission Rates:** | House & Gardens: £9.00 (£5.50 Garden Only), Child £4.50 (£2.70), Family £22.50 (£13.70) Groups £7.35, National Trust Members FREE. |
| **Group Rates:** | Minimum group size: 15 |
| **Facilities:** | Visitor Centre, Shop, Plant Sales, Restaurant, Teas, Free car parking, Bookable holiday cottage in garden. |
| **Disabled Access:** | Yes – partial. Toilet and car parking on site. Wheelchair loan available please call to book. |
| **Tours/Events:** | Jazz concerts, Aster open days, 1930s days, vintage car meetings, art days, Christmas opening, historical re-enactments. |
| **Coach Parking:** | Yes |
| **Length of Visit:** | 3 hours |
| **Booking Contact:** | Jane Scarff, Upton House & Gardens, Upton House, Banbury, Oxfordshire OX15 6HT. Telephone 01295 670266  Fax: 01295 671144 |
| **Email:** | uptonhouse@nationaltrust.org.uk |
| **Website:** | www.nationaltrust.org.uk |
| **Location:** | On the A422 between Banbury and Stratford upon Avon. Signposted from Junction 12 M40. |

Please quote this guide when making a booking

Waterperry gardens are steeped in history, with the famous, purely herbaceous border dating back to the 1930's when Beatrix Havergal established her Ladies Horticultural School. Running more than 200 feet along the length of the old kitche garden wall, the south facing border provides interest from early May to late September, using early, mid-season and late-flowering herbaceous plants and climbers.

New design elements have been incorporated into the 8 acre gardens over the years, including the colour border, showing how to use flowers, stems, autumn foliage and fruit in design. A formal knot garden reflects planting through the ages from Tudor to modern times and there's also a herb border and spectacular white and lavender wisteria arch. The Mary Rose Gardens show how roses can be used in design and there's a waterlily canal, herbaceous nursery stock beds from which all our cuttings are taken for the plants sold in the walled garden plant centre; island beds designed by nurseryman Alan Bloom; an alpine garden and riverside walk.

As well as an art gallery, small rural life museum and teashop, the garden shop sells a full range of garden sundries, gifts and books. Waterperry is an oasis of calm and beauty within easy reach of Oxford.

## Fact File

**Opening times:** March to October 10am to 5.30pm. November - February 10am to 5pm.

**Admission Rates:** January 1st to February 5th 2010. Adults & concessions £3.85. Children aged 16 & under free.
February 6th to October 31st 2010. Adults £5.90, concessions £4.70. Children aged 16 & under free.
November 1st to February 2011. Adults & concessions £4.20. Children aged 16 & under free.

**Group Rates:** January 1st to February 5th 2010. £3.85 for parties of 20 or more booked in advance.
February 6th to October 31st 2010. £4.70 for parties of 20 or more booked in advance.
November 1st to February 2011. £4.20 for parties of 20 or more booked in advance.

**Facilities:** Garden shop, Plant centre, Teas, Restaurant, Gallery, Museum

**Disabled Access:** Yes. Toilet and parking for disabled on site. Wheelchairs on loan.

**Tours/Events:** Tours can be arranged. Waterperry has a full programme of annual events from those with a horticultural theme to outdoor concerts and theatre. There's also a full programme of gardening, arts and crafts classes. Please visit our website www.waterperrygardens.co.uk for more information.

**Coach Parking:** Yes. Coach drivers also receive a meal voucher on booking.

**Length of Visit:** Approximately 3 – 4 hours.

**Booking Contact:** Main Office, Waterperry Gardens, Waterperry, Near Wheatley, Oxfordshire OX33 1JZ. Tel 01844 339254. Fax 01844 339883.

**Email:** office@waterperrygardens.co.uk

**Website:** www.waterperrygardens.co.uk

**Location:** 7 miles east of Oxford – junction 8 M40 from London. Follow brown signs. Junction 8a M40 from Birmingham.

Please quote this guide when making a booking

# Hodnet Hall Gardens

The gardens at Hodnet were started in 1922 when there was only a marshy hollow in front of the house. This was excavated, dams built and a chain of seven lakes and pools was created, all planted out with rare trees and shrubs. Rhododendrons and camellias thrive in the acid soil; iris and other bog plants enjoy this fairly high rainfall area and their position around the pools.

April is the perfect time to come and admire the camellias, crocuses and daffodils, not forgetting the magnificent Magnolia Walk. May and June showcases rhododendrons, lilacs, azaleas and bluebell woods. High summer is brimming with peonies, hydrangeas, roses and many other flowering shrubs, the colours lasting right through September. With 63 acres to explore there is something for everyone here.

The half-timbered restaurant serves lunches and teas amongst a unique collection of big game trophies.

## Fact File

| | |
|---|---|
| **Opening Times:** | 12 noon – 5 p.m.<br>April: 4th & 5th – Easter.  May: 2nd & 3rd (BH), 16th, 23rd, 30th & 31st (BH).<br>June: 6th (NGS), 13th & 27th.  July: 11th & 25th.  August: 1st, 15th, 29th & 30th (BH).<br>September: 12th & 26th |
| **Admission Rates:** | Adults: £4.50, Senior Citizens: £4.50, Children: £2.00 |
| **Group Rates:** | Minimum Group Size: 20.  Adults: £4.50, Senior Citizens: £4.50, Children: £2.00 |
| **Facilities:** | Restaurant – teas and lunches |
| **Disabled Access:** | Yes. |
| **Toilet On Site:** | Yes. |
| **Tours:** | Yes.  Booking required. |
| **Events:** | See website |
| **Coach Parking:** | Yes. |
| **Car Parking:** | Yes. |
| **Length of Visit:** | 1 hour minimum. |
| **Booking Contact:** | The Secretary<br>Hodnet Hall Gardens, Hodnet Hall, Hodnet, Market Drayton, TF9 3NN<br>Telephone No. 01630 685786.  Fax No. 01630 685853 |
| **Email:** | secretary@heber-percy.freeserve.co.uk |
| **Website:** | www.hodnethallgardens.org |

# Wollerton Old Hall Garden Shropshire

Photo Clive Nichols

Created 20 years ago around a Tudor house (not open), this quality garden has achieved the highest "Good Garden Guide" rating and RHS Partnership status. Designed by the owner, Lesley Jenkins, this outstanding garden combines a strong structure with clever planting combinations using perennials.

The early spring shows of anemones, hellebores and trilliums are followed by tulips, aquilegias and oriental poppies. The summer roses herald the arrival of the delphiniums which in turn give way to the dominance of stately hollyhocks and vibrant phlox. August sees the hot garden ignited which still burns when the asters and euonymus seed capsules arrive in September.

The garden has significant collections of rare perennials, salvias, paniculata phlox and clematis and many of these are available in the Plant Centre. The Tea Room provides excellent lunches, teas and evening meals with all the food being prepared freshly on the premises.

**Joint Tickets:** These are available for groups to visit Wollerton and the Trentham Estate on the same day for £10 per person.

## Fact File

**Opening Times:** Public days – Good Friday, every Friday, Sunday and Bank Holiday until end of September: 12 noon – 5 p.m.

**Admission Rates:** Adults/Senior Citizens: £5.50 per person, Children 4-15 years: £1.

**Group Rates:** Garden groups welcome by appointment on Tuesdays and Wednesdays. Minimum 25, Group rate £5.00 per person.

**Facilities:** Plant Sales, Lunches, Teas, large car park for cars.

**Disabled Access:** Easy wheelchair access for 80% of the garden. The remainder accessible with helper.

**Tours/Events:** Guided tours available: topic-specific garden tours with Head Gardener.
Lectures by garden personalities.
Evening Summer Strolls with candlelit garden and supper.

**Coach Parking:** Coaches welcome by appointment. Coach parking available on the lane outside the garden.

**Length of Visit:** 2 – 4 hours, depending upon level of plant interest.

**Booking Contact:** Diana Oakes.
Wollerton Old Hall Garden, Wollerton, Market Drayton, TF9 3NA.
Telephone: 01630 685760  Fax: 01630 685583

**Email:** info@wollertonoldhallgarden.com

**Website:** www.wollertonoldhallgarden.com

**Location:** The garden is brown-signed off the A53 between the A41 junction and Hodnet.

Please quote this guide when making a booking

Located in an area of outstanding natural beauty, the hilltop site of Claverton Manor, the home of the American Museum, takes full advantage of the spectacular views over the valley of the River Avon. The grounds total some 120 acres of which forty are open to visitors. A unique replica of George Washington's flower garden at Mount Vernon, Virginia is flanked by an Arboretum devoted to American trees and shrubs. Below this has been added the Lewis and Clark trail containing trees and shrubs discovered on the pioneering expedition across the States, now celebrating its 200th anniversary. The parkland, with its majestic old cedars, provides a circular walk through ancient meadows while above the house a path has been created through woodland. A small vegetable garden dye plant area and colonial herb garden give a flavour of early colonial plantings.

## Fact File

**Opening Times:** 13th March - 31st October: Tuesday to Sunday, Bank Holiday and every Monday in August. 12.00noon – 5.00pm

**Admission Rates:** House & Garden: Adult £8.00, Concession £7.00, Child (5-16) £4.50, Family £21.50. Grounds & Exhibition Gallery only: Adult £5.50, Concession £4.50, Child £3.50.

**Group Rates:** Pre-booked parties over 15 £6.00 each.

**Facilities:** Shop. Plant sales. Restaurant. Teas. Museum of American Decorative Art.

**Disabled Access:** Limited disabled access. Toilet and parking on site.

**Tours/Events:** Guided tours available. Visit www.americanmuseum.org for details on special events.

**Coach Parking:** Yes.

**Length of Visit:** 1½ - 2 hours

**Booking Contact:** Helen Hayden. The American Museum in Britain, Claverton Manor, Bath, Somerset, BA2 7BD Telephone: 01225 460503 Fax: 01225 469160

**Email:** info@americanmuseum.org

**Website:** www.americanmuseum.org

**Location:** Just along from the University of Bath. Signposted from Bath City Centre and A36 Warminster Road. Coaches MUST approach from city centre, up Bathwick Hill.

Please quote this guide when making a booking

Having undergone extensive redevelopment over the past few years, the Walled Gardens were recently officially opened by HRH Prince Edward. The Gardens lie within the grounds of a mediaeval priory, and many of its fine buildings remain.

The Gardens have classic and contemporary features such as the 'hot' herbaceous border, the blue garden a sub-tropical walk and a Victorian style fernery. There is also a botanical glasshouse, where arid, sub-tropical and tropical plants can be seen. Two smaller gardens within the walls, 'The Bishop's' and 'Australasian' gardens are areas of real tranquillity.

As well as ensuring the continuation of a garden on this historic site, the Gardens provide a dynamic learning environment for students, as well as a plant shop and newly opened tea room. They really are a gem waiting to be discovered!

## Fact File

**Opening Times:** Winter opening, Mon – Fri 10 a.m. – 4 p.m.
Summer opening, daily 10 a.m. – 5 p.m.

**Admission Rates:** Adults: £3.50, Senior Citizens: £2.50, Children: under-5s free; 5-16: £2.50

**Group Rates:** Minimum Group Size: 15, Adults: £6.00 (includes guided tour, tea/coffee and cake), Senior Citizens: £2.50, Children: £2.50

**Facilities:** Shop, plant sales, tearooms

**Disabled Access:** Yes.

**Toilet On Site:** Yes.

**Tours/Events:** Yes. Booking required.

**Coach Parking:** Yes, by prior arrangement

**Car Parking:** Yes.

**Length of Visit:** Can stay all day

**Booking Contact:** Jane Wagner
The Walled Gardens of Cannington, Church Street, Cannington, Nr. Bridgwater, Somerset TA5 2LS
Telephone: 01278 655042

**Email:** wagnerj@bridgwater.ac.uk

**Website:** www.canningtonwalledgardens.co.uk

**Location:** Cannington, nr. Bridgwater, Somerset. At village war memorial turn into Church Street, then first turning on left.

Please quote this guide when making a booking

Whilst in the Garden, many talk of a heightening of sensory acuity; colours, light, fragrance and sound serving to amplify the garden experience. The planting philosophy of the Trust allows the visitor to enjoy a connection with this sensory world, and year round the beds are planted with a care for colour and form. The favoured style is that of the traditional cottage garden. Recognisable favourites include delphiniums, hollyhocks, dahlias, calendula, violas, nicotiana, hardy geraniums, bells of Ireland, and mignonette. In Buckton's orchard, apple varieties such as Ashmeads Kernel, James Grieve, Laxtons Superb, Ribston Pippin, Blenheim Orange and Crispin are particularly well-represented. Particular aspects of the garden that the visitor can enjoy include the Well Head, the Lions Head, Arthurs Court and the Vesica Piscis, all offer the visitor a journey through this living Sanctuary that the Garden exudes and is well known for.

## Fact File

**Opening Times:** Open 365 days of the year including Christmas Day & Boxing Day
April 1st - 31st October, 10.00am to 5.30pm.  November 1st - March 31st, 10.00am to 4pm
We request no smoking, no alcohol, no mobile phones, no dogs please (except guide dogs)

**Admission Rates:** Adults £3.90, (gift aid donation included in price), £3.50 Standard Entrance
Senior Citizen £3.20, (gift aid donation included in price), £2.90 Standard Entrance
Children £1.90, (gift aid donation included in price), £1.70 Standard Entrance
Companionship From £15 entitles free entrance to gardens for a year (plus other benefits).

**Facilities:** Visitor Shop & plant sales.

**Disabled Access:** Yes. Motorised vehicle available on request.

**Tours/Events:** None in house. Outside tours welcome – booking desired.
Events are year round (refreshments available), please check the website or call for details.

**Car/Coach Parking:** 100 m away at Drapers

**Length of Visit:** I hour minimum, longer for a fuller enjoyment of the garden.

**Booking Contact:** Office/Gatehouse, Chalice Well Gardens, Chilkwell St, Glastonbury, Somerset, BA6 8DD
Tel. 01458 831154  Fax. 01458 835528

**Email:** info@chalicewell.org.uk

**Website:** www.chalicewell.org.uk

**Location:** The Chalice Well is situated at the foot of Glastonbury Tor, on the main road (A361) towards Shepton Mallet. Between May and September, a shuttle bus runs between the town center, (outside the Abbey), Chalice Well and the Tor, so you can park your car in one of the town center car parks if you wish. Chalice Well is 15 minutes walk from the town centre.

Please quote this guide when making a booking

# Cothay Manor & Gardens Somerset

Five miles West of Wellington, hidden in the high-banked lanes of Somerset, lies Cothay, built at the end of the Wars of the Roses in 1485. Virtually unchanged in 500 years, this sleeping beauty sits on the banks of the river Tone within its twelve acres of magical Gardens.

The Gardens, laid out in the 1920's, have been re-designed and replanted within the original structure. Many garden rooms, each a garden in itself, are set off a 200 yard yew walk. In addition there is a bog garden with azaleas and drifts of primuli, a cottage garden, a courtyard garden, river walk and fine trees. A truly romantic plantsman's paradise. Two stars in the Good Garden Guide.

## Fact File

**Opening Times:** Easter to September inc. Tues, Wed, Sun, & BH - 11am with last entry 4.30pm.

**Admission Rates:** Prices vary - Please visit our website.

**Group Rates:** Groups (20+) are welcome every day of the season by appointment. For further information please contact us, or download a booking form from our website. Click on Groups.

**Facilities:** Plant Sales, Cream Teas, (Groups 20+ catering by arrangement).

**Disabled Access:** Yes (Garden) Partial (House), Toilet and parking for disabled on site.

**Tours/Events:** On Sundays (during the season) at 1.45pm and 3pm a group from the general public will be guided round the Manor, 1 $\frac{1}{4}$ hours, otherwise the manor is only open to groups of 20+ by appointment throughout the year. For Events please visit our website.

**Coach Parking:** Yes.

**Length of Visit:** $1\frac{1}{2}$ - $3\frac{1}{2}$ hours

**Booking Contact:** The Administrator, Cothay Manor, Greenham, Wellington, Somerset, TA21 0JR
Telephone: 01823 672 283  Fax: 01823 672 345

**Email:** cothaymanor@btinternet.com

**Website:** www.cothaymanor.co.uk

**Location:** From junction 26 M5, direction Wellington, take A38 direction Exeter, $3\frac{1}{2}$ miles turn right to Greenham. From junction 27 M5 take A38 direction Wellington, $3\frac{1}{2}$ miles take 2nd turning left to Greenham.

# East Lambrook Manor Gardens Somerset

One of England's best-loved privately-owned gardens created by the late Margery Fish, celebrated plantswoman and gardening writer, between 1938 and 1969. Her talent for combining old-fashioned and contemporary plants in a relaxed and informal manner has created an extraordinary and unusual garden of great charm.

Now Grade-I listed and renowned as the premier example of the English cottage gardening style, it is noted for its many small paths dividing densely planted beds. It remains a true plantsman's garden, having over 85 varieties of rare snowdrop and extensive collections of hellebores and geraniums. New owners intent on improving the garden arrived in 2008 and work is underway on restoring Margery Fish's 'Green Garden', an area overgrown for more than 20 years.

The Margery Fish Plant Nursery stocks an increasing selection of hardy plants including geraniums, with many propagated from plants growing in the garden.

## Fact File

| | |
|---|---|
| **Opening Times:** | February, May & June daily 10a.m. - 5p.m. |
| | March-April & July-October: Tuesday-Saturday & Bank Holiday Mondays, 10a.m. - 5p.m. |
| **Admission Rates:** | Adults: £4.50, Senior Citizens: £4.50, Children under 16 free. |
| **Group Rates:** | Minimum Group Size: 10. Adults: £4.00, Senior Citizens: £4.00, Children under 16 free. |
| | RHS Members Free from 1st February - 31st March and from 1st September - 30th October. |
| **Facilities:** | Plant sales, teas. Malthouse Gallery has regular exhibitions. Excellent lunches available at C17 Rose & Crown pub directly opposite the garden. |
| **Disabled Access:** | Yes, partial. |
| **Toilet On Site:** | Yes, including a toilet for people with disabilities. |
| **Tours/Events:** | Yes, booking required. All group visits receive an introductory talk by Head Gardener/owner. |
| **Coach Parking:** | Yes. |
| **Car Parking:** | Yes. |
| **Length of Visit:** | 1-2 hours. |
| **Booking Contact:** | Mike Werkmeister, |
| | East Lambrook Manor Gardens, East Lambrook, South Petherton, Somerset TA13 5HH |
| | Booking Telephone No. 01460 240328 |
| **Email:** | mike@eastlambrook.com |
| **Website:** | www.eastlambrook.com |
| **Location:** | Four minutes from the A303 South Petherton roundabout which is just south of the A3088 Yeovil roundabout. |
| | Follow brown signs to East Lambrook. |

Please quote this guide when making a booking

Greencombe is intimate and unexpected. Set in woodland on a steep slope, looking north to Porlock Bay and the Severn Sea, it makes its own world of trees, ferns, moss and colour. Come in April for erythronium, early rhododendrons and camellias, in early May for fragrant rhododendrons, and mid to late May for knock-out azalea colour; come in June for roses, July for lilies, clematis and hydrangeas. Come any time for wonder and magic with the sea beyond.

Walking is easy because main paths go with the contours of the hill and are level. It is only 3½ acres.

This is Jo Swift's favourite garden and is among the few selected for his personal top choice by Patrick Taylor, the great garden guru. It is completely organic and has been so for over 40 years. Compost heaps and leaf tips are on show. Come and see.

You can make tea for yourself in our delightful Green Room and enjoy delicious home-made cakes.

## Fact File

| | |
|---|---|
| **Opening Times:** | 2 – 6 p.m. on Saturdays, Sundays, Mondays, Tuesdays & Wednesdays throughout April, May, June and July |
| **Admission Rates:** | Adults including Senior Citizens: £6.00, Under 16's: £1.00 |
| **Group Rates:** | Maximum Group Size: 40 |
| | Adults including Senior Citizens: £6.00, Under 16's: £1.00 |
| **Facilities:** | Garden Registry open to visitors to refresh themselves and refer to Garden Records, Greencombe plants for sale, Make your own Tea facilities. |
| **Disabled Access:** | Yes, with car parking on site. |
| **Tours/Events:** | Owner present for plant talk and answering questions. |
| **Coach Parking:** | Not here but 1/4 mile away. |
| **Length of Visit:** | 1-4 hours. |
| **Booking Contact:** | Joan Loraine |
| | Greencombe Gardens, Greencombe, Porlock, Somerset TA24 8NU |
| | Tel: 01643 862363 |
| **Email:** | none |
| **Website:** | www.greencombe.org.uk |
| **Location:** | About ½ a mile west of Porlock, off the B road to Porlock Weir, on the left. |

Please quote this guide when making a booking

# Hestercombe Gardens Somerset

Lose yourself in 40 acres of walks, streams and temples, vivid colours, formal terraces, woodland, lakes, cascades and views that take your breath away.

This is Hestercombe: a unique combination of three period gardens.  The Georgian landscaped garden was created in the 1750's by Coplestone Warre Bampfylde, whose vision was complemented by the addition of a Victorian terrace and Shrubbery and the stunning Edwardian gardens designed by Sir Edwin Lutyens and Gertrude Jekyll. All once abandoned, now being faithfully restored to their former glory:  each garden has its own quality of tranquillity, wonder and inspiration.

Free entry to our fabulous Courtyard Café and excellent shop; conference and business facilities, weddings, parties, year round events.

## Fact File

**Opening Times:** Open every day 10am - 6pm (last admissions 5pm).

**Admission Rates:** Adults £8.90*, Senior Citizen £8.30*, Children £1.00 per child up to 2 children, extra children £3.30 each.
*Includes 10% voluntary donation towards the continuing restoration.

**Group Rates:** Groups 20 or more £6.50.
Guided tours minimum 20 people £12.00.

**Facilities:** Visitor Centre with Courtyard Cafe, Shop, Plant Sales. Function Rooms.

**Disabled Access:** Partial. Toilet & parking for disabled on site. Wheelchairs on loan, booking advisable.

**Tours/Events:** A wide range of events including Themed Fairs, Food Markets, Childrens Trails and many other seasonal events.
Walks.  Garden tours available for groups.

**Coach Parking:** Yes

**Length of Visit:** Refreshment stop or part to full day out.

**Booking Contact:** Hestercombe Gardens, Cheddon Fitzpaine, Taunton, Somerset, TA2 8LG
Telephone 01823 413923 Fax: 01823 413747

**Email:** groupbookings@hestercombe.com

**Website:** www.hestercombe.com

**Location:** 4 miles from Taunton, Signposted from all main roads with the Tourist Information Daisy symbol.

Please quote this guide when making a booking

Set amongst glorious views of the Staffordshire countryside, this beautiful garden, created by local landowner, Colonel Harry Clive, for his wife Dorothy, embraces a variety of landscape features. They include a superb woodland garden etched from a disused gravel quarry, an alpine scree, a fine collection of specimen trees, spectacular summer flower borders and many rare and unusual plants to intrigue and delight.

A host of spring bulbs, quickly followed by a magnificent display of *Rhododendrons* and *Azaleas* start the season off. Meanwhile the summer season brings with it a wonderful set of flowering herbaceous and mixed borders to admire. Finally the summer gives way to a stunning autumn floral foliage and berry spectacle.

A fine tearoom, overlooking the garden, provides a selection of home baking and light lunches.

## Fact File

**Opening Times:** Saturday 20th March - Sunday 26th September.
New for 2010 Special openings out of season, see website for details
**Admission Rates:** Adults £5.50, Senior Citizen £4.75, Child Free.
**Group Rates:** Minimum group size: 20, Daytime £4.50, Evening £6.00.
Group leader/organiser & driver free entry & refreshments.
**Facilities:** Teas
**Disabled Access:** Yes, Toilet and parking for disabled on site. Wheelchairs on loan, booking necessary.
**Toilet On Site:** Yes.
**Tours/Events:** None
**Coach Parking:** Yes.
**Car Parking:** Yes.
**Length of Visit:** 2 hours
**Booking Contact:** The Administrator
The Dorothy Clive Garden, Willoughbridge, Market Drayton, Shropshire, TF9 4EU
Telephone: 01630 647237 Fax: 01630 647902
**Email:** info@dorothyclivegarden.co.uk
**Website:** www.dorothyclivegarden.co.uk
**Location:** On the A51, two miles south from the village of Woore.
From the M6 leave at Junction 15, take the A53, then the A51

Please quote this guide when making a booking

Redesigned by top designers Tom Stuart-Smith and Piet Oudolf are the stunning gardens and lake.

The vast perennial plantings provide breathtaking displays throughout the year.

What's new?
The gardens have recently been increased in size to include the mile long lake and circular lakeside walk. New Show Gardens, a beautiful new Garden Tearoom, the unique Barefoot Walk, and a special joint ticket to combine the garden with the Monkey Forest or the Premier Inn hotel; make Trentham one of the countries leading garden attractions.

Also set within the estate are 60 individual shops and restaurants, an award winning garden centre and 120 room Premier Inn Hotel.

**Joint Tickets:**  These are available for groups to visit Trentham and Wollerton Old Hall Garden on the same day for £10 per person.

## Fact File

| | |
|---|---|
| **Opening Times:** | (Northern Entrance) Summer 1st April - 1st Nov 2010 9am - 6pm (last admission) Exit by 8pm.  Winter 1st Nov 2010 - 1st April 2011 10am - 3pm (last admission) Exit by 4pm. |
| **Admission Rates:** | Summer (Reduced rates in Winter) Adults £7.25, (Groups £5.70 if paid in advance) Family £24.85, Concessions £6.20, (Groups £4.65 if paid in advance) Joint Garden Money Forest Adult £12.50, Groups £10.50 if paid in advance. |
| **Group Rates:** | Special group and school rates. Educational groups can now choose Bush craft and Forest School activities. |
| **Facilities:** | Trentham is a leading garden based visitor destination with an award winning garden centre, 60 individual shops and restaurants, Lake, Hotel, Corporate events, Monkey Forest and Aerial Extreme. |
| **Disabled Access:** | Yes with wheelchair loan available. |
| **Car Parking on site:** | Yes. Free. |
| **Coach Parking:** | Yes with Drop off, Meet and Greet, and incentives for Driver and Organiser. |
| **Tours/Events:** | Guided tours available. Booking required. Special events. |
| **Length of Visit:** | 1 or 2 days. Accommodation available on site in the 120 room Premier Inn Hotel. |
| **Special Events:** | Quilt Show, Summer Music Festival, Plant Festival, Seasonal Events. |
| **Booking Contact:** | Jackie Grico. Trentham Leisure Ltd. Stone Road, Trentham, Stoke-on-Trent, Staffordshire, ST4 8AX Booking tel number 01782 645 215 Booking Fax 01782 644 536 |
| **Email:** | jgrice@trentham.co.uk |
| **Website:** | www.trentham.co.uk |
| **Location:** | 5 mins from Jn 15 M6, Staffordshire. |

Please quote this guide when making a booking

Part of the magnificent grounds of Loseley Park, the original two and a half acre Walled Garden is largely based on a design by Gertrude Jekyll.

The Walled Garden features five exquisite gardens, each with its own theme and character. The award-winning Rose Garden is planted with over one thousand bushes, mainly old-fashioned varieties. The extensive Herb Garden contains four separate sections devoted to culinary, medicinal, household and ornamental. The Fruit and Flower Garden is designed to provide interest and bold, fiery colour throughout the season. The White Garden, in total contrast, is planted with white, cream and silver plants, with two water features, creating an idyllic and tranquil area. The Organic Vegetable Garden is spectacular with a huge variety and the Wild Flower meadow is an attractive display during the summer months. Other features include the magnificent vine walk, mulberry tree, ancient wisteria and moat which runs almost the entire length of the Walled Garden and is abundant with wildlife and pond plants.

## Fact File

| | |
|---|---|
| **Opening times:** | Gardens open: May - September, Tuesday - Sunday 11am - 5pm. |
| | Loseley House open (guided tours only): May - August, Tues - Thurs & Sun, 1pm - 5pm. |
| | May and August Bank Holidays. |
| **Admission Rates:** | Gardens only: Adults £4.50, Senior Citizens £4.00, Child £2.25. |
| | House & Gardens: Adults £8.00, Senior Citizen £7.50, Child £4.00. |
| **Groups Rates:** | Minimum group size: 10. Adults £7.00, Child £3.50 |
| **Facilities:** | Courtyard Tea Room & light snacks, Gift shop, Plant Sales. |
| **Disabled Access:** | Yes. Toilet and parking for disabled on site. Wheelchair on loan. |
| **Tours/Events:** | House tours and garden tours for groups by arrangement. |
| **Coach Parking:** | Yes |
| **Length of Visit:** | 4 hours |
| **Booking Contact:** | Group Co-Ordinator |
| | Loseley Park, Estate Office, Guildford, Surrey, GU3 1HS |
| | Telephone: 01483 405112   Fax: 01483 302036  General Information: 01483 304440 |
| **Email:** | groups@loseleypark.co.uk |
| **Website:** | www.loseleypark.co.uk |
| **Location:** | 3 miles south of Guildford via A3 and B3000. |

Please quote this guide when making a booking

# Painshill Park Surrey

Step into a 'living picture of paradise' and discover a Georgian landscape, created by the Hon. Charles Hamilton between 1738 and 1773 as a Living Work of Art... Enjoy 158 acres of award-winning authentically restored 18th century parkland complete with 14 acre lake, spectacular views across Surrey, an amazing crystal Grotto plus many more interesting and unusual follies.

From snowdrops to Autumn colour the pleasure grounds and plantings have something to offer the visitor throughout the year. Enjoy exploring the American Roots exhibition which tells an amazing story of the 18th century craze for new and exciting exotic plants from outside the British Isles and discover the NCCPG John Bartram Heritage Plant Collection of North American Trees and Shrubs.

Guided tours for pre-booked groups give a fascinating insight into Hamilton's vision and it's a great way to discover the pleasure grounds. We hold entertaining events and interesting talks throughout the year covering a wide range of subjects and sell Painshill Honey and Wine from the Vineyard.

## Fact File

**Opening Times:** Open all year. (Closed Christmas Day and Boxing Day) March - October 10.30am – 6pm or dusk if earlier (last entry 4.30pm) November – February 10.30am – 4pm or dusk if earlier (last entry 3pm). The Grotto has limited opening hours. Opened for groups by appointment.

**Admission Rates:** Adults: £6.60. Concessions: £5.80. Children (5 – 16): £3.85, under 5's: Free. Carer of Disabled Person: Free. Family Ticket (2A & 4C): £22.00. Dogs on a lead welcome.

**Group Rates:** Pre-Booked Adult Groups of 10+: £5.80 plus £1.00 per person for a Guided Tour. Free Entry & Refreshments for Group Organiser and Coach Driver.

**Facilities:** Visitor Centre & Gift shop, Licensed Tea Room (Group Menu available), Picnic Area, Education Visits, Classrooms, Meeting Room, Permanent Marquee (Weddings & Corporate).

**Disabled Access:** Yes. Accessible Route. Toilet and Parking on site. Free of charge pre-booked Wheelchair loan & Buggy Tours (Capacity Max. 3) available for disabled persons.

**Tours/Events:** Guided Tours/Introductory Talks for pre-booked Groups. Events throughout year, telephone or visit website for details. American Roots Exhibition and NCCPG Plant Collection.

**Coach Parking:** Yes. No Charge.

**Length of Visit:** 2 – 4 hours.

**Booking Contact:** Visitor Manager. Painshill Park Trust, Portsmouth Road, Cobham, Surrey KT11 1JE Telephone: 01932 868113 Fax: 01932 868001

**Email:** Info@painshill.co.uk **Website:** www.painshill.co.uk

**Location:** Just off M25/J10/A3 to London. Exit A245 towards Cobham. Entrance in Between Streets, 200m East of A245/A307 roundabout. Nearest Station Cobham/Stoke d'Abernon. The Surrey Parks & Gardens Explorer Bus Route 515/515A.

Please quote this guide when making a booking

Ramster is famous for its stunning collection of rhododendrons and azaleas, which flourish under the mature woodland canopy. Established in the 1900s by Gauntlett Nurseries of Chiddingfold, with influences from the Japanese gardens, it now stretches over twenty acres. April heralds the arrival of many varieties of daffodils, complementing the camellias, the early flowering rhododendrons and the stunning magnolias. The carpets of scented bluebells contrast exquisitely with the fiery display of azaleas and rhododendrons in May and the warmth of June brings forth the Mediterranean grasses, and the subtle pink climbing roses. In the bog garden a mass of colourful primulas cascade down the rill, and stepping-stones weave a path under the leaves of the giant gunnera.

Always peaceful and beautiful the changing colours are reflected in the pond and lake. Wildlife abounds throughout the season, including kingfishers, herons, ducks, geese and moorhens.

## Fact File

| | |
|---|---|
| **Opening times:** | 2nd April – 20th June 2010: 10.00 a.m. – 5.00 p.m. |
| **Admission Rates:** | Adults: £5.00, OAP £4.50, Children: Under 16 – free. |
| **Group Rates:** | Minimum Groups Size: 10 |
| | Group Adults: £4.50, Children: Under 16 – free. |
| **Facilities:** | Plant sales, homemade teas, sandwiches and snacks. |
| **Disabled Access:** | Yes. Toilet and car parking on site. |
| **Tours/Events:** | Guided tours available for groups of over 20, please book. |
| | Special Event: 25th April, Charity Plant and Local Food Fair 10.00 a.m. - 5.00 p.m. |
| | 20th June, Childrens Theatre in the Garden, Robin Hood. |
| **Coach Parking:** | Yes. |
| **Length of Visit:** | Between 2-4 hours. |
| **Booking Contact:** | Ramster Gardens, Petworth Road, Chiddingfold, Surrey GU8 4SN |
| | Telephone: 01428 654167  Fax: 01428 642481 |
| **Email:** | info@ramsterweddings.co.uk |
| **Website:** | www.ramsterweddings.co.uk |
| **Location:** | 1½ miles south of Chiddingfold on the A283 |

# Titsey Place Gardens Surrey

The Trustees are delighted to welcome visitors to Titsey Place and Gardens. The House which dates back to the 17th Century is home to four stunning Canaletto paintings, superb collection of porcelain and objets d'arts belonging to the Leveson Gower and Gresham families who have owned this beautiful mansion house in the North Downs. The gardens extend to some 15 acres and are a mix of formal lawns and rose gardens to informal walks around the two lakes. There is a modern Etruscan temple, walled kitchen garden and four miles of woodland walks.
For further information visit www.titsey.org or telephone 01273 715359.

## Fact File

| | |
|---|---|
| **Opening Times:** | 1 p.m. – 5 p.m. Mid-May to End September on Wednesdays and Sundays. Additionally open summer bank holidays. The garden only open on Easter Monday, plus all Saturdays (gardens only) 12th May to 29th September. |
| **Admission Rates:** | Adults: £7.00, Senior Citizens: £7.00, Garden only: £4.50. |
| **Group Rates:** | Please telephone for details |
| | Adults/Senior Citizens/Children: £8.50 |
| **Facilities:** | Picnic Area and Tea Room. |
| **Disabled Access:** | Yes, but garden only and not very easy. Toilet and parking on site. |
| **Tours/Events:** | Guided tours of house & garden, 1.30pm, 2.30pm & 3.30pm. Private tours available by arrangement. |
| **Coach Parking:** | Yes. By arrangement only. |
| **Length of Visit:** | 1 hour garden / 1 hour house. |
| **Booking Contact:** | Kate Moisson |
| | Titsey Place Gardens, Titsey Place, Oxted, Surrey RH8 0JD |
| | Telephone: 01273 715360  Fax: 01273 779783 |
| **Email:** | brighton@struttandparker.com |
| **Website:** | www.titsey.org |
| **Location:** | From the A25 between Oxted & Westerham turn left onto B629 and at the end of Limpsfield High Street turn left & follow signs to visitors car park. |

Please quote this guide when making a booking

Great Dixter was the birthplace and home of gardening writer Christopher Lloyd. Built c1450 it boasts the largest surviving timber-framed hall in the country which was restored and enhanced by Sir Edwin Lutyens.

The magnificent gardens are now the hallmark of Christopher who devoted his lifetime to creating one of the most experimental gardens in the country, including flower meadows, ponds and the famous Long Border and Exotic Garden. Great Dixter Nurseries offer a wide range of rare and interesting plants that can be seen in the fabric of the garden. Head Gardener Fergus Garrett will lead a number of educational Study Days during the year, please see website for details.

## Fact File

**Opening Times:** 1st April – 31st October Tuesday – Sunday and Bank Holiday Mondays
House: 2 – 5 p.m., Garden: 11.00 – 5 p.m.

**Admission Rates:** Adults House & Garden: £8.50, Children House & Garden: £4.00.
Adults Garden Only: £7.00, Children Garden Only: £3.50.

**Group Rates:** Min Group Size: 25, Adults: £7.00, Children: £3.00. Annual tickets available.

**Facilities:** Shop, Plant sales, Light Refreshments.

**Disabled Access:** Limited. Bookable wheelchair loan available.

**Toilets on site:** Yes.

**Tours/Events:** Guided tours available, booking required. Study Days, (Horticultural Lectures)

**Coach Parking:** Yes.

**Car Parking on site:** Yes.

**Length of Visit:** 2 hours.

**Booking Contact:** Isabelle Sambrook.
Great Dixter House & Gardens, Great Dixter, Northiam, Rye, East Sussex TN31 6PH
Telephone: 01797 252878 Ext 3.
Fax: 01797 252879

**Email:** groupbookings@greatdixter.co.uk

**Website:** www.greatdixter.co.uk

**Location:** Signposted from the centre of Northiam on the A28.

Please quote this guide when making a booking

# Gardens & Grounds of Herstmonceux Castle East Sussex

Herstmonceux is renowned for its magnificent moated castle, set in beautiful parkland and superb Elizabethan Gardens. Built originally as a country home in the mid 15th century, Herstmonceux Castle embodies the history of medieval England and the romance of renaissance Europe. Set among carefully maintained Elizabethan Gardens and parkland, your experience begins with your first sight of the castle as it breaks into view.

In the grounds you will find the formal gardens including a walled garden dating from before 1570, a herb garden, the Shakespeare Garden, woodland sculptures, the Pyramid, the water lily filled moat and the Georgian style folly.

The Woodland walks will take you to the remains of three hundred year old sweet chestnut avenue, the rhododendron garden from the Lowther/Latham period, the waterfall (dependent on rainfall), and the 39 steps leading you through a woodland glade.

## Fact File

| | |
|---|---|
| **Opening Times:** | 3rd April - 31st October, open daily. |
| **Admission Rates:** | Adults £6.00, Senior Citizen £4.95, Child £3.00 (5-15yrs). |
| **Group Rates:** | Minimum group size: 15 |
| | Adults £4.50, Senior Citizen £4.00, Child/Students £2.00 (5-15yrs). |
| **Facilities:** | Visitor Centre, Gift Shop, Tea Room, Nature Trail, Children's Woodland Play Area. |
| **Disabled Access:** | Limited. Toilet and parking for disabled on site. 1 Wheelchair on loan. booking advisable. |
| **Tours/Events:** | Guided Tours are conducted at an extra charge and subject to availablity. |
| | Please telephone for confirmation of tours before you visit. |
| **Coach Parking:** | Yes |
| **Length of Visit:** | 2 - 4 hours |
| **Booking Contact:** | Caroline Cullip |
| | Herstmonceux Castle, Hailsham, East Sussex, BN27 1RN |
| | Telephone: 01323 834457 Fax: 01323 834499 |
| **Email:** | c_cullip@isc-queensu.ac.uk |
| **Website:** | www.herstmonceux-castle.com |
| **Location:** | Located just outside the village of Herstmonceux on the A271, entrance is on Wartling Road. |

Legend has it that King John II, who became King of France in 1350, was held hostage in this house for some years. King John's Lodge is a listed Jacobean house surrounded by a garden for all seasons. Snowdrops and hellebores precede spring bulbs, wild orchids, primroses and violets. This exceptionally romantic garden is noted for its roses, especially those cascading over apple trees in the wild garden. The borders around the formal garden are planted with softly-coloured roses and clematis and herbaceous plants. The year ends with carpets of pink and white cyclamen. The five acre garden is surrounded by meadows with fine trees, grazing sheep and panoramic views. There are a number of water features including a lily pond and fountain in the formal garden, a wild pond and a secret pond in the woodland area. A propagation nursery and shop has now opened selling a wide range of unusual perennials and shrubs, statuary and iron work as well as a range of interesting garden equipment and gifts.

## Fact File

| | |
|---|---|
| **Opening Times:** | 10.00am – 4.00pm. Daily, closed from 24 December – 31 January |
| **Admission Rates:** | Adults: £3.50, Children (0-16yrs): Free |
| **Group Rates:** | Minimum Groups Size: 10 for concession price Adults: £3.00 |
| **Facilities:** | Shop, plant sales, teas, lunch by arrangement, B&B and holiday accommodation |
| **Disabled Access:** | Car parking on site and garden access |
| **Coach Parking:** | Yes |
| **Length of Visit:** | 1 hour |
| **Booking Contact:** | Jill Cunningham |
| | King John's Lodge, Sheepstreet Lane, Etchingham, East Sussex TN19 7AZ |
| | Telephone: 01580 819232  Nursery: 01580 819220 |
| **Email:** | kingjohnslodge@aol.com  or kingjohnsnursery@btconnect.com |
| **Website:** | www.kingjohnslodge.co.uk |
| **Location:** | 2 miles west of Hurst Green. A265 Burwash to Etchingham. Turn left before Etchingham Church into Church Lane which leads into Sheepstreet Lane after 1/2 mile. On the left after 1 mile, the entrance and parking is at King John's Nursery. |

A garden not be missed - Merriments Garden at Hurst Green offers everything for the "Garden Lover's" day out.

Set in 4 acres of gently sloping Weald farmland, this is a garden of richly and imaginatively planted deep curved borders, colour themed and planted in the great tradition of English gardening.  These borders use a rich mix of trees, shrubs, perennials, grasses and many unusual annuals which ensure an arresting display of colour, freshness and vitality in the garden right through to its closing in autumn.  Also in the garden are two large ponds, dry scree area, bog and wilder areas of garden planted only using plants suited for naturalising and colonising their environment.  It delights all who visit.

The extensive Nursery offers a wide choice of unusual and interesting plants for sale many of which can be seen growing in the garden.

## Fact File

**Opening times:** Easter to 30th September.
**Admission Rates:** Adults £4.50, Senior Citizens £4.50, Child £2.00.
**Group Rates:** Minimum group size: 15 (£4.00 per Adult)
**Facilities:** Gift Shop, Plant Sales, Restaurant, Wild Bird Centre.
**Disabled Access:** Yes.  Toilet and parking for disabled on site, Wheelchairs on loan booking advisable.
**Tours/Events:** None
**Coach Parking:** Yes
**Length of Visit:** 2 - 3 hours
**Booking Contact:** Taryn Murrells
Hawkhurst Road, Hurst Green, East Sussex.  TN19 7RA.
Telephone: 01580 860666 Fax: 01580 860324
**Email:** info@merriments.co,uk
**Website:** www.merriments.co.uk
**Location:** 15 miles north of Hastings just off the A21 at Hurst Green.

Please quote this guide when making a booking

Magical Michelham, set on an island approached through a 14th century gatehouse in the beautiful Cuckmere Valley. It is surrounded by the longest water-filled medieval moat in England.

The historic buildings include part of an Augustinian priory that over 800 years evolved into a splendid country house (reputedly haunted) surrounded by spacious gardens. The property also includes a fully restored watermill and a stunning Elizabethan Barn. Exhibitions, exciting events plus a working forge and rope museum are all part of what makes Michelham a fascinating day out for all family members. The various planting areas appeal to many as well, from the gentle Moat Walk around the island, to the Physic, Cloister and Kitchen Gardens and medieval Stew Pond filled with historically accurate plants.

The licensed restaurant serving hot meals and home-baked cakes, outside picnic area and plenty of free parking make Michelham Priory a place you'll want to return to again and again.

## Fact File

**Opening Times:** 1 Mar-1 Nov: Tues-Sun from 10.30am Closed Mondays except on Bank Holidays and in August Closing Times: Mar & Oct - 4.30pm, April-July & Sept, 5pm, August, 5.30pm Last admission 45 minutes before closing time.

**Admission Rates:** Adults £6.80, Student £5.80, OAP £5.80, Child £3.60, Disabled/Carer £3.60 each, Family (2+2) £17.50. Game Fair: Adults £8.00, Student £6.00, OAP £6.00, Child £5.00, Disabled/Carer £5.00 each, Family (2+2) £23.50

**Groups Rates:** Adults £5.00, Student £5.00, OAP £5.00, Child £3.15, Disabled/Carer £3.40 each. Game Fair: Adults £8.00, Student £6.00, OAP £6.00, Child £5.00, Disabled/Carer £5.00 each, Family (2+2) £13.50.

**Facilities:** Gift Shop, Restaurant, Plant Sales, Weddings.

**Disabled Access:** Yes. Toilet and parking for disabled on site. Loan wheelchairs available.

**Tours/Events:** Spring Garden Fair-April, Iron Age & Roman Event-May, Food Fair-June, Game & Country Fair-July, Crafts in Action; Sussex Guild-August, Medieval Weekend & Early Music Fair-September, Hallow'een-October

**Coach Parking:** Yes. Free meal voucher for Coach Drivers.

**Length of Visit:** 3 - 4 hours

**Booking Contact:** Michelham Priory, Upper Dicker, Nr Hailsham, East Sussex, BN27 3QS Telephone: 01323 844224 Fax: 01323 844030

**Email:** adminmich@sussexpast.co.uk

**Website:** www.sussexpast.co.uk/michelham

**Location:** 2 miles west of Hailsham & 8 miles north west of Eastbourne. Signposted from A22 & A27. (OS map 198 TQ558 093).

Please quote this guide when making a booking

## Pashley Manor Gardens East Sussex

'One of the finest gardens in England' award winning Pashley Manor Gardens offers a sumptuous blend of romantic landscaping, imaginative plantings and fine old trees, fountains, springs and large ponds. The moated Manor was once owned by the forebears of Anne Boleyn and it is possible she stayed here during her childhood. In 1543 the estate was sold to Sir Thomas May, who built the Tudor house you see today, the fine Georgian façade was added in 1720.

Pashley prides itself on its delicious homemade food and selection of licensed beverages which visitors can enjoy in the Garden Room Café with Terrace. In 2009 Pashley built a new reception/gift shop. The new gift shop caters for every taste from postcards and local honey to traditional hand painted ceramics and tapestry cushions.

Special Events include: Tulip Festival 23rd April – 3rd May; Sculpture in Particular 22nd – 31st May; Special Rose Weekend 11th – 13th June; Kitchen Garden Weekend 18th – 20th June; Lily Time mid July – Mid August; Sussex Guild Craft Show in late August and an exhibition and sale of Sculpture and Botanical Art lasting throughout the season.

Nicola Stoken Tomkins

### Fact File

**Opening Times:** 1st April - 30th September, Tuesday, Wednesday, Thursday, Saturday, Bank Holiday Mondays and Special Event Days 11am - 5pm.
**Admission Rates:** Adults £8.00, Children £5.00.
**Groups Rates:** Minimum group size 15, Adults £7.50. Tulip Festival £8.50 no concessions.
**Facilities:** New Gift Shop, Plant Sales, Licensed Café, Light Lunches and Afternoon Teas.
**Disabled Access:** Limited. Toilet and parking for disabled on site. Wheelchairs on loan, booking necessary.
**Tours/Events:** Pre-booked tours of garden available. Please call for special event details.
**Coach Parking:** Yes
**Length of Visit:** 2 1/2 hours - half day.
**Booking Contact:** Pashley Manor Gardens, Ticehurst, East Sussex, TN5 7HE
Tel: 01580 200888 Fax: 01580 200102
**Email:** info@pashleymanorgardens.com
**Website:** www.pashleymanorgardens.com
**Location:** On the B2099 between the A21 and Ticehurst village (Tourist brown-signed).

Please quote this guide when making a booking

This magnificent informal landscape garden was laid out in the 18th century by 'Capability' Brown and further developed in the early years of the 20th century by its owner Arthur G. Soames. The original four lakes form the centrepiece.

There are dramatic shows of daffodils and bluebells in spring, and the rhododendrons and azaleas are spectacular in early summer. Autumn brings stunning colours from the many rare trees and shrubs, and winter walks can be enjoyed in this garden for all seasons. Don't forget to visit our newly acquired parkland – perfect for a good walk with stunning views.

Whatever the season, Sheffield Park Garden offers a fantastic visit for all!

## Fact File

| | |
|---|---|
| **Opening times:** | Open all year, please telephone or check website for details. |
| **Admission Rates:** | Please call 01825 790231 or check our website www.nationaltrust.org.uk/sheffieldpark for current admission rates. |
| | NT members free. RHS members free, (individual members only) |
| **Group Rates:** | (pre-booked), Minimum Group Size: 15. |
| **Guided tour:** | £2.00 pp (inc. NT members), (Must be pre-booked) |
| **Facilities:** | Visitor Centre, Shop, Plant Sales, Restaurant (not NT) Munch Buggy (NT in garden) |
| **Disabled Access:** | Yes. Wheelchair loan available. PMV Loan, Yes booking required, book on 01825 790302 |
| **Toilets on site:** | Yes |
| **Car Parking on site:** | Yes |
| **Coach Parking:** | Yes |
| **Guided Tours:** | Yes, booking required. |
| **Length of Visit:** | 2 hours garden 2 hours parkland |
| **Special Events:** | Throughout the year - check website for details. |
| **Booking Contact:** | Jill Reeves, The National Trust Sheffield Park Garden, Sheffield Park, East Sussex TN22 3QX Booking Tel No.01825 790231, Booking Fax No. 01825 971264 |
| **Email:** | sheffieldpark.groups@nationaltrust.org.uk |
| **Website:** | www.nationaltrust.org.uk/sheffieldpark |
| **Location:** | 5 miles NW of Uckfield, on east side of A275 (between A272 and A22). |

Please quote this guide when making a booking

Borde Hill's botanically-rich Garden, traditional parkland, remarkable woods and peaceful lakes captivate visitors. Listed as of Grade II* historic importance, it effortlessly combines tranquil retreats with wide open spaces and outstanding views.

Created in the era of the Great Plant Hunters, the collection of fine trees and shrubs provides interest and inspiration for every horticultural enthusiast. The 17-acre formal garden has distinctive living 'rooms' each with their own unique style, offering seasonal colour and fragrance. These include the amazing Azalea Ring, the tranquil Garden of Allah, replanted Italian Garden, sumptuous Rose Garden with 500 David Austin roses and Round Dell, planted with sub-tropical lush plants.

Early spring-flowering bulbs, magnolias, camellias, rhododendrons and azaleas give way to exuberant summer borders of roses and herbaceous plants. These plantings extend into 200 acres, where the variety of micro-climates has contributed to the best collection of the tallest and largest girth 'champion' trees on privately-owned land in Britain.  All the family will enjoy Borde Hill with woodland walks, the wildlife ponds and lakeside picnics. Children can challenge themselves in the adventure playground or enjoy the variety of children activities.  Don't miss the Battle Proms 7th August.

## Fact File

| | |
|---|---|
| **Opening times:** | 22 March – 12 September and 23 – 31 October 2010, daily 10 a.m. – 6 p.m. (or dusk) |
| **Admission Rates:** | Adult £7.50, Senior Citizen £6.50, Child £4.50. |
| **Group Rates:** | Pre-paid £6.00 |
| **Facilities:** | Shop, Plant Sales, Restaurant, Teas, children's Adventure Playground, coarse fishing |
| **Disabled Access:** | Yes, wheelchair loan available (booking required) |
| **Toilets on site:** | Yes |
| **Car Parking on site:** | Yes |
| **Coach Parking:** | Yes |
| **Guided Tours:** | Yes, booking required |
| **Length of Visit:** | 2-4 hours |
| **Special Events:** | Full programme – see website for details |
| **Booking Contact:** | Borde Hill Garden, Balcombe Road, Haywards Heath, W. Sussex RH16 1XP |
| | Booking Tel No.01444 450326  Booking Fax No. 01444 440427 |
| **Email:** | info@bordehill.co.uk |
| **Website:** | www.bordehill.co.uk |

Please quote this guide when making a booking

# High Beeches Gardens                                    West Sussex

Especially colourful in spring and autumn, High Beeches is a romantic landscape, changing with the seasons. Discover 27 acres of beautiful and historic woodland and water gardens full of rare and unusual plants and trees. Wander down the winding paths, through open sunlit glades, enjoy stunning vistas and sit by tranquil ponds.

In spring enjoy daffodils along with camellias and many different magnolias, followed by bluebells throughout the woodland glades. The gardens are spectacular in May and early June, carpeted with amazing colour and fragrance from azaleas and magnificent rhododendrons.

The old wildflower meadow is full of wild orchids, cowslips, oxeye daisies and many other wildflowers throughout June and The National Collection of Stewartia flower at the end of June. In August the wonderful azure blue Willow Gentians bloom throughout the glades – High Beeches is the only site in the UK where these have naturalised.

In autumn the views alter again as the varied foliage changes to a splendid crescendo of crimson, copper, gold and green with one of the finest displays of autumnal colour in the country.

## Fact File

**Opening times:** 1 – 5 p.m. every day except Wednesday, 21 March – 31 October
**Admission Rates:** Adults: £6.00, Senior Citizens: £6.00, Children: Under 14 – Free
**Group Rates:** Minimum Group Size: 20. Adults: £5.50, Senior Citizens: £5.50, Children: Under 14 – Free
**Facilities:** Restaurant, Teas
**Disabled Access:** Limited – tearoom yes
**Toilets on site:** Yes
**Car Parking on site:** Yes
**Coach Parking:** Yes
**Guided Tours:** Yes, booking required.
**Length of Visit:** 2 hours
**Special Events:** See website.
**Booking Contact:** Sarah Bray, High Beeches Gardens, Handcross, West Sussex RH17 6HQ
Booking Tel No. 01444 400589. Booking Fax No. 01444 401543
**Email:** gardens@highbeeches.com
**Website:** www.highbeeches.com
**Location:** 1 mile east of the A223 at Handcross on the south side of the B2110 in mid-Sussex.

Please quote this guide when making a booking

# Leonardslee Lakes & Gardens West Sussex

Leonardslee is home to one of the most magnificent displays of rhododendron and azaleas and the fascinating miniature 1/12 scale model exhibition "Beyond the Doll's House". The gardens which nestle in a romantic valley with walks around seven beautiful lakes is one of the finest in Europe when the sumptuous rhododendrons overhang paths fringed with bluebells, making an earthly paradise full of fragrances. The Rock Garden is a kaleidoscope of colour with azaleas of every hue. "Beyond the Doll's House", an exhibition of Victorian life, is one of the most detailed examples in the world with a frontage of around 140ft. Discover the wildlife: wallabies, wildfowl and much more. Enjoy hot food in our licensed self-service restaurant and visit the gift shop and plant sale.

## Fact File

| | |
|---|---|
| **Opening Times:** | 1st April - 31st October 9.30am-6pm (last admission 4.30pm) |
| **Admission Rates:** | May (Weekends & Bank Holidays) £9.00; May (Weekdays) £8.00 |
| | April and 1st June - 31st October £6.50; Children aged 5-15 (Anytime) £4.00 |
| **Groups Rates:** | May (Weekends & Bank Holidays) £8.00; May (Weekdays) £7.00 |
| | April and 1st June - 31st October £5.50; Children aged 5-15 (Anytime) £3.50 |
| **Facilities:** | Shop, Licensed Self-service Restaurant, Plant Sales. |
| **Disabled Access:** | No |
| **Tours/Events:** | - |
| **Coach Parking:** | Yes (Free) |
| **Length of Visit:** | 4 - 5  hours |
| **Booking Contact:** | The Secretary, Leonardslee Gardens, Lower Beeding, Horsham, West Sussex, RH13 6PP |
| | Telephone: 01403 891212   Fax: 01403 891305 |
| **Email:** | info@leonardsleegardens.com |
| **Website:** | www.leonardsleegardens.com |
| **Location:** | 4 miles from Handcross at bottom of M23 via B2110, entrance is at junction of B2110 and A281, between Handcross and Cowfold. |

Please quote this guide when making a booking

Set in the High Weald with splendid views, the Nymans estate was created by the Messel family and their gardeners. The garden is a series of experimental designs with spectacular planting and all-year-round beauty, created in the changing fashion of early 20th century gardening. Both a horticulturalist's dream and a peaceful country garden, it's easy to lose yourself in its intimate and surprising corners.

The house, transformed into a gothic mansion in the twenties, burnt down shortly after, leaving romantic ruins. The remaining rooms are unexpectedly charming, filled with flowers from the garden reflecting the taste of Anne Messel, Countess of Rosse. Oliver Messel's television draped in stage curtains is one of the more curious objects inside.

Ancient woods beyond the garden dip into the valley, providing wonderful walks among avenues, wild flowers, lake and cascades

## Fact File

**Opening Times:** Garden All year round 10.00–5.00, Weds, Thurs, Fri, Sat, Sun
House 11 Mar – 1 Nov 11.00–4.00, Weds, Thurs, Fri, Sat, Sun
Woods, Restaurant*, Shop & Garden Centre All year round 11.00–5.00, Weds, Thurs, Fri, Sat, Sun.  Open Bank Holiday Mondays, *Restaurant closes at 4:30
Nymans closes at 4pm November-January. Closed 25 to 31 December.

**Admission Rates:** Adult £9.00, Child £4.50, Family 2 Adults + 3, £22.00, Family 1 Adult + 3 £13.50.

**Group Rates:** 15+, Adult £7.50, Child £3.50.

**Facilities:** Visitor Centre, shop, plant sales, restaurant, teas.

**Disabled Access:** Yes, wheelchair loan available, Toilets on site.

**Tours/Events:** Guided tours available.  All year round events, family activities, summer open-air theatre, horticultural workshops, compost demonstrations, bat walks & photography workshops.

**Parking:** Yes, coach and car parking available.

**Length of Visit:** 3 hours

**Booking Contact:** Nymans Administrator, Booking Telephone No. 01444 405250

**Email:** nymans@nationaltrust.org.uk

**Website:** www.nationaltrust.org.uk/nymans

**Location:** 5 miles south of Crawley. Foot: 5 miles by footpath from Balcombe.
Cycle: on the National Cycle Network route 20. Ferry: Dieppe or Le Harvre to Newhaven, then 40 mins by car / train. Bus: Metrobus 273 Brighton to Crawley, 271 Haywards Heath to Crawley. Both stop outside Nymans.
Both pass Crawley . Train: Balcombe 4 miles, Crawley 5 miles.
Road: on B2114 at Handcross, just off London to Brighton M23/A23.
Parking: free. Designated coach bays.

Please quote this guide when making a booking

One of the top twenty in Simon Jenkins' book "England's Thousand Best Houses", Parham is one of England's finest Elizabethan examples. Set in the heart of a deer park, with its dark fallow herd first recorded in 1628, the house sits below a completely unspoilt stretch of the South Downs. Its Pleasure Grounds, laid out in the 18th century, encompass specimen trees, a brick and turf maze built in 1991. They lead down to a peaceful lake overlooked by a summer house.

The spectacular four-acre walled garden, cultivated for many centuries, contains herbaceous and mixed borders of Edwardian opulence. Vibrant with colour, it is run on organic principles and designed for a long season, peaking in summer and in late autumn. With its herbs, vegetables, lavender, roses and fruit trees, the garden is a series of interlocking pictures, woven into each other with a tapestry-like effect in the English romantic tradition.

The Wendy House, built into the old garden wall, with its balcony, fireplace and parquet floor, was built in 1928 for the daughters of the Hon. Clive and Alicia Pearson, who bought the estate in 1922.

Parham is justly famous for its long tradition of flower arrangements which decorate every room in the house. Everything is cut from the garden, which won the HHA/Christie's Garden of the Year Award in 1990.

## Fact File

| | |
|---|---|
| **Opening Times:** | House: Easter Sunday - end of September, Wednesdays, Thursdays, Sundays & Bank Holiday Mondays, also Tuesdays & Fridays in August 2pm - 5pm. Gardens: Tuesday to Friday incl, Sundays & Bank Holiday Mondays 12 noon - 5pm. |
| **Admission Rates:** | See web site for 2010 rates. |
| **Group Rates:** | Discounted rates for group advanced bookings. |
| **Facilities:** | Restaurant, Gift Shop, Picnic Area, Plant Sales, Shop, Brick & Turf Maze, Wendy House. |
| **Disabled Access:** | Yes. Toilet and parking for disabled on site. |
| **Tours/Events:** | Parham Garden Weekend, 10th, 11th July 2010. |
| **Coach Parking:** | Yes. No Charge. |
| **Length of Visit:** | 1 - 2 hours (excluding house) |
| **Booking Contact:** | Parham House & Gardens, Storrington, Pulborough, West Sussex, RH20 4HS. Telephone: 01903 742021 or 744888 (information line)  Fax: 01903 746557. |
| **Email:** | bookings@parhaminsussex.co.uk |
| **Website:** | www.parhaminsussex.co.uk |
| **Location:** | Parham is located on the A283 midway between Storrington and Pulborough, Equidistant from the A24 or A29. |

Please quote this guide when making a booking

**In the heart of the South Downs National Park.**
A short lime avenue leads to the Topiary Garden with its amusing animals and birds in clipped box and yew. Beyond the stone balustraded bridge a riot of hollyhocks can be seen in high summer in front of the 15th century timber-framed house. Here visitors can still see the fine panelled interiors of a much-loved home.
Through the stone arch the yew tunnel leads to the mysterious ivy-clad Monks' Walk. The upper lawn is enclosed by herbaceous borders, while the lower lawn has clipped yew hedges and roses, with an exceptional example of the 'Living Fossil' tree, the prehistoric *Ginkgo Biloba*.

The five acres of gardens include the Victorian 'Secret' Garden, with its 40-metre fruit wall, heated pineapple pits and stove house. The Victorian potting shed now houses a Rural Museum of horticultural implements from the family farms. The Rose Garden commemorates the Queen's Golden Jubilee. The Terracotta Garden has a central fountain, complemented by colourful herbaceous borders. The unusual English Poetry Garden, in its semi-woodland setting, has a bust of lord Byron as its centrepiece, a long curved pergola, and poems displayed around the circular broadwalk for the pleasure of visitors.

## Fact File

| | |
|---|---|
| **Opening Times:** | May to end of September (House and Gardens). Public open afternoons Suns, Thurs, BH Mondays 2-6pm (last entry 5pm). Groups at other times by appointment. |
| **Admission Rates:** | Adults £7.00, Senior Citizen £6.50, Child £3.00. |
| **Group Rates:** | Groups (of 25 or more). Adults £6.50, Child £3.00. |
| **Facilities:** | Gift Shop, Teas, Car Park. |
| **Disabled Access:** | Partial. |
| **Tours/Events:** | Guided tours of House and Gardens for groups. |
| **Coach Parking:** | Yes. |
| **Length of Visit:** | 2 - 3 hours. |
| **Booking Contact:** | Jean Whitaker St Mary's House, Bramber, West Sussex, BN44 3WE. Tel: 01903 816205 Fax: 01903 816205 |
| **Email:** | info@stmarysbramber.co.uk |
| **Website:** | www.stmarysbramber.co.uk |
| **Location:** | 10 miles NW of Brighton off A283 in Bramber Village, 1 mile east of Steyning. |

Please quote this guide when making a booking

# Coughton Court

Created over the last decade the gardens are mature and varied.  Visitors can enjoy the delights within the different areas: The Courtyard with Elizabethan Knot Garden, The Walled Garden, The Courtyard, The Bog Garden, Riverside and Lake Walks amongst others.

Opened in 1996 the Walled Garden is a splendid example of individual 'garden rooms'. One of the most spectacular is the Rose Labyrinth, celebrated during the annual Rose Festival in June when it becomes rich with colour and perfume.  In 2006, this garden was given an "Award of Garden Excellence" by the World Federation of Rose Societies, the first time ever it has been awarded in the UK. There are beautiful 'hot' and 'cold' herbaceous borders containing plants, nurtured at Coughton Court, which are also on sale to visitors.

Thanks to the enthusiasm of the Throckmorton family, who have lived at Coughton Court for 600 years, the gardens are now considered to be some of the finest in the country.

## Fact File

**Opening Times:** Please call our info line on 01789 400777 or visit our website www.coughtoncourt.co.uk for details.

**Admission Rates:** Please call to confirm 2010 admission prices or visit our website.

**Disabled Access:** Yes (Gardens only), Toilet and parking for disabled on site.

**Tours/Events:** There is a programme of events from April to October (see website).

**Parking:** All Cars Free of Charge.  Coaches by prior arrangement.

**Length of Visit:** 3 hours

**Booking Contact:** Coughton Court, Alcester, Warwickshire, B49 5JA. Telephone: 01789 400777 Fax: 01789 764369

**Email:** office@throckmortons.co.uk

**Website:** www.coughtoncourt.co.uk

**Location:** Take the A435 from Alcester towards Birmingham, the House is signposted from the road.

Please quote this guide when making a booking

Although Ragley's 400 acres of parkland were designed by Lancelot 'Capability' Brown during the 18th Century, little is known about the gardens prior to 1873 when Victorian garden designer Robert Marnock created a formal flower garden intended to show off plants discovered in the new world.

This area of the garden is now a modern Rose Garden, completed in 2009, with the new design based around diversity by taking away the majority of the grass and planting trees, shrubs and perennials to encourage insects. This naturalistic approach is demonstrated throughout the Gardens which provide colour and interest throughout the year with areas such as a Spring Bulb Bank, Prairie Garden and Alpine Garden.

Other attractions at Ragley include a Woodland Walk, which takes visitors around the surrounding Parkland and provides some wonderful views of the countryside, a collection of 19th Century Carriages housed in the Stables and, of course, the Palladian House itself.

## Fact File

| | |
|---|---|
| **Opening times:** | 10 a.m. – 6 p.m. weekends and school holidays |
| **Admission Rates:** | (2008), Adults: £8.50, Senior Citizens: £7.00, Children: £5.00 |
| **Group Rates:** | Minimum Group Size: 20, Adults: £7.50, Senior Citizens: £6.00, Children: £4.50 |
| **Facilities:** | Teas, Light Refreshments |
| **Disabled Access:** | Yes.  Wheelchair loan available – booking required |
| **Toilets on site:** | Yes |
| **Car Parking on site:** | Yes |
| **Coach Parking:** | Yes |
| **Guided Tours:** | Yes, booking required. |
| **Length of Visit:** | 2 hours for gardens, plus further 2 hours to visit woodland walk and house |
| **Booking Contact:** | Carol Handy, Ragley Hall, Alcester Warwickshire, B49 5NJ<br>Booking Tel No.01789 762090,  Booking Fax No. 01789 768691 |
| **Email:** | ragley@ragleyhall.com |
| **Website:** | www.ragleyhall.com |
| **Location:** | Ragley is situated 2 miles southwest of Alcester, off the A435/A46 |

Please quote this
guide when
making a booking

Ryton Gardens is home to Garden Organic, the UK's leading organic growing charity showcasing ten acres of stunning organic display gardens. These demonstrate all aspects of domestic horticulture including herbs, roses, lawns, shrubberies, herbaceous planting and vegetable and fruit growing.

The gardens are full of information for gardeners on organic techniques including composting and pest and disease control. The grounds also boast a large conservation area with native trees and wild flowers, a bee garden, living willow structures and the world's first public biodynamic garden.

The Vegetable Kingdom, an interactive visitor centre, houses Garden Organic's world renowned Heritage Seed Library which conserves hundreds of threatened vegetable varieties.

The site is also home to an award winning restaurant and shop where organic, local and sustainable produce, including delicious home cooked food, gifts and products, are available to buy.

## Fact File

| | |
|---|---|
| **Opening Times:** | 9am - 5pm all year round |
| **Admission Rates:** | Adults £6.00 (admits 1 child free), Concessions £5.50, £3.00 for additional child, members go free. |
| **Facilities:** | Visitor centre, award winning shop & restaurant, garden café, plant sales, picnic area, large car park. |
| **Disabled Access:** | Disabled toilet and parking facilities. Mobility scooters available – booking necessary. Braille Guidebook. |
| **Tours/Events:** | Annual programme of events. Garden tours and group visits available to book. |
| **Coach Parking:** | Yes. |
| **Length of Visit:** | Half a day |
| **Booking Contact:** | Garden Organic, Ryton Gardens, Wolston Lane, Coventry, CV8 3LG. Telephone: 02476 303517  Fax: 02476 639229 |
| **Email:** | enquiry@gardenorganic.org.uk |
| **Website:** | www.gardenorganic.org.uk |
| **Location:** | Just off the A45 on the road to Wolston, five miles south east of Coventry. |

Please quote this guide when making a booking

Beside the Abbey Church in Malmesbury and straddling the River Avon, this truly spectacular 5 acre garden has brought praise from around the world.

These are just some of the comments from our visitors' book:

"I thought I'd seen all the best gardens in the world – until now!"
"The loveliest truly English garden on the planet!"
"This garden alone made my visit to the UK worthwhile"

With over 1000 years of history, burial place of an English King, knot gardens, herb gardens, river walk, monastic fishponds, waterfall over 2000 different roses (largest collection in the UK) over 100,000 tulips, 10,000 different plants with constant colour from March to November, these 5 acres are a must see garden and history experience with approx. half an hour drive from Bath.

p.s. you can even get married here!

## Fact File

| | |
|---|---|
| **Opening Times:** | 11am - 5.30pm 21st March - 31st October |
| **Admission Rates:** | Adults £6.50, Concessions £5.75, Children £2.50 |
| **Group Rates:** | Minimum Group Size: 20. £5.50 per person. |
| **Facilities:** | Plant Sales, Teas. |
| **Disabled Access:** | Yes. |
| **Tours/Events:** | Plays, Demonstrations, Sculpture and Exhibitions. Also licensed for Civil Marriage/Partnerships, See website for additional information. |
| **Coach Parking:** | Yes. |
| **Length of Visit:** | 2 hours minimum |
| **Booking Contact:** | Geraldine Wilkins. Abbey House Gardens, Market Cross, Malmesbury, Wiltshire, SN16 9AS Tel: 01666 827650, Fax: 01666 822782 |
| **Email:** | info@abbeyhousegardens.co.uk |
| **Website:** | www.abbeyhousegardens.co.uk |
| **Location:** | In Malmesbury town centre. Off A429 between M4 junction 17 (5miles) and Cirencester (12 miles). Coaches drop passengers in centre of town, 3 minute level walk from garden. Cars follow signs for long stay car park from Malmesbury town centre. Garden is 5 min walk across the bridge, up the Abbey steps and entered left of Cloister Garden. |

Please quote this guide when making a booking

# Bowood Rhododendron Woodland Garden Wiltshire

The Bowood Rhododendron Woodland Garden is a sixty acre Aladdin's cave of ericaceous plants. It surrounds Robert Adam's Mausoleum built in 1762, which overlooks Capability Brown's great park. It lies on a seam of greensand fed by multiple springs. The peak flowering season is from April, through to early June. In late April, the under storey is carpeted with bluebells. Towering above are magnificent scented Loderi and Kewensis with huge pink trusses, followed in May and June, by the earliest known hardy hybrids introduced in 1854, many of which are unique to this garden. Plants thrive in this microclimate. A group of Lacteum, brought back as seed by Mr. Roy Lancaster in 1981, are now twelve feet high, and flower profusely.

The rides through this woodland garden cover approximately four miles. Visitors should allow at least two hours to explore this paradise. Also visit Bowood House, Gardens and Arboretum, which are reached by a separate access and car park. So why not make it a day out?

## Fact File

| | |
|---|---|
| **Opening times:** | 11.00 – 18.00 Mid April – early June |
| **Admission Rates:** | Adults: £5.90, Senior Citizens: £5.60, Children: FOC |
| **Facilities:** | Toilets. |
| **Disabled Access:** | Limited, bookable wheelchair loan available. |
| **Tours/Events:** | None. |
| **Coach Parking:** | Yes |
| **Length of Visit:** | Minimum of 2 hours |
| **Booking Contact:** | Mr Will Long |
| | Bowood House, Calne Wiltshire SN11 0LZ |
| | Telephone:01249 812102 |
| | Fax: 01249 821757 |
| **Email:** | houseandgardens@bowood.org |
| **Website:** | www.bowood.org |
| **Location:** | Off A342 between Derry Hill and Sandy Lane. 8 miles south of Junction 17, M4. |

Please quote this guide when making a booking

Alfred Parsons designed Arts and Crafts gardens to complement restoration of the manor in 1905-1912. He kept the large lawn but designed terraces, walls, flagged paths, topiary pavilions beside a lily pond, and cedar over a gazebo with swept roof in local stone: creating subtle frameworks for the future.

Snowdrops and aconites sparkle around the springfed lower moat; daffodils, tulips and Queen Anne's lace follow in the orchard. A charming rill is fed from the upper moat or mill pond. Roses flourish: Caroline Testout and Bennetts' Seedling in the forecourt, Old Blush China in the churchyard, Natalie Nyples surrounds the well, Rambling Rector and Sanders White climb in apples, and The Fairy tumbles in profusion to the lower moat.

In autumn asters flower below the terrace, Virginia creeper then willows flame at the entrance. Robert Fuller gave his Manor to the National Trust in 1943, it is now home to his grandson's family who have replanted the gardens. The house and garden feature in the new film 'The Other Boleyn Girl'.

## Fact File

| | |
|---|---|
| **Opening Times:** | Garden open Tuesday, Wednesdays, Thursday, 11am - 5pm. Manor Admission by guided tour Tuesday – Thursday 11, 12, 2, 3 & 4 Sunday: Garden open 2pm – 5pm. Manor tours at 2, 3 & 4. |
| **Admission Rates:** | Adults: £7.20 (Garden only: £4.80) Senior Citizens: N/A, Children: £3.60 (Garden only: £2.40), Family: £18.40 |
| **Group Rates:** | Minimum Group Size: 15 Adults: £6.10, Senior Citizens: N/A, Children: £3.10 |
| **Disabled Access:** | No – photo album available. Garden partly accessible. Car parking and toilet on site. |
| **Tours/Events:** | Yes. |
| **Coach Parking:** | Drop-off point |
| **Length of Visit:** | Whole visit: 1 hour, 30 minutes. |
| **Booking Contact:** | Mrs. R. Floyd Great Chalfield Manor & Garden. Nr. Melksham, Wiltshire SN12 8NH Tel: 01225 782239 |
| **Email:** | greatchalfieldmanor@nationaltrust.org.uk |
| **Website:** | www.nationaltrust.org.uk/greatchalfieldmanor |
| **Location:** | 3 miles south-west of Melksham, off B3107, via Broughton Gifford Common. |

Please quote this guide when making a booking

# Iford Manor - The Peto Garden Wiltshire

Romantically sited overlooking the valley of the River Frome, close to Bradford-on-Avon, Iford Manor is built into the hillside below a hanging beechwood and fine garden terraces. The house was owned during the first part of the last century by Harold Peto, the architect and landscape designer who taught Lutyens, and who expressed his passion for classical Italian architecture and landscaping in an English setting. After many visits to Italy he acquired statues and architectural marbles. He planted phillyrea and cypress trees and other Mediterranean species to add to the plantings of the eighteenth century and to enhance the Italian character of the garden.

The great terrace is bounded on one side by an elegant colonnade and commands lovely views out over the orchard and the surrounding countryside. Paths wander through the Woodland and garden to the summerhouse, the cloister and the casita and amongst the water features.

## Fact File

| | |
|---|---|
| **Opening Times:** | 2pm - 5pm Sundays April and October. |
| | 2pm - 5pm Tuesdays - Thursdays, Saturday, Sunday and Bank Holiday Mondays, May to September. Mornings and Mondays and Fridays reserved for group visits by Appointment. |
| **Admission Rates:** | Adults £4.50, Senior Citizen £4.00, Child over 10 yrs £4.00. |
| **Group Rates:** | Minimum group size: 8 |
| | Adults £5.00, Senior Citizen £5.00, Child over 10 yrs £5.00 for visits outside normal hours. |
| **Facilities:** | House Keeper's Cream Teas at weekends. Cake "du jour" on weekdays. Group refreshments by arrangement. |
| **Disabled Access:** | Yes, Toilet and parking for disabled on site. |
| **Tours/Events:** | By appointment |
| **Coach Parking:** | Yes. |
| **Length of Visit:** | 1-1½ hours |
| **Booking Contact:** | Mrs Elizabeth Cartwright-Hignett |
| | Iford Manor, Bradford on Avon, Wiltshire BA15 2BA |
| | Telephone: 01225 863146 Fax: 01225 862364 |
| **Website:** | www.ifordmanor.co.uk |
| **Location:** | Follow brown tourist signs to Iford Manor:- 7 miles south of Bath on A36 Warminster Road & ½ mile south of Bradford on Avon on B3109. |

Often referred to as "Paradise", Stourhead is an exquisite example of an English landscape garden. It was once described by Horace Walpole as 'one of the most picturesque scenes in the world'.

Visitors can discover the inspiration behind Henry Hoare II's world famous garden, laid out between 1741 and 1780 and enjoy breathtaking views all year round.

The garden is dotted with Classical temples including the Pantheon and the Temple of Apollo, which provide a dramatic backdrop to the majestic lake, secluded valley and magnificent trees.

Stourhead House, an 18th century Palladian Mansion, is situated at the top of the gardens surrounded by lawns and parkland.

The Stourhead Estate extends east to King Alfred's Tower, a 160 foot folly 2½ miles from the House which affords stunning views across three counties, and is the perfect place for picnics. Visitors can also enjoy breathtaking walks across Whitesheet Hill's chalk downs, and explore the mature woodland packed with an exciting range of trees, and a rich array of native wildlife.

## Fact File

**Opening Times:** Garden open all year daily 9am-7pm.
House open Friday-Tuesday 13th March-31st October, 11am-5pm, last entry 4.30pm
King Alfred's Tower open daily, 13th March-31st October, 11am-5pm, last entry 4.30pm.

**Admission Rates:** Garden & House: Adults £12.80*, Child £6.40*. Garden or House: Adults £7.70*, Child £4.20*.
King Alfred's Tower: Adult £3.10*, Child: £1.60*. National Trust members free.
*Includes a voluntary 10% donation but visitors can however, choose to pay the standard prices which are displayed at the property and on the website.*

**Group Rates:** Minimum group size 15: Garden & House £11.20, Garden or House £6.70.
King Alfred's Tower £2.60. National Trust members free.

**Facilities:** Visitor Centre, Shop, Plant Centre, Self-service Restaurant, Farm Shop, Spread Eagle Inn, Art Gallery, Ice Cream Parlour, Licensed Civil Ceremony venue.

**Disabled Access:** Toilets, parking, Shuttle Bus service March to October. Sympathetic hearing scheme, Assistance dogs welcome and wheelchairs. Self-drive mobility vehicle subject to availability. Stair-climber available with advance booking.

**Tours/Events:** Please contact us for details of all our events and tours.

**Coach Parking:** Yes.

**Length of Visit:** Recommend Minimum 3 hours.

**Booking Contact:** Georgina Mead. Stourhead Estate Office, Stourton, Nr Mere, Warminster, Wiltshire BA12 6QD
Tel: 01747 841152  Fax: 01747 842005

**Email:** stourhead@nationaltrust.org.uk

**Website:** www.nationaltrust.org.uk/stourhead

**Location:** Stourhead is in the village of Stourton, off the B3092, 3 miles northwest of Mere (A303) or 8 miles south of Frome (A361).

Please quote this guide when making a booking

# Arley Arboretum & Gardens

Arley Arboretum is one of the oldest privately owned arboretums in Great Britain. It boasts more than 300 species of trees in formal and informal plantings and gardens. Nestling in the Severn Valley and overlooking the river, it has been growing and maturing in this idyllic setting for two centuries.

Spring in Arley is a magical time of growth and renewal. A carpet of spring flowering bulbs drives away the winter gloom. The arboretum is filled with birdsong and the bustling activity of its many residents. Explore the stunning Magnolia garden and enjoy the Azaleas and Rhododendrons in bloom. In summer the herbaceous borders in the walled garden and the planters in the Italian garden are a riot of colour?

Autumn is a wonderful time of year in the arboretum. The leaves turn a kaleidoscope of colours, and cover the ground with a rich and exotic carpet. Visitors can enjoy the spectacle of the acers in their autumn glory and the Barbican Tower with its scarlet waistcoat and fine display provided throughout the arboretum.

## Fact File

| | |
|---|---|
| **Opening Times:** | Wednesday to Sunday 11 a.m. – 5 p.m. |
| **Admission Rates:** | Adults: £5.00, Senior Citizens: £5.00, Children aged 5-16: £1.00. |
| **Group Rates:** | Minimum Group Size: 10. Adults: £4.50. Senior Citizens: £4.50, Children: £1.00. RHS Members Free on Thursdays only. |
| **Facilities:** | Tea room, open to non visitors. |
| **Disabled Access:** | Yes. |
| **Toilet On Site:** | Yes. |
| **Tours/Events:** | Yes. Booking required. |
| **Coach Parking:** | Yes. |
| **Car Parking:** | Yes. |
| **Length of Visit:** | Minimum 1½ hours to all day. |
| **Booking Contact:** | Mrs. Norah Howells<br>Arley Arboretum & Gardens, Arley estate Office, Upper Arley, Nr. Bewdley, Worcs. DY12 1XG<br>Booking Telephone No. 01299 861368 |
| **Email:** | info@arley-arboretum.org.uk |
| **Website:** | www.arley-arboretum.org.uk |
| **Location:** | Between Kidderminster and Bridgnorth on the A442 and is brown-signed from this road. |

Please quote this guide when making a booking

Croome was 'Capability' Brown's first complete landscape, making his reputation and establishing a new style of garden design which became universally adopted over the next 50 years. Stroll through winding shrubberies to discover temples, statues and a lakeside garden, or enjoy longer walks through our estate. Learn about the secret work of RAF Defford in our restored WWII building, or simply relax and enjoy a slice of cake in our 1940s-style canteen.

The outer eye-catchers, acquired in 2009, and the elegant park buildings were designed by Brown, Robert Adam and James Wyatt. Croome Court, sold by the Coventry family in 1948, is at last reunited with the parkland, allowing visitors to appreciate the 6th Earl of Coventry's vision for the estate as a whole. The house is presented empty of contents, giving visitors an opportunity to follow the restoration progress over the coming years.

## Fact File

**Opening Times:** Park, Tea-room and Shop:
1 January – 14 February, Saturday and Sunday 10am-4pm.
20 February – 31 October, Daily 10am-5:30pm
6 November – 19 December, Saturday and Sunday 10am-4pm
26 December – 31 December, Daily 10am-4pm
Court:
20 February – 31 October, Wednesday to Monday 11am-4:30pm
6 November – 19 December, Saturday and Sunday 11am-3:30pm

**Admission Rates:** Adult £6, Child £3, Family £15

**Group Rates:** Minimum of 15 people £5.25

**Facilities:** 1940's style Canteen, Toilets, Shop.

**Disabled Access:** Gardens are fully accessible and flat access car park is available on request.
Manual wheelchair and powered mobility vehicle available for loan.

**Tours/Events:** Full programme of events, please contact us for more information.

**Coach Parking:** Yes. Pre-booking is essential.

**Length of Visit:** Approximately 2 hours.

**Booking Contact:** Please call us on 01905 371006.
Croome Park Estate Office, Builder's Yard, High Green, Severn Stoke, Worcs, WR8 9JS

**Email:** croomepark@nationaltrust.org.uk

**Website:** www.nationaltrust.org.uk/croomepark

**Location:** 9 Miles south of Worcester. Signposted on A38 and B4084.

Please quote this guide when making a booking

# Spetchley Park Gardens Worcestershire

This is a beautiful 30 acre Victorian garden, surrounded by glorious countryside and boasting an enviable collection of worldwide plant treasures. You can enjoy the fantastic vistas and stunning architecture that not only inspired Edward Elgar to write one of his great compositions from the gardener's cottage but was also home to convalescing American pilots during World War 2

The wonderful display of spring bulbs in April and May, together with flowering trees and shrubs are followed in June and July by the large selection of roses, whilst July, August and September reveal the great herbaceous borders in all their glory. This is a garden for all seasons

Having explored the gardens you can enjoy the peaceful surroundings of the Tea room or, for the more adventurous walk around the 150 acre deer park with its herd of red and fallow deer.

## Fact File

| | |
|---|---|
| **Opening times:** | 21st March - 30th September. Wednesday - Sunday 11am - 6pm, 1st - 31st October. Saturdays and Sundays 11am - 4pm. Bank Holiday Mondays 11am - 6pm. Last admissions one hour before closing. |
| **Admission Rates:** | Adults £6.00, Senior Citizen £5.50, Under 16s free. Adults Season Tickets £25.00 |
| **Group Rates:** | Minimum group size: 25 Adults £5.00, Senior Citizen £5.00, Child £1.90. |
| **Facilities:** | Tea Room, plant sales and small gift shop. |
| **Disabled Access:** | Partial. Parking for disabled on site, Booking necessary for parties. (Access restricted, please telephone contact details below for advice). |
| **Tours/Events:** | Please check website for details. |
| **Coach Parking:** | Yes. |
| **Length of Visit:** | 2 hours minimum. |
| **Booking Contact:** | Berkeley Estate Office, Ham, Berkeley, Gloucestershire GL13 9QL. Tel: 01453 810303 Fax: 01453 511915 |
| **Email:** | hb@spetchleygardens.co.uk |
| **Website:** | www.spetchleygardens.co.uk |
| **Location:** | 2 miles east of Worcester on A44, leave M5 at either junctions 6 or 7 |

Please quote this guide when making a booking

# Burton Agnes Hall & Gardens Yorkshire

**Winners of 2005 HHA Christies Garden of the Year Award**

Burton Agnes is a magnificent Elizabethan Hall surrounded by lawns, topiary yew bushes and beautiful award winning gardens. The eastern aspect of the house showcases a classical pond with beautiful fountains and a newly created pebble mosaic. To the right of the house lies an Elizabethan walled garden, home to over 3,000 different plants, a potager of herbs and vegetables, fruit beds and even a maze! Contained within the walled garden is also a National Collection of campanulas, a fantastic knot garden with coloured theme gardens and giant board games.

## Fact File

**Opening Times:** Gardens, shops and cafe open 6th - 28th February, daily 11am to 4pm
Hall, gardens, shops and cafe open 1st April to 31st October, daily 11am to 5pm
Christmas Opening 14th November to 22nd December, daily 11am to 5pm

**Admission Rates:** Adults £4.00, Senior Citizens £3.50, Children £2.50

**Group rates:** 10% discount for groups of 30+

**Facilities:** Elizabethan Hall and gardens with courtyard shops, cafe and plant sales

**Disabled Access:** Yes, toilet and parking on site.

**Tours/Events:** Guided tours available on request.
Snowdrop Opening   6th-28th Feb
Orchid Weekend  6th & 7th March
Easter Egg Hunt 4th & 5th April
Gardeners' Fair 12th and 13th June
Michaelmas Fair 30th and 31st October
Christmas Opening 14th Nov - 22nd Dec

**Coach Parking:** Yes

**Length of Visit:** 1 1/2 to 2 hours

**Booking Contact:** The Estate Office, Burton Agnes Hall, Burton Agnes, Near Driffield, East Yorks, YO25 4NB.
Telephone: 01262 490324

**Email:** office@burtonagnes.com

**Website:** www.burtonagnes.com

**Location:** On A614 between Driffield and Bridlington.

Please quote this guide when making a booking

The early 18th Century green gardens of 35 acres (14ha) have been described as "the supreme masterpiece of the art of the landscape gardener". Peace and tranquillity reign supreme in this classical English setting – a rare survivor of a style of gardening using the natural landscape.

The designer is unknown although it has been suggested that either Switzer or Bridgeman, or both, may have been involved. The parterres to the North and South of the house were added in the middle of the 19th Century and along with the conservatory are the only additions that have been made to the garden since it was landscaped in the middle of the 18th Century. Explore at leisure the great lawn and level terraces, temples, yew tree walk, woodland walks and the scented 'secret garden' around the conservatory.

## Fact File

| | |
|---|---|
| **Opening Times:** | Sunday 4th April – 31st October. Closed 23rd and 24th June. Parkland Centre: 11.00a.m. – 5.30p.m. Garden: 11.00a.m. – 5.30p.m., Last Admission 4.30p.m. House – by Guided Tour only. Tours: 12.30p.m., 1.30p.m., 2.30p.m. & 3.30p.m. |
| **Admission Rates:** | House & Gardens: Adult: £8.25, Concession: £6.25, Child 10-16 yrs: £3.75 (under 5's Free) Family (2 adults & 2 children 5-16 yrs): £17.00, E.H. Members: £4.50. Gardens & Parkland: Adult: £5.00, Child 10-16 yrs: £2.00 (under 5's Free). Parkland: Adult: £3.00, Concession: £4.50, Child 5-16 yrs: £3.00 (under 10's Free). Season Ticket: Family (2 adults & 2 children 5-16 yrs) £35.00, Adult: £20.00 |
| **Group Rates:** | House & Gardens (15 or more): £5.75. Gardens & Parkland (15 or more): £4.00 or Group Guided Tour £5.00 |
| **Facilities:** | Visitor Centre, Shop, Restaurant, Teas. |
| **Disabled Access:** | No, only partial to the garden. Bookable wheelchair loan available. |
| **Toilets on site:** | Yes. |
| **Tours/Events:** | Guided tours available, booking required. |
| **Coach Parking:** | Yes. |
| **Car Parking on site:** | Yes. |
| **Length of Visit:** | 3 hours. |
| **Booking Contact:** | Mrs. E M Williams, House Manager, Duncombe Park, Helmsley, York, YO62 5EB Telephone: 01439 772625  Fax: 01439 772114 |
| **Email:** | liz@duncombepark.com |
| **Website:** | www.duncombepark.com |
| **Location:** | 1 mile from A170 entrance in the centre of Helmsley. |

Please quote this guide when making a booking

# Fountains Abbey and Studley Royal Water Garden North Yorkshire

Yorkshire's first World Heritage site is a truly remarkable place encompassing nearly 900 years of history.

Once wild and wooded, this landscape was transformed into one of England's most spectacular Georgian water gardens by the Aislabie family. Conserved to look much as it would in the 18th century, this elegant ornamental garden is adorned with neo-classical statues, temples and follies which appear reflected in long mirror-like stretches of water. Take in the formal geometric design with beautifully contrived vistas, majestic sweeping avenues and breathtaking surprise views. Let yourself be transported to another era where peace and tranquillity reign.

The perfect complement to the garden is 12th century Fountains Abbey, landscaped into the garden as the ultimate surprise view. Lose yourself in the passages, staircases and towers of the largest, best-preserved monastic ruins in the country, and marvel at a unique relic of ancient craftsmanship

## Fact File

**Opening Times:** April - Sept 10am - 5pm, October - March 10am - 4pm.
Closed Fridays in November - January and closed 24th and 25th December.

**Admission Rates:** Adults £8.50, Child £4.55, Family's £21.60,
NT/EH Members Free. Under 5's Free.

**Groups Rates:** Group discounts and bespoke tours available, call the Group Visits Organiser on 01765 643197.

**Facilities:** Shop, Tea Room, Restaurant, Kiosk and Play Area.

**Disabled Access:** Yes. Toilet and parking for disabled on site.
Personal Mobility Vehicles on loan, booking necessary.

**Tours/Events:** Guided Tours for groups, must be pre booked, telephone 01765 643197.
Annual events programme, please enqire for details.

**Coach Parking:** Yes

**Length of Visit:** 1 1/2 hours minimum.

**Booking Contact:** Fountains Abbey, Ripon, Yorkshire, HG4 3DY
Telephone: 01765 608888   Fax: 01765 601002

**Email:** fountainsenquiries@nationaltrust.org.uk

**Website:** www.fountainsabbey.org.uk   www.nationaltrust.org.uk

**Location:** 4 miles west of Ripon of B6265 to Pateley Bridge, signposted from A1,
10 miles north of Harrogate A61.

Please quote this guide when making a booking

# RHS Garden Harlow Carr

## North Yorkshire

Wander through tranquil surroundings in this stunning 58 acre garden and pick up the latest tips and techniques for your own borders...or simply relax with family and friends on a leisurely stroll.

Find inspiration in the innovative Main Borders with their creative combinations of mixed perennials, grasses and roses, beautifully combined with sustainable practices and admire the dramatic Rose Revolution Borders - planting with a contemporary twist! Meander through 200 years of gardening history in the Gardens through Time, take practical ideas from the raised beds in the extensive Kitchen Garden, enjoy the beautiful Streamside Garden and the enticing Scented Garden.
The garden offers interest for all seasons from spring bulb displays, through rich summer & autumn colour to the frosted silhouettes of winter.

Year-round events include activities for all the family - outdoor theatre, guided walks, workshops, demonstrations. Visit the extensive RHS Shop & Plant Centre, and linger over delicious goodies in Bettys Café Tea Rooms.

## Fact File

**Opening Times:** 9.30am - 6pm (4pm Nov - Feb incl.) with last entry 1 hour before closing.
**Admission Rates:** (2009 prices) Adults £7.00, Child (6-16yrs) £2.50 (under 6 Free).
**Groups Rates:** Minimum group size 10, Adults £6.00.
**Facilities:** Largest Gardening Bookshop in the north, Bettys Cafe Tea Rooms, RHS Gift Shop & Plant Centre, Library.
**Disabled Access:** Yes. Toilet and parking for disabled on site. Wheelchairs on loan, booking necessary.
**On The Website:** A full programme of events is available from the gardens or from the website.
**Coach Parking:** Yes
**Length of Visit:** 2 hours
**Booking Contact:** The Admin Department
RHS Garden Harlow Carr, Crag Lane, Harrogate, HG3 1QB
Tel: 01423 565418 Fax: 01423 530663
**Email:** harlowcarr@rhs.org.uk
**Website:** www.rhs.org.uk/harlowcarr
**Location:** Take the B6162 Otley Road out of Harrogate towards Beckwithshaw. Harlow Carr is 1.5 miles on the right.

Please quote this guide when making a booking

These substantial walled gardens and wooded pleasure grounds are well worth visiting in all seasons: massive herbaceous borders, Victorian Kitchen garden with rare vegetable collection, the National Hyacinth Collection, herb and shade borders, extensive hothouses and thousands of snowdrops, bluebells, daffodils and narcissi. A stroll around the lake takes you through the deer park, where fallow deer graze beneath the boughs of living oak trees, now believed to be over a thousand years old. This walk also offers the best views of the 14th century castle. Children will have fun spotting the faces on several of our older trees.

Guided tours of the castle give you a chance to view the civil war armour, secret priests hiding hole and splendid furnishings. On site facilities include ample free parking, wc's (including disabled), tea room, historic inn with beer garden and gift shop selling plants.

## Fact File

| | |
|---|---|
| **Opening Times:** | Daily - Throughout the year 9am - 5pm (dusk in the winter months). |
| **Admission Rates:** | Gardens, Adults £5.50, Concession £5.00, Child £3.50. (under 5 yrs Free) |
| **Group Rates:** | Minimum group size 25 people to qualify for group rate. Gardens, Adults £4.50, Child £3.00. |
| **Facilities:** | Gift Shop, Plant Sales, Tea Rooms, Restaurant, Children's play area. |
| **Disabled Access:** | Yes. Toilet and parking for disabled on site. Mobility Scooter, booking necessary. |
| **Tours/Events:** | Guided tours of gardens by prior arrangement only. |
| **Coach Parking:** | Yes |
| **Booking Contact:** | Jenny Carter Ripley Castle Gardens, Ripley, Nr Harrogate, North Yorkshire, HG3 3AY Telephone: 01423 770152  Fax: 01423 771745 |
| **Email:** | enquiries@ripleycastle.co.uk |
| **Website:** | www.ripleycastle.co.uk |
| **Location:** | Three miles north of Harrogate on the A61. |

Please quote this guide when making a booking

Set within the 18th century walls of the original kitchen garden for Scampston Hall, the 4 acre Walled Garden has been completely redesigned by internationally acclaimed plantsman, Piet Oudolf, to produce a stunning garden with an unashamedly contemporary feel. Amongst nine contrasting garden rooms is a striking perennial meadow and a reflective silent garden. The 400m border walk contains many unusual spring and autumn flowering shrubs and bulbs.

A self-guided Woodland Walk provides visitors with the opportunity to visit the traditional gardens around the Hall. This includes a splendid 19th century Rock Garden and 'Capability' Brown lakes and park.

In-house propagated plants for sale, along with an excellent on-site restaurant, helps to make this a modern plantsman's paradise.

Scampston Hall, open during the summer, is home to a superb collection of paintings, porcelain and furniture including pieces by Gainsborough, Scott and Chippendale.

Please ask about our special group package with nearby Jackson's Wold Garden.

## Fact File

| | |
|---|---|
| **Opening Times:** | 2nd April – 31st October: 10 a.m. – 5 p.m. |
| **Admission Rates:** | Walled Garden: Adults: £5.00, Children (12-16): £2.50. Under 12: free. |
| | Woodland Walk: Adults £3.00, Children (12-16): £1.50. Under 12: free. |
| **Group Rates:** | Minimum Group Size: 15, Cost (Walled Garden): £4.50 including a free plant list. |
| **Facilities:** | Restaurant/teas, shop, plant sales, toilets. |
| **Disabled Access:** | Yes. Bookable wheelchair loan available |
| **Car Parking on site:** | Yes |
| **Coach Parking:** | Yes |
| **Tours/Events:** | Introductory talk available for pre-booked groups of 15+. |
| **Length of Visit:** | 1½ - 2 hours |
| **Special Events:** | Spring Plant Fair Sunday 6th June 2010 |
| | Autumn Plant Fair Sunday 10th October 2010 |
| | Annual events programme. Please enquire or see website for details. |
| **Booking Contact:** | Anne Ainsley, |
| | The Walled Garden at Scampston, Scampston Hall, Malton, North Yorkshire YO17 8NG |
| | Telephone No. 01944 759111   Fax No. 01944 758700 |
| **Email:** | info@scampston.co.uk |
| **Website:** | www.scampston.co.uk |
| **Location:** | 5 miles east of Malton on the north side of the A64. |
| | Just east of the village of Rillington. |

Please quote this guide when making a booking

---
153

## Stillingfleet Lodge Garden & Nursery                    Yorkshire

Walking around Stillingfleet Lodge Garden and Nurseries is a journey through one woman's passion for plants. Vanessa Cook, who is usually on hand to offer planting advice, held the National Collection of Pulmonaria and now turns her attention to trees as well as unusual perennials and climbers. She has created a charming country garden that combines cottage garden planting with traditional herbaceous borders. Abundant displays of shady planting and inspiring plant combinations with the emphasis on texture and shape, weave throughout a series of gardens creating a haven of peace. Interest continues around every corner with a wildflower meadow, wildlife pond, rare breeds of poultry and a contemporary rill garden which is a tranquil delight. Homemade cakes and refreshments are available in the converted barn. Complete your trip with a visit to the well-stocked nursery.

### Fact File

| | |
|---|---|
| **Opening times:** | April 3rd 2010 - Sept 30th 2010, Wednesday and Friday 1.00 p.m. – 5.00 p.m. |
| | 1st and 3rd Saturdays and Sundays of each month 1.00 p.m. – 5.00 p.m. |
| **Admission Rates:** | Adults: £4.00, Senior Citizens: £4.00, Children: 5 – 16 years: £0.50 |
| | RHS Members Free – on Wednesday afternoons |
| **Group Rates:** | Minimum Group Size: 15 |
| | Adults: £4.00, Senior Citizens: £4.00, Children: 5 – 16 years: £0.50 |
| **Facilities:** | Visitor Centre, Plant Sales, Teas |
| **Disabled Access:** | Yes |
| **Toilets on site:** | Yes |
| **Car Parking on site:** | Yes |
| **Coach Parking:** | Yes – 200 yards away |
| **Length of Visit:** | 1½ - 2 hours |
| **Special Events:** | Courses for RHS and listed on the website. |
| **Booking Contact:** | Vanessa Cook, Stillingfleet Lodge Garden and Nursery, Stewart Lane, Stillingfleet, York YO19 6HP |
| | Booking Tel No.01904 728506. Booking Fax No. 01904 728506 |
| **Email:** | vanessa.cook@stillingfleetlodgenurseries.co.uk |
| **Website:** | www.stillingfleetlodgenurseries.co.uk |
| **Location:** | 6 miles south of York on B1222. Brown sign opposite the church. |

Please quote this guide when making a booking

A wonderful and romantic garden located in the vale of York, not too far from most of the stunning areas of North Yorkshire countryside.

The garden has beautiful terraces, an exotic bamboo border, Edwardian fernery and overlooks the parkland which is bordered by a Woodland Walk. In the late spring the bluebells add to the attraction and from the Woodland Walk you can enter the garden under a tunnel of yellow provided by the Laburnum Walk.

As we progress into summer old fashioned shrub roses and the herbaceous borders burst into colour. Other highlights include a fine old Ice House and magnificent specimen trees, an Austrian Pine being just one of many to note.

A visit to Sutton Park is an ideal way to relax and unwind.

## Fact File

| | |
|---|---|
| **Opening times:** | April – September: daily 11 a.m. – 5 p.m. |
| **Admission Rates:** | Adults: £3.50, Senior Citizens: £3.00, Children: £1.50 |
| **Facilities:** | Shop, Plant Sales, Teas |
| **Disabled Access:** | Yes. Wheelchair loan available – booking required. |
| **Toilets on site:** | Yes |
| **Car Parking on site:** | Yes |
| **Coach Parking:** | Yes |
| **Guided Tours:** | Yes, booking required. |
| **Length of Visit:** | 1 - 1.5 hours |
| **Booking Contact:** | Elaine Ellis, Sutton Park, Sutton on the Forest, York YO61 1DP Booking Tel No. 01347 810249, Booking Fax No. 01347 811251 |
| **Email:** | suttonpark@statelyhome.co.uk |
| **Website:** | www.statelyhome.co.uk |
| **Location:** | 8 miles north of York on B1363 in the village of Sutton on the Forest |

Please quote this guide when making a booking

# Samares Manor Gardens Jersey, Channel Islands

These exceptional gardens were originally designed and constructed in the 1920s by wealthy shipping line owner, Sir James Knott. Inspired by an enthusiasm for plants and a special interest in the Orient, he created a rich diversity of planting which included many rare and special plants: a Japanese Garden, rock and water gardens, formal gardens, large ponds with islands and camellia plantations are the result of his passion.

In recent years there has been a programme of restoration, development and diversification. This included the introduction of the internationally renowned herb garden, the inspiration of designer, John Brookes. Sited in the south facing walled garden it contains hundreds of culinary, medicinal and fragrant plants. Manor activities include daily talks on herbs, a plant trail that highlights seasonal specialities and children's competitions. The manor house and the rural life museum are also open to the public.

## Fact File

| | |
|---|---|
| **Opening Times:** | 3rd April – 16th October 2010: 9.30 a.m. – 5 p.m. |
| **Admission Rates:** | Adults: £6.75, O.A.P: £6.20, Children over 5 / Student: £2.35. |
| **Group Rates:** | Minimum Group Size: 10 |
| | Adults: £5.95, O.A.P: £5.65, Children over 5 / Student: £2.25. |
| **Facilities:** | Shop, plant sales, restaurant, Jersey Rural Life and Carriage Museum, Toilets. |
| **Disabled Access:** | Yes.  Bookable wheelchair loan available (1 only) |
| **Car Parking on site:** | Yes |
| **Coach Parking:** | Yes |
| **Tours/Events:** | Guided tours available.  Booking required. |
| **Length of Visit:** | 3 hours minimum |
| **Special Events:** | Samarés Summer Festival and Jersey Rose Show: 26th & 27th June 2010. |
| **Booking Contact:** | Sally Fleming, Samarès Manor, St. Clements, Jersey JE2 6QW |
| | Booking Telephone No. 01534 870551  Booking Fax No. 01534 768949 |
| **Email:** | enquiries@samaresmanor.com |
| **Website:** | www.samaresmanor.com |
| **Location:** | From St. Helier, drive to Georgetown crossroads and follow road signs to St. Clements (A4, A5). Pass New Veterinary Hospital, bear right and turn left at traffic lights St. Clements' inner road. Pass the Roman Catholic Church on the right. Entrance to Samarès Manor is 500 yards on the left. Watch for the flags. |

Please quote this guide when making a booking

# Scotland

'What a desolate place would be the world without a flower! It would be a face without a smile, a feast without a welcome.'

**A.J. Balfour**

From the grandeur of the Royal Botanic Gardens in Edinburgh to the positively sub-tropical plant collection at Logan, there are Scottish gardens to suit all tastes in the following pages. Discover the romantic delights of Dunvegan Castle Gardens and Armadale Castle Gardens on the Isle of Skye, the 200 year-old magnificence of the gardens at Bolfracks in Perthshire and the beautiful loch-side setting for the gardens at Castle Kennedy near Stranraer, to name just a few.

**Benmore Botanic Garden - Argyll**

## Armadale Castle Gardens - Clan Donald Skye          Isle of Skye

Armadale Castle Gardens & Museum of the Isles has a spectacular setting within the Sleat Peninsula of the Isle of Skye called the 'Garden of Skye'.

The forty acre Garden is set around the ruins of Armadale Castle. The warm, generally frost free climate of the west coast of Scotland - a result of the Gulf Stream - allows these sheltered gardens, dating back to the 17th Century, to flourish.

Wander over the expanses of lawn leading from the ruined Armadale Castle to viewpoints overlooking the hills of Knoydart. Terraced walks and landscaped ponds contrasting with wildflower meadows bring the natural and formal side by side. The Nature Trails provide another dimension to this garden experience. In May during the bluebell season, a carpet of blue around the Arboretum creates a visual and fragrance sensation that is so prevalent around the gardens at that time of year.

### Fact File

| | |
|---|---|
| **Opening Times:** | 9.30am - 5.00pm (last entry 5pm), 7 days Thursday 1st April to Saturday 23rd October. |
| **Admission Rates:** | Adults £6.95, Concessions £4.95, Child £4.95, Family £20.00. |
| **Groups Rates:** | Minimum group size: 8. £4.50. |
| **Facilities:** | 40 Acres of Woodland Garden and mature Trails, Museum of the Isles, Restaurant, 3 Shops. |
| **Disabled Access:** | Yes, Toilet and Parking for disabled on site. Electric Wheelchairs on loan, booking necessary. |
| **Tours/Events:** | Guided walks on request. Audio tour available in Museum Of The Isles - French, German, Italian, Spanish, English and Gaelic, also available, a visually impaired tour in English. |
| **Coach Parking:** | Yes |
| **Length of Visit:** | 2 hours |
| **Booking Contact:** | Mags MacDonald<br>Armadale Castle, Armadale, Sleat, Isle of Skye, IV45 8RS<br>Telephone: 01471 844305 Fax: 01471 844275 |
| **Email:** | office@clandonald.com |
| **Website:** | www.clandonald.com |
| **Location:** | 2 minutes from Armadale/Mallaig Ferry. 20 miles from Skyebridge on A851. |

Please quote this guide when making a booking

# Benmore Botanic Garden                                              Argyll

Benmore with its magnificent mountainside setting is a joy to behold.  Its 120 acres boast a world-famous collection of flowering trees and shrubs including over 300 species of rhododendron and over one third of the world's hardy conifer species plus fine collections from North and South America, the Orient and the Himalaya.

Visitors are welcomed by an impressive avenue of Giant Redwoods, arguably one of the finest entrances to any botanic garden in the world.  Established in 1863, these majestic giants now stand over 50 metres high.

The Garden is glorious throughout the seasons, from the vibrant blooms of rhododendrons and azaleas in early spring, striking Eucryphias of late summer and breathtaking displays of rich autumn fruit and foliage.

Trails throughout the Garden lead to beautiful spots such as the restored Victorian Fernery, the Formal Garden with its distinctive Puck's Hut and hillside woodlands to a dramatic viewpoint at 450 feet (140m) overlooking the surrounding mountains and Holy Loch.

## Fact File

| | |
|---|---|
| **Opening times:** | Open daily from 10 a.m. 1 March – 31 October.  Closing: 5 p.m. (March and October) and 6 p.m. (April – September). |
| **Admission Rates:** | Adult: 5.00, Senior Citizens: £4.00, Children: £1.00, Family: £10.00 |
| **Group Rates:** | Minimum Group size: 11.  For rates contact the Garden. |
| **Facilities:** | Shop, Plant Sales, Restaurant/Teas, Courtyard gallery hosting events & exhibitions, audio tours |
| **Disabled Access:** | Yes, partial |
| **Toilets on site:** | Yes |
| **Car Parking:** | Yes |
| **Coach Parking:** | Yes |
| **Wheelchair Loan:** | Yes, No Booking Required for Wheelchairs |
| **Guided Tours:** | Yes, every Tuesday/Wednesday/Thursday/Sunday at 2 p.m., no booking required |
| **Length of Visit:** | |
| **Special Events:** | Restored Victorian fernery now open. |
| **Booking Contact:** | Benmore Botanic Garden, Dunoon, Argyll PA23 8QU Booking Tel No. 01369 706261.  Booking Fax No. 01369 706369 |
| **Email:** | benmore@rbgc.org.uk |
| **Website:** | www.rbge.org.uk/benmore |
| **Location:** | Dramatically set within the Loch Lomond and The Trossachs National Park and the Argyll Forest Park, on the A815 seven miles north of Dunoon on the Cowal Peninsula. |

North facing and steep, Bolfracks is a challenge to garden. There has been a graden here for 200 years. Owned by the same family since the 1920's, each generation has made their changes to it.

As you arrive you sweep up a long drive that in spring is just a stream of golden daffodils. An enticement to visit!

The garden is divided into a wild garden and a formal rose and herbaceous garden. The Wild garden follows a burn up, where you see marvellous spring bulbs, Hellebores, Azaleas, Rhododendrons, Meconopsis, Gunnera, Lysichiton, Primula and then wonderful autumn colours from the collection of specimem trees. We are now proud owners of a Wollemi Pine There are wonderful views across the Tay Valley.

The formal garden has a good selection of roses, clematis, specimem trees and a new herbaceous border and peony beds. There is a wonderful Peony delavyii and a well established Prunus pissardi hedge.

Bolfracks is a graden planted with love by the current owner's uncle. Recent years have seen some much needed changes and renovation. As always, this is an ongoing process

## Fact File

**Opening times:** April – October, Daily 10 a.m. – 6 p.m.
**Admission Rates:** Adults: £4.00, Child free.
**Facilities:** Toilet facilities, plants for sale, catering possibilities for groups.
**Disabled Access:** Limited
**Tours:** By arrangement.
**Coach Parking:** Yes Please call for details.
**Length of Visit:** 2 hours
**Booking Contact:** Mr & Mrs R. A. Price
Bolfracks Estate Office, Aberfeldy, Perthshire PH15 2EX
Telephone: 01887 820344, Fax: 01887 829522
**Email:** info@bolfracks.fsnet.co.uk
**Website:** www.bolfracks.com
**Location:** 2 miles west of Aberfeldy on A827 towards Loch Tay

Please quote this guide when making a booking

# Castle Kennedy & Gardens

Located in beautiful scenery between two large natural lochs, the Gardens extend to seventy five acres of landscaped terraces and avenues. With the romantic and ruined 16th century Castle Kennedy over looking a walled garden and a 2 acre round pond at one end, and Lochinch Castle at the other, these world famous gardens are uniquely outstanding.

In close proximity to the sea on two sides, the Gardens are greatly influenced by the Gulf Stream, and contain many fine specimens of trees, Rhododendrons and tender exotic plants. Originally designed in 1722 by the 2nd Earl of Stair, Field Marshal and Ambassador to France, who was greatly influenced by the gardens of Versailles, the gardens are full of adventure and history.

Four carefully planned walks of different lengths and interest have been designed for visitors. These reveal the full garden experience throughout the seasons including the Daffodils, Magnolias and Rhododendrons early in the year to the beautiful herbaceous borders later in the summer, as well as many woodland and loch-side walks.

## Fact File

| | |
|---|---|
| **Opening Times:** | Weekends February, March & October, 1st April - 30th September, seven days a week, 10am- 5pm. Rest of the year by appointment. |
| **Admission Rates:** | Adults £4.00, Senior Citizen £3.00, Child £1.00 |
| **Groups Rates:** | Minimum group size 20 <br> 10% discount on normal admission rates. |
| **Facilities:** | Gift Shop, Tea room, Plant Sales |
| **Disabled Access:** | Partial. Toilet and parking for disabled on site. |
| **Tours/Events:** | Tours by special appointment. Annual events include an Easter Egg Hunt, Plant Fair, Family Trails as well as open-air Theatre Productions in the gardens |
| **Coach Parking:** | Yes |
| **Length of Visit:** | 1 - 4 hours |
| **Booking Contact:** | Castle Kennedy Gardens, Stair Estates, Rephad, Stranraer, Dumfries & Galloway, DG9 8BX <br> Gardens Tel: 01581 400225 Telephone: 01776 702024   Fax: 01776 706248 |
| **Email:** | info@castlekennedygardens.co.uk |
| **Website:** | www.castlekennedygardens.co.uk |
| **Location:** | Approximately 5 miles east of Stranraer on A75. |

Please quote this guide when making a booking

# Dawyck Botanic Garden

With over 300 years of tree planting Dawyck is truly one of the worlds finest arboreta, boasting some of the tallest trees in Britain, as well as exotic conifers and the unique Dawyck Beech. Set amidst a picturesque glen in the heart of the Scottish borders, these majestic trees form a splendid backdrop to the abundance of native and exotic plants on display.

The Garden is a magical place throughout the year, from swathes of snowdrops and daffodils in early spring to breathtaking displays of azaleas, rhododendrons and pools of blue Himalayan poppies in early summer.

In autumn the foliage bursts into vivid hues of red, orange and gold and provides a magnificent backdrop of colour.

Dawyck's new state-of-the-art visitor centre greatly enhances the visitor experience at this renowned botanic garden.

## Fact File

| | |
|---|---|
| **Opening times:** | Open daily from 10 a.m. 1 February – 30 November. Closes 4 p.m. February & November; 5 p.m. March & October; 6 p.m. April – September. |
| **Admission Rates:** | Adults: £5.00, Senior Citizens: £4.00, Children: £1.00 |
| **Group Rates:** | Minimum Group Size 10. Adults: £4.50, Senior Citizens: £3.60, Children: £0.90 |
| **Facilities:** | Visitor Centre, Shop, Plant sales, Restaurant Teas, studio for exhibitions and events |
| **Disabled Access:** | Yes. Wheelchair loan available. |
| **Toilets on site:** | Yes |
| **Car Parking on site:** | Yes |
| **Coach Parking:** | Yes |
| **Booking Contact:** | Vicky Brunt, Dawyck Botanic Garden, Stobo, Near Peebles, Scottish Borders, EH45 9JU Booking Tel No.01721 760254 Booking Fax No. 01721 760214 |
| **Email:** | dawyck@rbge.org.uk |
| **Website:** | www.rbge.org.uk/dawyck |
| **Location:** | 28 miles south of Edinburgh on the B712, 8 miles southwest of Peebles in the Scottish Borders. |

Please quote this guide when making a booking

# Dunvegan Castle Gardens Isle of Skye

Any visit to the Isle of Skye is incomplete without savouring the wealth of history offered by Dunvegan Castle & Gardens, the oldest continuously inhabited castle in Scotland and ancestral home of the Chiefs of clan MacLeod for 800 years.

Dunvegan Castle's five acres of formal gardens began life in the 18th century. In stark contrast to the barren moorland and mountains that dominate Skye's landscape, the gardens are a hidden oasis featuring an eclectic mix of plants, woodland glades, shimmering pools fed by waterfalls and streamsflowing down to the sea. After experiencing the Water Garden with its ornate bridges and islands replete with a rich and colourful plant variety, wander through the elegant surroundings of the formal Round Garden featuring a Box-wood Parterre as its centrepiece

For more information about our opening times and our Friends of Dunvegan Castle membership scheme, please visit www.dunvegancastle.com

## Fact File

**Opening times:** 1 April – 15 October 10 a.m. – 5.30 p.m.  16 October – 31 March: open by appointment
**Admission Rates:** Garden: Adults: £5.50, Senior Citizens/Students: £4.50, Children: £3.00
**Group Rates:** Garden: Minimum Group Size: 10.  Adults: £4.50, Senior Citizens: £4.50, Children: £3.00
**Facilities:** Shop, Café, seal boat trips, fishing and loch cruises, Dunvegan Castle
**Disabled Access:** Yes.
**Toilets on site:** Yes
**Car Parking on site:** Yes
**Coach Parking:** Yes
**Booking Contact:** Macleod Estate Office, Dunvegan Castle & Gardens, Dunvegan, Isle of Skye, Scotland, IV55 8WF
Booking Tel No.01470 521206.  Booking Fax No. 01470 521205
**Email:** info@dunvegancastle.com
**Website:** www.dunvegancastle.com
**Location:** 1 mile north of Dunvegan on the northwest corner of Skye.

Please quote this guide when making a booking

This exotic Garden, justifiably described as a plantsman's paradise, is home to a spectacular collection of bizarre and beautiful plants. This majestic corner of Scotland is warmed by the Gulf Stream and the climate provides perfect growing conditions for southern hemisphere plants.

Famed for its tender collections, Logan's Walled Garden is a showcase for colourful blooms throughout the season. Adding to the summer colour are Osteospermums, gazanias and diascias – all half-hardy perennials from southern Africa. The Woodland Garden is a haven for the weird and wonderful, from the groves of eucalyptus to the Gunnera Bog and the evocative Tasmanian Creek planting. Visitors who venture to the highest point of the Garden will be rewarded with magnificent views over the Rhins to the Galloway Hills and beyond.

Over 1,800 different plant species, including around 120 that are threatened in the wild, can be seen thriving within Logan's 24-acre site.

## Fact File

**Opening times:** Open daily from 10 a.m. 15th March - 31st October. (Sundays only in February 4 p.m.) March & October 5 p.m. April - September 6 p.m.
(Sundays only in February), 5 p.m. March & October; 6 p.m. April – September

**Admission Rates:** Adults: £5.00, Concessions: £4.00, Children: £1.00, Family £10.00

**Group Rates:** Minimum Group Size: 11, 10% discount.

**Facilities:** Visitor Centre, Shop, Plant Sales, Restaurant, Teas, Audio guides

**Disabled Access:** Yes

**Toilets on site:** Yes

**Car Parking on site:** Yes

**Coach Parking:** Yes

**Guided Tours:** Yes, 10.30a.m. every second Tuesday of the month (April – September) pre-booked tours available.

**Booking Contact:** Richard Baines, Logan Botanic Gardens, Port Logan, Stranraer, Dumfries & Galloway DG9 9ND
Booking Tel No.01776 860231. Booking Fax No. 01776 860333

**Email:** logan@rbge.org.uk

**Website:** www.rbge.org.uk/logan

**Location:** 14 miles south of Stranraer in the Rhins of Galloway, off the B7065.

Please quote this guide when making a booking

# Royal Botanic Garden Edinburgh Scotland

Established in 1670, the Royal Botanic Garden Edinburgh has developed into a world leading centre of horticultural excellence and its 70 magnificent acres are home to seven per cent of all known plants.

At the heart of the Garden stands the iconic Palm House - the tallest of its kind in Britain. Within the Glasshouses you will enjoy a fascinating journey through the tropical and temperate regions of the globe as you wander through ten distinct climatic zones.

Reflecting the international research and conservation work of RBGE, the Garden is home to the largest collection of wild-origin Chinese plants outside China. See, too, the Scottish Heath Garden, recreating the plantings and landscape of the Scottish highlands; the world-famous Rock Garden; the stunning 165-long Herbaceous Border, backed by an outstanding century-old Beech Hedge and don't miss the Queen Mother's Memorial Garden – an inspirational tribute to a much-loved royal.

## Fact File

| | |
|---|---|
| **Opening times:** | Open daily from 10 a.m. (except 25 December and 31 January), closing 4 p.m. November – February; 6 p.m. March & October; 7 p.m. April to September |
| **Admission Rates:** | Adults: Free, Senior Citizens: Free, Children: Free. A charge applies to the glasshouses |
| **Disabled Access:** | Yes. Wheelchair loan available – booking required. |
| **Toilets on site:** | Yes |
| **Car Parking on site:** | On street, metered Mon-Fri. Weekend free. |
| **Coach Parking:** | On street, metered Mon-Fri. Weekend free. |
| **Guided Tours:** | Yes. |
| **Length of Visit:** | Guided tours depart daily at 11 a.m. & 2 p.m., April – September. Booked tours for groups available throughout the year |
| **Special Events:** | The John Hope Gateway Biodiversity and Information Centre now open |
| **Booking Contact:** | To book guided tours, please contact The Education Department. Booking Tel No.0131 248 2937. Booking Fax No. 0131 248 2901 |
| **Email:** | education@rbge.org.uk |
| **Website:** | www.rbge.org.uk |
| **Location:** | One mile north of Princes Street on the A092, with entrances on Arboretum Place, Inverleith Row and Inverleith Place. |

Please quote this guide when making a booking

# Wales

# Ireland

*'Once I saw two flowers blossom in a garden 'neath the hill, One a lily fair and handsome, and one a rose with crimson frill; Erect the rose would lift its pennon and survey the garden round, While the lily-lovely minion meekly rested on a mound.'*

**Reverend Daniel Evans**

From Cardiff Bay to the mountains of Snowdonia, Wales is a country of contrasts and this can be clearly seen through the diversity of its gardens. Historic garden restorations such as at Aberglasney, modern garden creations like the stunning National Botanic Garden of Wales, Dewstow with its caves and grottoes, the magnificent collections of trees and shrubs at Bodnant and the beautiful herbaceous borders at Dyffryn are just some of the Welsh delights within this book.

*'Autumn is over the long leaves that loves us and over the mice in the barley sheaves; Yellow the leaves of the rowan above us And yellow the wet-wild strawberry leaves'.* The falling of the leaves.

**William Butler Yeats.**

The weather is soft in Ireland, seldom offering extremes of heat or cold, just copious gifts of gently falling rain and mild airstreams enabling every landscape, plant and garden to green and grow. Irish gardens are like no other; they too are soft and gentle, full of atmosphere and a fecundity of foliage. The following pages provide just a little taster of some of the finest Irish gardens including Cashel House, Lisselan and Benvarden.

**Aberglasney Gardens - Carmarthenshire**

**Lisselan Gardens**

# Aberglasney Gardens                         Carmarthenshire

Aberglasney is one of the finest gardens in Wales. The Gardens have wonderful horticultural qualities and a mysterious history. Within the ten acres of garden are six different garden spaces including three walled gardens. At its heart is a unique and fully restored Elizabethan /Jacobean Cloister Garden and a parapet walk, which is the only example that survived in the UK. The Garden contains a magnificent collection of rare and unusual plants which are seldom seen elsewhere in the country.

The Mansion and Garden will continually be improved over the years, the result is a world renowned Garden set in the beautiful landscape of the Tywi Valley. There is a Café in the grounds, which serves delectable light lunches and snacks. In the summer, tea can be taken on the terrace overlooking the Pool Garden. There is also a shop and plant sales area. The creation of a winter garden in 2005 called the Ninfarium (after the mediaeval garden near Rome) is situated in the ruinous central courtyard of the Mansion. It provides a unique garden environment, displaying a wonderful range of exotic sub-tropical plants.

## Fact File

| | |
|---|---|
| **Opening times:** | Summer: 10am - 6pm (last entry at 5pm). |
| | Winter: 10.30am - 4pm (last entry at 3pm). |
| **Admission Rates:** | Adult/OAP £7.00, Child £4.00, Family £18.00. |
| **Groups Rates:** | Groups 10+ |
| | Adult/OAP £6.50. |
| **Facilities:** | Shop, Plant Sales, Cafe. |
| **Disabled Access:** | Yes.  Toilet and parking for disabled on site.  Wheelchairs on loan, booking necessary. |
| **Tours/Events:** | Guided tours on request. |
| **Coach Parking:** | Yes |
| **Length of Visit:** | 2 - 4 hours |
| **Booking Contact:** | Bookings Department. |
| | Aberglasney Gardens, Llangathen, Carmarthenshire, SA32 8QH |
| | Telephone: 01558 668998   Fax: 01558 668998 |
| **Email:** | info@aberglasney.org.uk |
| **Website:** | www.aberglasney.org |
| **Location:** | Four miles outside Llandeilo off the A40. |

Bodnant Garden is one of the finest gardens in the country not only known for its magnificent collections of rhododendrons, camellias and magnolias but also for its idyllic setting above the River Conwy with extensive views of the Snowdonia range.

Visit in early Spring (March and April) and be rewarded by the sight of carpets of golden daffodils and other spring bulbs, as well as the beautiful blooms of the magnolias, camellias and flowering cherries.  The spectacular rhododendrons and azaleas will delight from mid April until late May, whilst the famous original Laburnum Arch is an overwhelming mass of yellow blooms from mid-may to mid-June. The herbaceous borders, roses, hydrangeos, clematis and water liles flower from the middle of June until September.

All these, together with the outstanding October autumn colours make Bodnant truly a garden offering interest for all the seasons.

## Fact File

| | |
|---|---|
| **Opening Times:** | 20th Feb - 31st Oct 10-5pm.  1st Nov - 21st Nov 10-4pm. Last entry 30mins prior to closing. |
| **Admission Rates:** | Adults £7.90, Child £3.95 (5-16yrs) |
| **Groups Rates:** | Minimum group size 15. |
| | Adults £6.85. |
| **Facilities:** | Tearoom, Car & Coach Park. Garden Centre, Art & Craft Studios (Not NT). |
| **Disabled Access:** | Yes accessible toilet and parking on site.  Wheelchairs on loan. |
| **Tours/Events:** | Phone for details |
| **Coach Parking:** | Yes |
| **Length of Visit:** | 2 hours + |
| **Booking Contact:** | Ann Smith |
| | Bodnant Garden, Tal Y cafn, Nr Colwyn Bay, Conwy.  LL28 5RE |
| | Telephone: 01492 650460  Fax: 01492 650448 |
| **Email:** | ann.smith@nationaltrust.org.uk |
| **Website:** | www.bodnant-garden.co.uk |
| **Location:** | 8 miles south of Llandudno and Colwyn Bay just off A470, signposted from the A55, exit at junction 19. |

Please quote this guide when making a booking

Established since 1989, Cae Hir Gardens were entirely envisaged, designed and created by just one man, Dutchman Wil Akkermans. Over the past 20 years his labour of love has matured into one of Wales' most acclaimed gardens, being featured in both of 2009's prestigious "The Gardens of Wales" and "Discovering Welsh Gardens" books. In 2004 Cae Hir also proudly accepted an invitation by the RHS to become a partner garden. This acclaim comes as a result of Wil's creativity and originality in his pioneering approach to blending the wild with the cultivated.

- "What a truly magnificent garden ... so beautifully landscaped. I have not seen a garden quite like it anywhere." *Gordon and Ivy Morris, July 2009.*
- "Eat your heart out Monty Don." *Joe Frostman, June 2009.*
- "Delicious cream tea, a wonderfully relaxing garden, nice people – what more could you ask of a Sunday afternoon!" *Liz, Austria, July 2009.*

## Fact File

| | |
|---|---|
| **Opening Times:** | Easter to October, daily from 10 a.m. – 5 p.m. |
| **Admission Rates:** | Adults: £5.00, Senior Citizens: £5.00, Children: £1.00 |
| **Group Rates:** | Minimum Group Size: 10-24 or 25+, Adults: £4.50 or £4.00, Senior Citizens: £4.50 or £4.00 Children: N/A. |
| **Facilities:** | Shop, plant sales, tearoom |
| **Disabled Access:** | Yes, partial |
| **Toilets:** | Yes. |
| **Tours/Events:** | See website |
| **Car Parking:** | Yes. |
| **Coach Parking:** | Yes. |
| **Length of Visit:** | 2-3 hours |
| **Booking Contact:** | Julie Whittington Akkermans Cae Hir Gardens, Cribyn, Lampeter, Ceredigion SA48 7NG Telephone. 01570 470839 |
| **Email:** | caehirgardens@googlemail.com |
| **Website:** | www.caehirgardens.com |
| **Location:** | West from Lampeter or east from Aberaeron on the A482. In Temple Bar turn onto the B4337 towards Llanybydder. The gardens are two miles down the road in Cribyn (left-hand side). |

Please quote this guide when making a booking

# Dewstow Gardens & Grottoes · Monmouthshire

THE secret is out . . . Dewstow's Hidden Gardens and Grottoes are rapidly becoming one of the most fascinating tourist attractions in South Wales. Situated just a few miles from the M4 motorway and the two Severn Bridges, the Dewstow estate offers a magical oasis of calm, set in the magnificent Monmouthshire countryside.

The "lost" gardens, which date back to the late 1890s, became buried by tons of soil around the time of the Second World War but were rediscovered by new owners in 2000. Now, due to a painstaking and meticulous renovation programme, Dewstow's buried treasure has been unveiled once again and is being viewed and enjoyed by a long line of enchanted visitors.

Dewstow, now Grade One listed, features a stunning series of gardens, pools, water features and ornamental areas just waiting to be explored at your leisure. Don't miss the chance to take a fascinating journey back in time in this subterranean wonderland before relaxing with some refreshments in our delightful tea room.

## Fact File

| | |
|---|---|
| **Opening Times:** | Open Daily from March 20th until 17th October 2010. 10.00am – 4.30p.m. |
| **Admission Rates:** | Adults: £6.00, Senior Citizens: £5.00, Children: £3.50. |
| **Group Rates:** | Minimum Group Size 15, Adults: £5.00, Senior Citizens: £5.00, Children: £3.50. |
| **Facilities:** | Plant sales, teas. |
| **Disabled Access:** | No. |
| **Toilets on site:** | Yes. |
| **Tours/Events:** | Guided tours available, booking required. |
| **Coach Parking:** | Yes. |
| **Car Parking on site:** | Yes. |
| **Length of Visit:** | 2 hours approximately. |
| **Booking Contact:** | Liz, Dewstow Gardens, Caerwent, Monmouthshire NP26 5AH |
| | Telephone: 01291 430444 |
| | Fax: 01291 425816 |
| **Email:** | gardens@dewstow.co.uk |
| **Website:** | www.dewstow.co.uk/gardens.htm |

Please quote this guide when making a booking

# The Dingle Garden

The Dingle garden is set in the heart of glorious mid-Wales. The four acre garden is mostly the work of Barbara Joseph who over the years, created a secluded and beautiful area which serves to inspire garden lovers everywhere.

The R.H.S. partner garden is south-facing with paths that wind down the slope to a lake and small waterfall. The beds are colour themed to look good all year round. Spectacular autumn foliage, including many unusual trees, shrubs and acers, along with an acre primrose wood in spring are special features. This peaceful haven, teeming with wildlife is the ideal spot for a relaxing wander at any time of year.

The Dingle Nursery runs alongside the garden and offers for sale a huge variety of common and rare plants and trees, many of which grow there.

## Fact File

**Opening Times:** 9 – 5 every day. Only closed for one week at Christmas
**Admission Rates:** Adults: £3.00, Senior Citizens: £3.00, Children: Free, R.H.S. members free.
**Group Rates:** No reduction for groups (free tea and coffee included in the price)
**Facilities:** Small shop with free tea and coffee available.
**Disabled Access:** Very limited. 1 wheelchair available for booking. Car Parking and toilet on site.
**Tours/Events:** No guided tours. Talk for groups.
**Coach Parking:** Yes.
**Length of Visit:** 1 – 3 hours.
**Booking Contact:** Jill Rock, The Dingle Garden, Frochas, Nr. Welshpool, Powys. SY21 9JD
Tel: 01938 555145 Fax: 01938 555778
**Email:** info@dinglenurseryandgarden.co.uk
**Website:** www.dinglenurseryandgarden.co.uk
**Location:** 2 miles north of Welshpool, off the A490.

Please quote this guide when making a booking

Set in the heart of the Vale of Glamorgan countryside, Dyffryn is one of Wales' largest and most important Edwardian Gardens. The impressive 55 acres are a result of the unique collaboration of landscape architect Thomas Mawson and avid plant collector Reginald Cory.

Dyffryn boasts a magnificent double herbaceous border, a Victorian fernery, a rose garden, a stumpery, a rockery and also an extensive tree collection in the arboretum. As you stroll the beautiful grounds you will also discover a series of intimate garden rooms, such as the Pompeian Garden, Lavender Court and the Reflecting pool.

This outstanding garden has been undergoing considerable restoration works with assistance from the Heritage Lottery Fund. The extensive project is due to conclude this year with the exciting revival of the walled garden and the reinstatement of the magnificent glasshouses.

## Fact File

**Opening Times:** Site open throughout the year. 1st March – 31st October 10am – 6pm.
1st November – 28th February 10am - 4pm.

**Admission Rate:** 1st March – 31st October Adults £6.50, Concession £4.50, Child £2.50, Family £17.00.
1st November – 29th February Adult £3.50, Concession £2.50, Child £1.50, Family £8.50.

**Group Rates:** Discount on groups of 15 and over, please contact for more details.

**Facilities:** Visitor centre, Tearooms, Play area and plant sales all before the pay barrier

**Disabled Access:** Majority of gardens is wheelchair friendly.
Wheelchairs available to loan, advanced booking is preferable.

**Tours/Events:** Tours available to groups by prior arrangement at an additional charge. Tours with Head Gardener held throughout the year, please contact for more details.
Varied programme of seasonal events and activities held throughout the year.

**Coach Parking:** Yes

**Length of Visit:** 2 – 3 hours

**Booking Contact:** Dyffryn Gardens, St Nicholas, Vale of Glamorgan, CF5 6SU.
Tel: 029 2059 3328, Fax: 029 2059 1966

**Email:** dyffryn@valeofglamorgan.gov.uk

**Website:** www.dyffryngardens.com

**Location:** Exit M4 at J33 to A4232(signposted Barry). At roundabout take 1st exit (A4232). At junction with A48/A4050 exit the A4232 at Culverhouse Cross Take 4th exit A48 (signposted Cowbridge). Turn left at lights in St Nicholas.
Dyffryn is on right after approx. 1 1/2 miles.

Please quote this guide when making a booking

Glansevern Hall was built, in Greek Revival style, by Sir Arthur Davies Owen at the turn of the 18th/19th Century.

It looks down on the River Severn from an enclosure of gardens set in wider parkland. Near the house are fine lawns studded with herbaceous and rose beds and a wide border backed by brick walls. A Victorian orangery and a large fountain face each other across the lawns. The large walled garden has been ingeniously divided into compartments separated by hornbeam hedges and ornamental ironwork. There is a rock garden of exceptional size, built of limestone and tufa, which creates a walk-through grotto. A little further afield, woodland walks are laid out around the 4 acre lake and pass through a water garden which, especially in May and June, presents a riot of growth and colour.

Glansevern is noted for its collection of unusual trees.

## Fact File

| | |
|---|---|
| **Opening times:** | May to September every Thursday, Friday, Saturday and Bank Holiday Monday 12.00 noon - 5.00 pm Groups on any other day, booking necessary. |
| **Admission Rates:** | Adult £5.00, Seniors £4.50, Children under sixteen Free. |
| **Facilities:** | Tea Room & Light Lunches (all Homemade), Plant Sales, Art Gallery. |
| **Disabled Access:** | Yes. Toilet and parking for disabled on site. |
| **Tours/Events:** | Guided walk indentifying the large number of unusual trees. |
| **Coach Parking:** | Yes |
| **Length of Visit:** | 1 ½ hours |
| **Booking Contact:** | Neville Thomas Glansevern Hall Gardens, Berriew, Welshpool, Powys, SY21 8AH Telephone: 01686 640644 Fax: 01686 640829 |
| **Email:** | glansevern@yahoo.co.uk |
| **Website:** | www.glansevern.co.uk |
| **Location:** | Signposted at Berriew on A483 between Welshpool and Newtown, North Powys, 4 miles S W of Powis Castle. |

Please quote this guide when making a booking

## National Botanic Garden Of Wales           Carmarthenshire

The remarkable National Botanic Garden of Wales is a very special place. The largest single-span Glasshouse in the world designed by Norman Foster, poised in the landscape like a giant raindrop is home to some of the most endangered plants on the planet from six Mediterranean climate regions, Western Australia, Chile, the Canaries, California, southern Africa and the Mediterranean basin. It helps protect and conserve what is considered to be the best collection of its kind in the world. The Tropical House located in the unique and historic double-walled garden is bursting with palms, pineapples, coconuts, cardamom and scores of orchids. The Garden lies on land that was once a magnificent Regency water park, many of the original features having been restored. Discover lakes, ponds, walks; theatre; licensed restaurant; shop; gallery; bog garden, apiary; Physicians of Myddfai Exhibition and Apothecaries' Garden; children's play area and discovery centre. Land surrounding the Garden has been designated a National Nature Reserve.

## Fact File

| | |
|---|---|
| **Opening times:** | 10 a.m. – 6 p.m. BST/10 a.m. – 4.30 p.m. BWT. (Closed Christmas Day) |
| **Admission Rates:** | Adults: £8.00, Senior Citizens: £6.50, Children: Under 16: £4.00, Under 5s: Free Family: 2 Adults + 4 Children £19.50 |
| **Group Rates:** | Minimum Group Size: 10. Adults: £7.00, Senior Citizens: £5.50, Children: £3.00 RHS members free – between 1st October and 31st March |
| **Facilities:** | Shop, Plant Sales, Licensed Restaurant, Café, 360 degree Multimedia Theatre, Conference Centre, Children's Playground, Activity Centre. |
| **Disabled Access:** | Yes. Wheelchair loan available FOC, booking advisable. |
| **Toilets on site:** | Yes |
| **Car Parking on site:** | Yes |
| **Coach Parking:** | Yes |
| **Guided Tours:** | Yes, booking required. |
| **Length of Visit:** | 4-6 hours |
| **Special Events:** | Full events programme |
| **Booking Contact:** | National Botanic Garden of Wales, Llanarthne, Carmarthenshire, SA32 8HG Booking Tel No.01558 668768. Booking Fax No. 01558 668933 |
| **Email:** | info@gardenofwales.org.uk |
| **Website:** | www.gardenofwales.org.uk |
| **Location:** | One hour's drive from Cardiff, two hours from Bristol. Just off the A48 which links directly to the M4 and on to the M5. |

Please quote this guide when making a booking

# Picton Castle Gardens & Gallery

## Pembrokeshire

Soak up a special magic as you walk beneath some of the largest and oldest trees in West Wales. The 40 acres of walled and woodland gardens around Picton Castle include a tree fern glade, a restored dew pond and the new jungle garden planted with gingers, banana trees and other vibrant exotics. Unique to Picton are Rhododendrons bred here, plus rare species like Embothrium, Eucryphia and an avenue of myrtles.

Massive Redwoods and oaks dominate the Avenues. Around them, rare trees and flowering shrubs include the largest Rhododendron 'Old Port' in existence, a particularly fine Dawn Redwood (a conifer presumed extinct until rediscovered in remote Chinese valley in 1941) and numerous rare conifers from all over the globe.

Scent and colour rule the Walled Garden, where a vast collection of border plants create riotous summer colour. Equally tantalising is Maria's Mediterranean Restaurant, in the Victorian courtyard.

## Fact File

| | |
|---|---|
| **Opening times:** | 29th March to 31st September daily 10.30am – 5.00pm.  Entrance to the Castle by guided tour only between 11.30am – 3.30pm.  Check website for dates and times of February and October half term opening and occasional winter weekend openings. |
| **Admission Rates:** | Gardens & Gallery: Adults £4.95, Senior Citizens £4.75, Children 5 – 15: £2.50 With Castle tour Adults £7.45, Seniors £7.25, Children £4.00 |
| **Group Rates:** | Reductions on Castle tours for pre-booked groups of 20 or more. RHS Members Free from April – September |
| **Facilities:** | Shop, plant sales, restaurant, teas, art galleries, castle tours, children's play area, picnic area, toilets. |
| **Disabled Access:** | Yes.  Free wheelchair loan available. |
| **Car Parking on site:** | Yes |
| **Coach Parking:** | Yes |
| **Tours/Events:** | Guided tours to Castle only.  Booking only required for large groups on Castle tours |
| **Length of Visit:** | 2 hours for castle tour and Walled Garden, plus 2 hours for 40 acres of woodland gardens. |
| **Special Events:** | See website for information. |
| **Booking Contact:** | Dai Evans Picton Castle Gardens & Gallery, Picton Castle, Haverfordwest, Pembrokeshire SA62 4AS Telephone & Fax No. 01437 751326. |
| **Email:** | info@pictoncastle.co.uk   Website www.pictoncaste.co.uk |
| **Location:** | OS Ref: SN011 135; two miles south of the A40. Follow brown tourist signs located on the A40 about 3 miles east of Haverfordwest, |

Please quote this guide when making a booking

The eighteenth-century house is set on wide open lawns leading down to the Bush River crossed by a fine Victorian iron bridge some 36 metres long. A walk through the surrounding parkland leads to a pond surrounded by azaleas, magnolias, rhododendrons, Japanese maples and Irish yews and a lushness of gunneras, irises, darmeras and other moisture-loving plants. The walled garden, where brick-faced walls are lined with espaliered apple and pear trees and a formal rose garden centred on a small pool and fountain is flanked on one side by a formal box parterre, provides a touch of old-world elegance. On the other side of the fountain a framework was constructed to give support to a mixture of climbers – wisteria, clematis etc, a variety of ivies and the pink and cream-splashed Actinidia kolomikta, while the gravel paths are lined with old cottage garden favourites like lupins, peonies and roses, punctuated by clipped cones and pyramids of yew and box. An open arch in the walls leads through to a one-acre kitchen garden abundant with fruit trees, vegetables and herbs, all contained within immaculately maintained box hedges. There is also a small plant sales area.

## Fact File

| | |
|---|---|
| **Opening Times:** | 12 – 5 p.m. from 1st June – 30th August. Open in May by arrangement. |
| **Admission Rates:** | Adults: £4.00, Senior Citizens: £4.00, Children: free under 14 |
| **Group Rates:** | Minimum Group Size: 10. Adults: £3.00, Senior Citizens:, Children: free under 14 RHS Members 2 for 1. |
| **Facilities:** | Plant Sales, Teas, small museum of old farm implements etc. |
| **Disabled Access:** | Yes. |
| **Toilet On Site:** | Yes. |
| **Tours:** | Yes. Booking required. House opened for groups by arrangement. |
| **Coach Parking:** | Yes. |
| **Car Parking:** | Yes. |
| **Length of Visit:** | 1-2 hours |
| **Booking Contact:** | Benvarden, 36 Benvarden Road, Ballybogey, Co. Antrim, BT53 6NN. Tel. 028 20741331 Fax. 028 20741955 |
| **Email:** | mail@benvarden.com |
| **Website:** | www.benvarden.com |
| **Location:** | On B67 Coleraine Ballycastle road. Brown tourist signs. 10 miles from Giants Causeway and Bushmills.. |

Please quote this guide when making a booking

# Cashel House Hotel & Gardens

Cashel house is a gracious country house owned by the McEvilly family. The gardens are an informal country house style based on a number of woodland glades. The garden contains profusion of roses both old fashioned and modern along with many herbaceous plants with naturalised day lilies, astilbes and primulas. Also camellias, magnolias, azaleas, eucryphia and many more. Our own herb and fruit gardens, stud farm and garden school are also on site.

## Fact File

**Opening times:** 10.30 – 5 p.m. each day from 12 February – 1 December.

**Admission Rates:** Adults: £5.00, Senior Citizens: £3.00, Children and students: £3.00 RHS members free

**Group Rates:** Minimum Group Size: Adults: 40/50, Senior Citizens: 30/40, Children: 8/10

**Facilities:** Plant Sales, Restaurant, Teas, Garden, Courses

**Disabled Access:** Part of the garden, all of the house, booking required for wheelchairs

**Toilets on site:** Yes

**Car Parking on site:** Yes

**Coach Parking:** Yes, for small coaches 20 – 60 persons

**Guided Tours:** Yes, booking required

**Special Events:** Garden courses, 2 or 3 days or one day, see leaflet attached

**Booking Contact:** Kay McEvilly, Cashel House Hotel & Gardens, Cashel, Connamara, Co. Galway Booking Tel No. 353 95 31001.  Booking Fax No. 353 95 81077

**Email:** res@cashel-house-hotel.com

**Website:** www.cashel-house-hotel.com

**Location:** West coast of Ireland, 40 miles from Galway, 8 from Roundstone, 8 from Carna, 12 from Clifden

*"The rockery is the glory of this garden. It is one of the most beautiful features in the country, breathtaking and definitely worth travelling to see."*
*Quote by Shirley Lanigan, O'Brien guide to Irish Gardens.*

Lisselan Gardens was designed in the 1800s and laid out in Robinsonian style, enhancing the natural features and contours provided by the valley and the river Argideen flowing throughout. Many unusual plants and shrubs not geographically associated with this region can be seen in our gardens.

Take a breath of 'fresh air' as you walk along the natural paths, bridges and flagstone pathways to lead you on an exploration of intrigue in this spectacular garden.
The rockery, Rhododendron garden, water garden, Azalea gardens, shrubbery and Fuchsia garden, are some of the features which can be seen at Lisselan Gardens.

## Fact File

| | |
|---|---|
| **Opening Times:** | 8 a.m. – dusk |
| **Admission Rates:** | Adults: €6.00, Senior Citizens: €5.00, Children under 12 free |
| **Group Rates:** | Any group size catered for.  Please contact for a quote, Children under 12 free. |
| **Facilities:** | Shop, plant sales, light refreshments available. |
| **Disabled Access:** | Yes. |
| **Toilet On Site:** | No, but one in house nearby |
| **Tours/Events:** | Guided tours available. Booking required. |
| **Coach Parking:** | Yes. |
| **Car Parking:** | Yes. |
| **Length of Visit:** | Approx 1½ hours. |
| **Booking Contact:** | Sandra Healy |
| | Lisselan Gardens, Lisselan, Clonakilty, West Cork, Ireland |
| | Booking Telephone No. +353 23 8833249 |
| | Booking Fax No. +353 23 8834605 |
| **Email:** | info@lisselan.com |
| **Website:** | www.lisselan.com |
| **Location:** | Lisselan Gardens is situated on N71 |

Please quote this guide when making a booking

# Index

# Index